To Renate

Know your Truth.
Choose your Truth.
Live your Truth.
BE YOU.

Above anything else I deeply appreciate this book being in your hands.
Once you will have read its content you will understand what it means to me

This edition is a self published effort and in my case, this implies there was no professional editing
I am therefore convinced a profusion of mistakes will have gone unnoticed.
I ask for your indulgence and invite you to contact me with your findings so that the next edition may be improved

REVISIONS@ANNIEPAQUETTE.COM

Left Right Then Center

A Story from the Middle

By-Einna Publishing

First published in Canada in 2012 by

By-Einna Publishing

The following people mentioned in the book have graciously granted permission to include their name, website, or excerpts: Gavin Carruthers, David Deida, Huuyaah, Jonathan Field, Jade Wa'hoo Grigori, Benoit Paquette, Richard and Xwalacktun.

Inquiries were made to determine whether the brief quotes from movies, television programs and other sources, as well as mentions of books, required permission ; the result was that they did not. If an error was made, I apologize, and ask to be informed so that I may make the corrections for subsequent editions.

CATALOGUING-IN-PUBLICATION DATA AVAILABLE FROM LIBRARY AND ARCHIVES CANADA 2012

LEGAL DEPOSIT: LIBRARY AND ARCHIVES CANADA 2012
ISBN: 978-0-9881501-0-2
1st edition: August 2012

Set in Adobe Garamond and Gotham HTF

Printed by Maranda Digital Print Inc., Vancouver, BC, Canada
Bound by Metropolitan Fine Printers, Vancouver, BC, Canada

Book and jacket design by Maude Paquette-Boulva
www.maudepaquette.com

To Rollande, my mother

A gentle paragon

Of unconditional love

In the gentle morning breeze
I listened to the winds
That carried the sounds of my soul

In the quiet evening breeze
I surrendered to the whispers
To the whispers of my soul

Where they lead I will follow
I will follow them there
I will follow them where

PROLOGUE

Weeks prior to going to print, two women passed through my home and saw a phrase from this book posted on my wall. They were quick to express their appreciation and asked if they could borrow the saying to inspire a friend who was sick.

When my niece read the manuscript, she told me that in the middle of a chapter, she had been inspired to email someone that was once dear to her but with whom she had lost touch.

On both occasions, my heart overflowed with joy and my resolve to finish was revived because such are my reasons for writing this book; the stories that it tells are incidental. My most fervent desire is that reactions of the heart such as these are multiplied infinitely.

There are two personal vocabulary and pronominal choices I wish to clarify before you begin reading. The first concerns the word "God", which appears often throughout the following pages. Personally, I favor the term not for its religious connotation but because it evokes the mystique, the boundless, the indefinable. It could just as well be replaced by Higher Power, Greater Consciousness, Creator, Life, Wisdom of the Universe, or simply, the Universe – another term I use frequently and interchangeably. I consider God as an omnipresent observer – and life-force, within us and around us – akin to that from quantum physics' Copenhagen Interpretation, which states that nothing exists until it is observed. Ergo, "something" must be observing. Finally, as an intangible ubiquitous presence, I consider God neither an "it, nor a "he" or a "she", but will refer to *it* as "he".

And this brings me to my second particularity: Ego, whom I also think of and will refer to as "he" rather than "it". In my circle, Ego is the chatty one in my head; the one that needs, wants, makes me feel guilty, unsatisfied, who blames others and is quick to beat himself (or me) up. He carries emotional baggage and opens up his suitcases at the most inconvenient of times – he seems quite confused about which wardrobe is appropriate for which situation. Of course, he's not all bad; he is also well versed in my history, skilled at planning and organizing, and knowledgeable of how to maneuver in the material world. This anthropomorphism assigns him a personality, which makes for much more satisfying interactions and animated discussions: I can tell him to back off or I can choose to negotiate, reconcile or collaborate. He is impossible to jettison and so, in the end, we both bring goodwill to the relationship.

The last thing I will mention is that I guarantee redundancies. These will occur not as a result of poor editing, but as authentic reflections of my mind's meanderings.

Everything and anything else you may need to know, you will find out, uncensored, as you read this book.

ANNIE PAQUETTE
VANCOUVER, 2012

OCTOBER

READY, SET, GO

OCTOBER 1ST, 2011

THE WHISPER

Saturday morning, another week has gone by, and I'm still waiting, literally holding my breath *(which yields to guilt because I practice yoga and know the benefits of breathing, such as making the energy flow or, well, keeping me alive).* I keep the faith, knowing that dawn always follows the night, but this has been a night of Alaskan proportions! Truth be told, I have grown occasionally cynical of happy endings, but then my true nature cannot help but believe: I will reach the fullest expression of myself and find my best place in the world. I am an Energizer Bunny of the spirit: Nothing can stop me.

I am poised for the next chapter of my life. No, actually, I have started it. I am past the point of being poised: I've jumped already. I have gotten my badges of resilience, endurance, resourcefulness, preparedness, perseverance and courage. I have leapt into a formidable gorge without a security net – the Universe (God) certainly seems to ask pretty big leaps from those who, unbeknownst to them, were entrusted with long legs.

AUGUST 18TH 2010

Standing on the pier at the North Shore Esplanade, this is my first morning ever in Vancouver. I have flown from the East coast to attend an ultimate business meeting, hoping a local yoga company will want to market the fitness products I have invented.

Seals are relishing their morning treats, ducks are quietly gliding past, waves are dancing about. Suddenly, my flesh is swept with chills, hairs on my arms rise up: the wind is whispering, "Welcome home."

"Whaaat?"

I surrender to what I hear; moisture fills my eyes, and it has nothing to do with the brisk ocean air. I know: *This is where my next home will be.*

But how the hell am I going to do it?

AUGUST 11TH 2011

Standing on my porch this morning, contemplating the alluring frosted peak of Mount Baker, I breathe and stretch gently. I am home, in Vancouver.

My 2010 meeting was not a success, I cried bitterly after being turned down, once more. So much had been riding on this; my future had depended on it. But even in the midst of my tears, I knew that perhaps the real goal had not been, after all, to make a deal with this company, and that maybe my trip had been a success because I had heard the whisper of my soul and now knew where I was heading in my life: Vancouver.

But having chosen to hear the disturbing murmurs of this voice was, and still is, neither a simple nor restful thing. But listen I did, and I acted too.

I am here in Vancouver against many odds, and certainly against all logic, reason and good sense.

On my way back to the East coast after that meeting, I made a stop in Seattle to see a friend for a few hours before my flight. After sharing the essentials of my ongoing plight, as well as my profound yearning and aspirations, she asked me one pointed question, "Do you think you've had enough?" I remember the fullness of the pause on my end: a pause during which years of brooding and incubation were finally going to produce their progeny. I felt the shell crack, my head thrusting upward to draw its freeing first breath: the chick had hatched. Gently I answered her question with a meaningful "Yes. I have."

Throughout the flight and upon my return, one word was echoing in my head: Enough. The time had come. The time had come for me to do something about the fact that I was not living the life I wanted to live *(and hadn't for ages)*; it was time to dare changing my living situation *(perhaps I'll share the details over tea one day)*. Drastic and intimidating steps would need to be taken; regardless, I knew I had to find a way to move on, which incredibly now implied moving to Vancouver.

One of the difficulties I was facing was that my belongings were haplessly scattered in storage units in Arizona, Massachusetts and Quebec *(maybe we can make that strong coffee instead of tea)* and I was painfully aware that I did not have a penny to my name to make any kind of move, let alone across the country *(oh dear, we'll need margaritas)*.

In order to follow through with my new plan, the priority was to address my absence of funds, which meant finding a job; something quite foreign to me since I had worked on my own projects all my life *(the latest of which, the fitness products, still not generating any money: hence the need for a job)*. The first order of business was to tackle the Everest that was drafting an up-to-date résumé; a task I poured myself into and successfully completed. The next peak to conquer was accepting to become an employee *(perhaps* that *was the Everest – the résumé was maybe camp III)*. Being a veteran captain of my own ship, the prospect of giving the helm was, to say the least, unsettling, and my willingness to do so attested to my newfound determination and direction. Having come to peace with this undesirable prospect (of becoming an employee) for my greater good, I then promptly and intensely began making general contacts and job inquiries in Vancouver.

For months on end I researched, networked, applied, emailed, and conversed. But nothing came of any of it. I was told by one of those contacts that Vancouver was a 1st and 2nd degree city and that people hired people they knew. It was suggested that I should find my way there first, start networking and expect that within six months *(given my numerous skills and talents)*, work would come and money would flow. BUT, how could I envision those months without revenue?

Here was the big picture, without the background stories:

1 I would be moving on 100 % credit *(something my new landlord would not like hearing)*. And I mean 100 %: No RRSP, 401(k), investments-I-don't-want-to-touch, royalties, bursting wool sock, stuffed mattress or rainy day reserve *('cause now would be a real good time to pull out that umbrella!)*.

2 Although quite accomplished professionally, I have no diploma and my work experience is so varied that finding a title for what I do, and thus a job, was and still is, a challenge.

3 My health is not something I have been able to rely on for the last 30 years.

Nine months had now passed, spring had come around, and I was still living out of my numerous suitcases *(we'll get around to tea, coffee or margaritas)* between my mother's condo in Ste-Ville*, Quebec, and a friend's house in Massachusetts, without a solution in sight. I had unsuccessfully scrambled to find a few thousand dollars to allow me to make my move with a semblance of security, until one morning in April, chatting with my Mom over coffee, it dawned on me: This

* The province of Quebec is home to a plethora of cities boasting canonized names. You can't go very far without rubbing elbows with sainthood. "Ste-Ville" is actually not a town, but could just as well be, and my mother does live in St-something, but I choose not to disclose which one in particular.

is what I have been doing for years, waiting for one event or another to unfold and provide me with the financial freedom to move on. None of the outcomes have gone my way. And here I am again, knowing precisely what I am supposed to do *(if you call listening to an inner voice a reliable source)* yet still letting it be conditional to money *(which is arguably a rather necessary commodity in this world)*. I think I'm going to have to be dangerously proactive and reverse the sensible way of doing things: I am going to move away on credit and trust life to unfold as I hope it will.

So it was decided the next day, during a drive on the quiet roads of Vermont, that I was going to "do it." I found I was determined to follow "the voice" I had heard last summer on the docks; it had moved me to my core and I had felt it was my truth that had spoken. Despite many doubts and fears and questions *(Why is this being asked of me this way? And who's asking?)*, I could still bring myself back to that moment of clarity, and check in: Yes, still my truth.

I proceeded to make a pact with the powers that be: "Okay, I will listen one ultimate time to what you are asking me to do even though what I am hearing is nuts *(Can't tests be easier? And why does it seem we need to be tested?)*. I gamble all: my future, my health, my life. I accept the challenge and hope the secret terms of the pact will bring me joy, doing what I am meant to do, and allow the greatest possibilities for who I am to manifest themselves."

And here I am today, in Vancouver, waiting for those terms to be revealed.

Last month, I went to the farmer's market in West Vancouver and one of the merchants asked me what made me move to the other coast. Confidently he asked, "Love or job?" and I answered, "Neither, but hoping for both. It was the intuition that my life would unfold here, that brought me." The honey-and-garlic man* looked at me inquisitively so I proceeded to tell him the story of how one morning last summer, the wind, the waves and the mountains had conspired to whisper to me. I also told him that now, I really needed a job. He exclaimed, "A job? You don't need a job! All you have to do is talk, talk, talk; just tell your story!"

So here I am, telling my story.

I have listened to my inner voice and now, I am looking for my voice in the world.

Sometimes life's whispers may seem discordant with our life's apparent capabilities. Although acting upon those whispers will surely turn out to be a perilous foray into faith's dense thicket of mysteries, the promise that they are guiding us closer to our fullest expression in the world can be irresistibly alluring.

OCTOBER 2ND, 2011

WORLDLY NEWS

Although the honey-and-garlic man's words were inspiring, I did, and do, need a job. Now that I have done the deed and moved to Vancouver, the reality is: I need to make money and fast. I can believe and dream as much as I want of this new life – where I find my

* The first crop of Siberian garlic is exquisite.

true expression and money ensues as a natural consequence of having listened to a divine whisper – but the real world's clock is ticking, and it's ticking way too fast for my accruing debt *(where is Einstein when you need to slow down time?).*

Since I have been here, I have met more people than during the past five years of my rather reclusive life. I have been networking and putting myself out there like never before *(and liking it, much to my surprise).* This new social disposition was adopted upon the day of my arrival by having a friend of a friend of my girlfriend's boyfriend, who has now become my friend, pick me up at the airport. I continue to actively pursue this unfamiliar lifestyle because I wish to develop a sense of community; something I have yearned for all my life but that has eluded me to date. This new chapter of mine is presenting me with the perfect opportunity to create the life I have aspired to have. And of course, the more people I meet, the better chances I have at finding a job.

To be honest though *(which I plan on being throughout this book),* I had believed that the Universe would have shown support for its obedient pupil – sparing me from unduly stress – and provided me with some financial security prior to my move or shortly thereafter. I had secretly hoped that complying with the instructions I had received would be sufficient "proof" of my loyalty, and that once I had surrendered, my prayers for assistance would be answered. Well, apparently not. I have now been here for over two months and no sign of the Universe's appreciation. Apparently, I still haven't surrendered enough or something. I must be walking on stilts! *(You know: the long legs for the big leap of faith over the gorge of uncertainty?)*

And if not showing support by supplying me with money to facilitate my move, then at least I thought the Universe would have lent me a hand in finding a job once I go here. It's not like that demand was in the order of a miracle: I do have broad work experience, I am committed and dedicated, and if I may say so myself, I bring to the table some wooing charismatic charms (!). You can understand that given all this, I naively pictured the task to be more of a snap.

I have been told that I am an impatient woman, hmm... could it be? Really, I did not think the idea of finding a job was so unrealistic *(yes, I have been tuned-in to the current woes of our economy but I am not one to let statistics limit my aspirations).*

It is through the daunting, eye opening, soul searching, cathartic, and therapeutic process of writing my résumé last fall, that I discovered – despite my absence of diploma or proper title – that I had acquired some marketable skills in the course of my professional life. I was an art director in television and radio advertising, worked in marketing, distribution, and graphic design. I have been celebrated as a Canadian artist and was granted USA residency on that merit *(I am Canadian, born and raised in a suburb on the island of Montreal – yes, it's an island).* I have designed the architecture, interior and landscape of a million dollar residential project, which appeared in a magazine. I have lead wellness retreats, and invented two yoga/fitness products – I'm not a dud. I am a multi-talented autodidact with a vastly diverse entrepreneurial career driven by creative zeal. In a way, my current penniless, unemployed situation is kind of an enigma, a whimsy of nature. But however it came to be, it is my current hand in this high stakes poker game.

Anyway. At this point, I have been at once toying with and haunted by the idea that I may have to resort to working in a coffee shop or restaurant. There have even been moments when I have smiled at the romantic appeal of the notion. It would be a good story to tell one day: "I had lost everything, moved across the country on credit with a shaky health and worked in a coffee shop for 10 dollars an hour... and then, my faith and perseverance paid off and my life turned around when..." – good one! It makes sense though, right? Better $ 10/hour than nothing? But the dilemma is that this wage will not delay the inevitable *(the end of my credit)* for very long; my monthly payments considerably exceed this kind of small stipend.

Also, I have to admit that the psychological process of accepting to be a waitress at my age – given my skills, gifts and aspirations – is a challenge *(to say the least)*. I'll get over it, but it is a challenge. And not only that, of all absurdities, I am scared that I will not be able to do it! Yes, really, after all the colossal tasks I have undertaken in my life and the litany of challenges I have overcome, I am scared of not being capable of making coffee for clients!

Beyond the psychological challenge, I have found an approach that makes the prospect of working as a barista, kind of acceptable: Obviously, it can't really be about the money – although it still somewhat has to be. So what it is, is actually about being seen. Being out there in the public will create many opportunities to meet people and allow chemistry to initiate interest and discussions, instead of the impersonal, hard-sale, cold-call emails I have been sending – as poetically and invitingly as I may have written them.

Yes, I need to change my strategy, or at least try it for a while. Up to now, I have been using will as my tactic: selling myself and pushing ideas in every creative and gutsy way possible, and it has not worked for me. Yet, I have been obstinately doing the same thing over and over again because I was taught that hard work, perseverance and single-mindedness towards your goal will bring you what you seek. But again, it hasn't worked for me! What's the definition of insanity? Doing the same thing over and over, and expecting different results? ... right.

I adhere to a theory that such an outward strategy may work for 80% of people, but that for 20% of us, the key is to prepare and wait: "Build it and they will come. Forget your will and surrender for a while. Let you 'do the being' instead of the talking."

This idea of working in a coffee shop in order to be seen does resonate with me a lot more than the principle of working in a coffee shop as a demonstration of humility and willingness to start at the bottom. Stepping on your ego may be an important process for many, perhaps the 80 %? but it doesn't feel true for me. With my recent extensive soul searching, I have realized that ego-suppression is not the actual reason for this type of experience in my journey. So I've been thinking about the coffee shop move in the new light of being seen.

Should I or should I not? Do I have the guts, or don't I?

THE PUPPY AND THE BOULDER

The other day at the beach *(yes, a skip and a hop will get me to the beach and I have the mountain trails at the end of my street! – although I have been saying that I live in Vancouver, I am actually in North Vancouver, across the water from the city, where the mountains line the shore. Since it is part of the greater Vancouver area, I will resume saying Vancouver when referring to my place of residence)* there was this cuddly little puppy wearing a bright red jacket. He had climbed onto a boulder and could not muster the courage to come down. His master was in front of him, prompting him, lovingly calling him, enticing him with treats he would put down at the foot of the rock, trying to make the puppy anticipate the joy of having the courage to take the step.

The dog knew he had to get off the rock but he was terrified. He would take one step forward then back away, come closer to the edge, look down, and wince with fear. He would look around, realizing he was stuck with no other way down. To the onlookers, it was obviously a tiny little step. But to him, his whole world was at stake and nothing was more insurmountable in that moment. Even the promise of a delicious treat could not convince him to jump. It took forever, his master patiently waiting.

Then suddenly, he did it! He took the leap! *(just a step, really)* and within a second, he was chewing on his treat, apparently having already forgotten all about the fear that constituted his entire world just seconds ago and wondering what all the fuss had been about. "Why didn't I do it earlier?" he seemed to think. "It was no big deal." And so he rejoined his master and momentarily started onto his next life discovery challenge: walking on pebbles.

So it is that the Puppy-with-the-red-jacket was my teacher!

Soon after seeing the puppy, I made my way to a local coffee shop I had spotted earlier. I met with the manager who, even though he was not hiring, offered me a job if I wanted it.

You would think that was it, right? The lesson was learned, the message received, like the puppy, I had taken the step. But oh no! We humans are more complicated than this *(I am anyway)*. Here is how it went: Since my next ten days were already booked with networking engagements, settling-in tasks, car insurance appointments, *et cetera*, I told the manager I would get back to him after that particular stretch of time. He was fine with this. Well the stretch came and went, and with it, a few hopeful bites for a "professional" job. Of course I felt my righteous duty was to pursue those leads, which I did, in remarkable ways... and nothing came of them. And this is how I succeeded in putting aside the coffee shop hot potato again.

After spending yet a few more days re-questioning for the umpteenth time if, really, I was "supposed" to go work at a coffee shop, well of course, three weeks had now passed. My credit was even more eaten away, thus raising the level of urgency as well as that of my stress. After further anxiety-filled reflection *(I am very proficient at this)* I figured I could use just a few more days *(can you believe it?)*: one last chance to try to find a "real" job for better money. There were still a few more emails to write and people to approach. Of course nothing came out of that either. What was I thinking? Hadn't I already understood what I was supposed to do?

Finally, a few days ago, having reached my limit of such dog-trying-to-catch-its-tail mind-numbing thinking, I reached a place on inner peace and was able to look at this whole deal as one simple little step. "Think of the puppy Annie, just jump!"

And so I calmly called the coffee shop to tell the manager that I could be over in half an hour to discuss a working schedule. Well, guess what, he had now gone on vacation for two weeks! Jeez! There went my mind into a tailspin again: What was I supposed to read into this? That all I was meant to do was to accept the idea but that the Universe would not "require" me to actually work in a coffee shop? Or was it that this was not the right shop for me? Or could it be that I had to prove *(to whom I wonder again)* the depth of my resolve and apply at other coffee shops? Or, was it simply that it was what it was, and that there was nothing to read into it? Sometimes a cigar is just a cigar.

That's when it happened. Suddenly, I had enough: Enough of attempting to decipher the cryptic messages of an oft-unfathomable Universe. I signed myself off for a few days.

THIS BOOK

And this is where I stand today: in the midst of taking a break from my overwhelming penchant for being a decoder, interpreter and analyst of the invisible world. My conclusion was that I absolutely needed to chill in order to clear my mind. My health had been taking a beating, and this had been compounding the stress further. It had to stop.

And so, two days ago, I wisely decided that for the next two weeks – until the manager's return – I would pretend that my job was to write my story and dedicate myself to it exclusively. And this is the reason you are reading my words. Writing a book has been a dream of mine for over ten years and for the near future, I will indulge.

With these pages, I am choosing my heart's desire over my head's reason, and seeing where that leads. This is the time. This is the place. By engaging myself in something I love, I hope to find inner peace and clarity. Many have claimed that when you reach for a goal born from your heart, the whole universe conspires to support you.

Here I am, summoning the universe, once more.

When your ego's chatter begins to feel like a spin cycle and you can no longer make any sense of which way is up and which way is down, remove yourself from the mix and hang yourself up to dry in the outdoor breeze for a while. Soak in the sun, focus on one thing you love, and see how you feel afterwards.

(I'm right there with you. How's it hanging?)

OCTOBER 3RD, 2011

TO WRITE OR WHAT TO WRITE

Last night, as I was attempting to fall asleep, I began questioning the validity of this smart idea of mine of pretending to be a writer. I began to wonder if there was anything in there for a reader to enjoy or if my story was, in truth, insipid to anyone but myself. I wondered if I was I just telling my sad-story-exciting-life-adventures as a self-serving exercise. Was there in fact something valuable in my life warranting writing about it? So early in my process, doubts submerged me.

I started thinking that perhaps I should rework these very first pages and insert some clever bits so that an eventual reader would actually get something out of it. I should be teaching something, shouldn't I? But then I wondered: Would it still be authentic? Would beefing up my thought process after the fact in order to present what I think would appeal to the public be like pretending to be someone I am not? Within seconds, I had my answer: if I am to write my story, I'm going to be real. Anything else would blatantly defeat the very purpose of the exercise: Following my heart and finding my true voice in the world.

I actually do have a string or two of pearls of wisdom to share. I have acquired them through a lifetime of questions, observation and reflection. I have been known to say that figuring out life has been my full-time job for the past fifteen years, and that prior to that it was a part-time job. Not only have I had to deal with a serpentine life but I have had to put up with a mind that just wouldn't stop thinking and a soul that just wouldn't stop searching. Some people find me exhausting *(to put it kindly)* and many have wished that – at least for my own benefit and peace of mind – I would just "live" and stop thinking for a while. But eh, that's just who I am.

Some seem to be inspired though, or curious, or in the least, entertained. Like watching the Roadrunner: you know he'll hit a wall or something, but also that he will undoubtedly pull out of the rubble, faithfully beep-beep on his way again, and that he will be returning next week. Some devoted followers tend to stay tuned to my story and even occasionally ask to be updated. "So, what is going on with you now?" "What is Annie up to these days?" "What unlikely thing happened to you since we last talked, what boulder was dropped on your head, and what cliff did you fall off of and how did you pick yourself up, again?" They know I will inform them, succinctly and insightfully, and that within fifteen minutes they will have an honest and complete account of where I have been and where I stand today. I will tell them my story with verve, sprinkled with humor, bits of self-deprecation, confessed ridicule of repetitious patterns and idiosyncrasies, and of course, joy and sorrow.

Then, not unlike the Roadrunner, I will faithfully continue on – mostly with a smile on my face, light in my soul and bounce in my steps – all the while being keenly aware that this bucolic slow-motion-illuminated-meadow-scene will often be interrupted by a stubbed toe, a bee sting, an allergic reaction, the fury of a hurricane and an occasional earthquake.

What can I say? I have practiced standing in the margins, reflecting, and making mental notes since I was five years old. I remember "play time" in kindergarten, when all the other kids would run to the chests of toys and dolls. I remember clearly just standing there thinking: "This is so silly. Don't they know this is not real life? How come they can just go and 'play' with objects and make up stories?" I certainly couldn't. Inevitably, I would go see the teacher and she would either give me tasks, or ask me to prepare the next activity with her.

In 1st grade, the teacher had made me sit at a desk close to hers because while others were playing, or perhaps doing exercises I had already completed, she would have me prepare, or even create, the next one. I also remember that in second grade, because I was ahead with the work, the teacher asked me if there was any project I would like to do. I replied, "Why don't I organize Olympics for the entire 1st to 6th grade?" And I did. With the activities, the rules, the spreadsheets, the two-day schedule. I even madc medals out of a birch log sawed in slices *(by me, at seven years old!)*, with a burnt-on Olympic torch symbol. The medals were varnished and hung on a red, blue and white nylon ribbon.

All this is to say, I have never been part of the pack *(the full impact of which is a whole other story to be told while laying on a couch one day)*, which has consistently put me in the position of observer: reflecting, considering, analyzing, pondering, and trying to reconcile with the mysterious nature of humans.

Now, where was I going with this? Right. The fact that last night, I was already questioning what I was writing *(a rather ominous presage for someone considering writing an entire book)*. By the way, a mind laden with uncertainty about what I could or should be writing about is nothing new to me.

As I mentioned before, I have thought for many years that one day, I would write a book. And I have, over time, taken notes towards its eventual concretization – notes that, ironically, are currently neatly boxed in a storage unit near Ste-Ville, Quebec. *(I am happy to inform you that my American storage units were emptied last spring prior to moving here and that their contents uneventfully crossed the border – to my great relief – and were at last reunited under one roof, in their country of origin, after a ten-year separation.)*

I had a feeling it would be some kind of life-teaching book, most likely based on personal experiences. But having read a multitude of books about people with extraordinary lives, unusual experiences, or remarkable knowledge, I felt rather inadequate, ill-equipped or even pretentious to think that I could stand amongst their ranks. Authors of worthy books have either studied under notable masters, discovered life-changing principles, delved into the realm of metaphysics, unearthed ancient wisdom, travelled to remote areas, lived amidst mystical tribes, or have defied improbable odds and surmounted mind-boggling obstacles. I had done none of these things. The thoughts that would linger in my head sounded like this: "I actually don't really have any 'real knowledge' to share. I am an expert at nothing. What am I going to talk about in this book of mine?"

And then one day, years ago, it came to me almost in a flash *(no, no, no voices this time)*: I was simply supposed to write about my life. And the real illumination was that I did not need any other "acquired knowledge". Who I was sufficed. "Teach what you know" is what I heard *(okay, maybe a little bit of a voice)*. But what *did* I know? What was I going to say? I had then believed the book would be about my enduring faith and perseverance and how one day, finally, I had triumphed over my life's challenges. I had figured my story was going to inspire people to keep going and believing because, in the end, everything works out for the tireless seeker, and I was to be a living example of that. Problem was, my life was still murky and not yet a proof of anything. I mean, a life-story should really only be shared publicly if it can offer expert guidance or a proven strategy to success.

THIS IS IT!

So the book was shelved in my mind, in a cubbyhole somewhere. I would still journal and write, and even sometimes mention my future book *(I actually listed it as a work-in-progress in last year's résumé!)* but without real intent. And then in 2006, I met Richard, the love I had been waiting for all my life. It was a magical, spiritual, karmic, otherworldly everything. This glorious union gifted me the greatest moments of almost euphoric illuminations when I would literally feel I was stretching the fabric of the universe through the power of Love. The event of our encounter could be described in one action-word, "Finally", spoken through a deep exhale of relief and gratitude. And it came with equally big obstacles.

At that time I thought: This is the book I am going to write! I will write about how true love overcomes everything, about our struggles, and about our emergence at the end of the tunnel, together, ready to serve the world with what we have learned and conquered. Service was our expressed common goal.

In fact, I did begin writing that story, even started writing the happy ending with retrospective analysis *(get it? I was writing as if I was in a future that did not exist yet, reflecting upon the past events with the wisdom I had acquired from what had not yet happened! I told you I had a slightly overactive, relentless mind!).*

NOT

Well, that wasn't to be either. What happened was that for three and a half years, my darling and I bravely battled with the harrowing circumstances of this incredible love, for Richard travelled with an entourage of personal demons. I dealt with pain, betrayal and disillusion because in the end, my love was a homeless drunk, the king of his street kingdom, and he remains so to this day. This was the lowest point in my life. It felt as though I had had my most fundamental belief crushed: true love did not conquer all. And that realization very nearly destroyed me.

I mean, what kind of joke was the Universe playing on me? It had at last granted me the kind of love I had always believed was possible on this planet, but had eluded me to this day, only to slowly rip it away from me in the most cruel fashion: I would have to watch my greatest kindred soul self-destroy. Witnessing this unraveling proved unbearable to me, because in my mind, there was no other reason to live than my belief in the ultimate power of Love. I would eventually learn that love goes beyond our earthbound personal stories.

The experience was filled with great suffering, deep insights, life lessons and personal growth. But in 2009, it is the weight of the pain that, compounded with other circumstances of my life, tipped the scale of my downfall. My health degenerated so seriously that I almost did not survive. I became so frail I could hardly walk but most importantly, my eyes had lost their light. I had been beaten down before by illness and discouragement, but this time, I could not find the smallest spark within me to reignite my life-fire. Through one of fate's poetic ironies, it was Richard who, after having disappeared from my life for nine months, ultimately reentered it long enough to bring me back from the brink of nothingness. It was to be our last hurrah *(a story for another day)*.

Needless to say, this did not constitute my anticipated happy ending. And so, again, I did not write my book.

THE GIFT

Years found me wondering ever more how and when this book would ever come about, as I still firmly believed it was destined to be one day. It was as if I could sense its existence in the ether, just waiting for the propitious moment to materialize: waiting for my cue to come to life.

Even though I had embraced the general concept of "teaching what you know", I still struggled with the eventual content of the book. What will my book be? What is it that I have to offer the world? What is my gift? This pivotal question, posed two year ago, brought me a step closer to understanding what it was that I had to share. My answer was: My gift is my journey and my awareness throughout my journey. My gift is my ability to articulate, communicate and share my soulful human experience for the benefit of others.

All I needed now was for some form of nameable success to arise: some favorably decisive event that would clearly mark the day my life fatefully changed course: the day when at last, my ship smoothly glided along the enlightened path of an enchanted sunrise.

Up until a few days ago, I remained steadfast in my belief that I had to have emerged from my life's struggles prior to telling my story. I did feel though, that I was getting closer to D-day. I was foreseeing that this yet unrevealed, blessed, momentous event was around the corner and would appear after perhaps just a little while longer in this prophetic city *(I had, after all, answered a divine whisper).* From that place of triumph, I could finally undertake the anticipated task of writing my story of perseverance and tell of the ineluctable well-deserved happy ending.

I had by then fully come to terms with the fact that indeed, I had not had an extraordinary life to share, at least not in the usual sense of the word: I hadn't been raised by a pack of wolves, or been stranded on the ocean for 90 days, or found God at the top of the Everest; I had not grown up surrounded by iconic celebrities or amongst royalty, and had not heroically raise myself from the ghetto. On the other hand, I also knew for sure that I was given an exceptional knack for living each moment with intensity and awareness, as well as an enduring, inextinguishable desire for self-expansion and betterment. And this had the makings of an extraordinary existence. I concluded my gift was not my story: my gift was how I lived my story.

A STORY FROM THE MIDDLE

That's when some radical idea hit me: How interesting would it be to share my story now, as it is unfolding and without the comfort of a happy ending or the benefits of hindsight? Now that would be authentic. I could chronicle the ups and down *(since from experience, I know there is a good chance it will resemble a mad roller coaster ride)* of the ongoing quest for my true voice while still in the muddy middle of it. No embellishments or revisionist history, which writing after the fact would inevitably entail. Just the naked truth of an uncensored human experience. A truthful account including both mundane and exciting days, just as the real world covers the gambit. A kind of unscripted literary reality show *(how refreshing)*: a journey in which people could undoubtedly recognize themselves precisely because it lacks the glitz of extraordinary circumstances, whether financial, social, or geographical. It would include life's unavoidable cliffhangers, blows and cheers, and would certainly keep me hooked and even spellbound since I will be wholeheartedly invested in what is to happen next.

So two days ago, I concluded that yes, my story is relatable and worth telling now, as I seek the expression of my full potential – just as so many of us do – and I will tell it in the form of a diary. If I reach a happy ending, this book will turn out to be a worthy roadmap. And who knows, there may not ever be the proverbial successful ending with financial rewards and notability; but perhaps a truly successful life is a life lived. And that, I have done in spades: That map, I can draw with my eyes closed.

We too often tend to measure success by worldly accomplishments, quantifiable achievements, size of bank accounts, social standing or celebrity. Perhaps the true measure of success lies within the openness of one's heart, their eagerness to grow into the best of themselves, their willingness to experience life fully and courage to do so, and their ability and strength to keep going, no matter what. Perhaps success is to live the life we have with earnestness, integrity and awareness. Perhaps a truly successful life is a life LIVED, at every moment.

OCTOBER 4TH, 2011

I KEEP CHANGING MY MIND AND I'M PROUD OF IT

Since I arrived in Vancouver, I have been open to change and unforeseen opportunities. I have put on some new habits and I'm trying them on to see how they fit. My move across the country represents a new volume of my life; not just a new chapter, it's a whole new book. And I want this one to tell the story of when I found my true voice, and used it to fulfill my life's purpose.

Until now, well, let's just say I have been wondering: When does the fun start? Until now, I feel I have been studying being a human being. I have attended life-school for nearly 47 years with a double, even triple class load, which resulted in not much time to play. All work and no play... well, I am ready to graduate, bring my knowledge to the world, and have some fun doing it.

But to get there, I need to juggle my aspirations with the material realities (paying the rent and eating), and it makes for an acrobatic show!

As I mentioned, I have been enjoying considering every possibility to make my new life come true. It is essential that I keep myself open, but this requires quite a process *(for me anyway)*. Every morning *(day, evening and night)*, I think, reflect, write, sulk *(too often)* and panic *(also)*. I chat with my Mom sharing what I think I will try today, what resulted from yesterday, what has changed since yesterday, which thoughts evolved, which transformed, what was silly to think, what needs to be trashed, and what needs to be reconsidered. It's actually kind of funny if I look at it as an observer: the number of days when I thought I had found "it" – the beginning of the solution, the path, the error of my previous ways – are plenty; pretty much every single day has come with an illumination, a crossed out plan, and a freshly hatched one.

THE HOKEY POKEY DANCE

So I wonder what work I should do, what could be my title, where I would be happy, what I could be recognized and hired for. Should I work full-time in any "professional job" for a while, or should I work in a café and not do something I don't like? After all, at my age I want to find meaningful work that represents who I am, but I do need money now, so how about the coffee shop? Well that won't even pay my rent, but I would be seen and meet people. I also question what strategy I should use, which tone to use in my letters and the length those letters should have *(they used to be long, now perhaps they should be short)*. I wonder what group I should join, think that groups really aren't my thing, that groups actually felt good last time, that I'm really too tired for groups. I think that I really should exercise everyday, no, I should not push too hard right now. I should do activities even if I'm tired, but then I should listen to my body when it tells me it's tired – if not I'll get sick again.

You get the slightly neurotic picture? It's funny. Not restful, but kind of funny. Like the Hokey Pokey dance: right hand in, right hand out, shake it all about and turn yourself around. And I like it for this moment because I feel I am allowing myself to be carried by the flow of energies moving in and around me, until I find my new "home". Granted, it's a little dizzying and not for everybody, but through it all, I am making headway. Since I am trying for a new life, I feel rigidity would not serve me. Flexibility and receptivity are more appropriate tools until the right pieces come together.

I am not in the least embarrassed by my ever-changing thinking: I love feeling that what I think I know is malleable and not a fixed thing. Mind you, I have to make sure to edit myself slightly when I talk with people because if I don't, I have noticed I tend lose my audience! Got to give this mind of mine in small doses, get them used to it, expecting it and then wanting it! *(Dear God, I'm a pusher.)*

I think we should all allow ourselves to sway in the wind! There is no shame in it; there is merit. And the breeze can be rather refreshing.

I used to have a boyfriend who took pride in saying he had not changed in years. He would blame our troubles on me because I, unlike him, was changing. He also used to say, in a self-congratulatory way, "You can't teach an old dog new tricks." And I hated it: it made me want to cry. I would try to explain that his premise was wrong, that he could not blame me for changing, that it was healthy, that an old dog should learn new tricks. But I had not grown into myself yet, and did not possess the right tools to argue convincingly, and he was older and way more articulate than I was. During our time together; I learned a lot but not in the healthiest way. In the end, I wanted to change; he did not want me to.

Over the years, as I did grow more fully into myself *(strange expression isn't it, had I grown into another's self before? Now that I think of it, that's exactly it)*, I have become more aware of my own beliefs and of who I am: I have become outspoken. What I know, I can express. It hasn't always been that way. I used to have a tendency to make the opinions of others my own. I believe this was the result of low self-esteem due in part to being bullied when I was young.

Consequently, I lacked screens between me and what others, those who had authority or seniority over me, would express. I was in such need of an inclusive identity that my mind was like an open window through which everything could blow in, and sort of become part of me. "Sort of" because these external thoughts did not sit right with me; but nonetheless I accepted *(invited?)* these aliens in the Temple of my Self, even pulled them a chair at my table, and let them get comfortable. I did not like their company, but they filled the seats. It took me a long time to realize they did not belong and to kick them out.

I imagine this is why most people over 40 will say they would never go back in time, not unless they could bring their wiser older self with them and give it the job of bouncer at the door of their inner temple.

Nowadays, I know what I know. And this includes knowing that some of what I know remains influenced by my life's external conditioning. And this is where there is room for fun. Although I usually have an opinion on things and can articulate and debate my point of view with gusto, I have discovered the joy of being proven wrong! I love the feeling of – after having put out an idea – listening to the other side, pausing, and noticing a shift inside me. It is almost a physical sensation and I can observe the phenomenon: I am changing my mind. This usually makes me smile big time; I find it exhilarating. Among friends, I can shamelessly admit what's going on: "You are right, it is so funny that I was thoroughly convinced and unyielding, when in fact, I was full of it!" Again, in less familiar circles, showing a little discretion is advised unless you want to be regarded as something of a flake.

What I *know* at my core does not change but my opinions can. And it pleases me when I allow myself the joyful freedom to change my mind.

Opinions can change as new knowledge and experiences are acquired. Wise is the one who has the humility to admit to oneself, and others, that their point of view has morphed or even radically changed. Where would progress be without such flexibility?*

* This begs to question why politicians are so afraid to admit they have changed their minds, and why we are so quick to blame them if they do. In my opinion, only incompetent leaders stick to their guns no matter what. If someone's mind is exactly the same today as it was ten years ago, it is actually not a good sign.

OCTOBER 5TH, 2011

THE VISITOR

This morning, I woke up in a truly crappy mood. I have an ill feeling of disdain towards myself in the pit of my stomach. I am disgusted by my own behavior last night and deeply frustrated with my situation. Here is what led me to this seriously uncomfortable state.

Last night my cousin came over. He was passing through Vancouver for the second time since I have moved here. The first time, I gently blew off his invitation to meet because I had just moved, was not settled in and frankly, I was in my bubble of newness and I did not want it burst by anything familiar. I was consciously enjoying seeing everything around me with fresh eyes, reminding myself many times a day to fully embrace this experience because so soon, it would all be familiar. Obviously, family was out of the question.

He had called during the day proposing we meet. He had suggested I take the Seabus (from the north shore to downtown) ; he would pick me up at the docks and treat me to dinner. Sounds harmless enough right? Quite a nice invitation actually. Nonetheless, I decided to tell him I was not in the right frame of mind to be chatty – which, being vaguely aware of my situation, he understood – and that I was physically not well enough for an outing. He gently suggested that getting out of my house would be a partial cure for my ill. I replied that I knew that, that he was right, but that it was still too much for me. We ended up compromising: he would bring sushi over to my place.

So I had my first visitor. It still took effort at my end to gather some enthusiasm. Not that I don't like him, I just don't like the content of my conversations these days. In the course of the past few weeks, as the level of stress has risen in my head, my inner and outer dialogues have been getting more and more dismal. As a result, my newly discovered social butterfly tendencies have reversed to their cocoon stage. I am pretty much back to being a blond recluse. Sure, I still believe I did the right thing moving here and that I'm in the right place, but the balance between fear and faith has been shifting.

I know, you would think: "Well, just talk about other stuff, get out of your little sorry world and just enjoy some purposeless conversation." But nowadays my situation has totally obnubilated my mind and if I chat mindlessly, I feel fake.

After giving him the grand tour of my one bedroom garden suite *(the ground floor of a private residence – a very common dwelling situation in Vancouver given the skyrocketing real estate value)*, we set up the table with all the weird Japanese foods he had generously brought over for me to try, and sat down. Slowly, we started to talk, and I eventually, inevitably, went on and on about how I was struggling and how the stress was getting to me. He shared innocuous stories of other people's travels and business coups and I told him that although I was happy for my friends and cousins success, it was difficult for me to hear about their financial security and freedom. I also admitted that I did not like the fact that it was beginning to make me jealous and envious.

My real self loves rejoicing in other peoples' good fortune, but at this point, I'm getting... bitter. And I don't like it. I also really don't like that it has come to the point where almost anytime I interact with someone, I now have an angle. And this unappealing angle is: What can they do for me? It's like I always have an ulterior motive lurking because I am so needy these days: money needy, job needy... and recognition needy. And this is not who I am – although unfortunately, it is whom I have temporarily become.

By the end of the night, I literally felt sick and nauseous. He had suggested I get on welfare, I had complained, whined, felt sorry for myself, got teary eyed, tried to sell my ideas to get financing from him, prompted him to contact some rich friends for me... frankly, enough to make me throw up. I don't want to do this anymore. I am not this story. I am not pitiful; I am extraordinary, and I have an extraordinarily uncommon type of guts and courage. I am tired of playing the role of poor Annie because it clashes with the very healthy opinion I have of myself. And I am proud of how I have lived my life. It's just that I am in a difficult *(long)* interlude, in a void between what was and what will be. I am smack in the middle of a pregnant pause and I am hormonal!

THE BIG BANG THEORY

That is the fabulous evening that caused my delightful sunny disposition this morning. The only, tiny thread of silver lining was that I had a brief but delicious morning dream in which a gorgeous man and I were in the first stages of flirting! *(Yes, hanging in by a very ephemeral tenuous thread.)*

Brooding as I sipped my coffee, I went to my computer and saw a bulk email from a creative website entitled: *Uncertainty, Innovation, and the Alchemy of Fear*. Whoa! Hold on! That's for me this morning. The article was based on a new book by Jonathan Fields that came out yesterday, and which is entitled: *Uncertainty: Turning Fear and Doubt Into Fuel for Brilliance*. The same author, I learn, as *The Career Renegade (inviting title!)*. Here are a few bell-ringing words I read:

> The ability to live in "the question" long enough for genius to emerge is a touchstone of creative success. [...] Problem is, with rare exception, when faced with the need to live in the question, most people (...) experience anything from unease to abject fear and paralyzing anxiety. [...] There may, in fact, be a very thin slice of [individuals] who arrive on the planet more able to go to and even seek out that uncertainty-washed place that destroys so many others.

I am one of those. I have willingly sought this "uncertainty-washed place" sensing it was to be the petri dish of my new life. Granted, I am not an expert at maintaining serenity while trudging in the middle of this gooey mixture, but I can't shake the belief that my mind's bubbling neurosis is stirring a new mix of elements from which will emerge my new life. Am I about to experience Annie's Big Bang? At my core, I believe so. But yesterday's nauseating episode is still a part of me, and although I am here because I have faith, my despair is so very raw.

ECCENTRIC DESTINATION

For a moment, I float off into a little reverie in which I envision this place of uncertainty as a remote country where fear and anxiety reign, where few visit and only the bravest reside long enough for the alchemy of transformation to occur. Most travel agents will advise against travelling there *(hence the reason I have not had many supporters of my foolhardy choice of destination)* because the lack of security will definitely not provide you with a relaxing experience: This is not where you will let your hair down and sip on a margarita at the beach *(even the shores are storm-ridden)*. It is not for the *Dolce Vita* seekers, not for the faint at heart and one should proceed at their own risk. On the flip side, and here comes the alluring propaganda:

> IF YOU ARE A PROPONENT OF THRILLS AND THE UNKNOWN, IF YOU ARE AN ADVENTUROUS TYPE AND THINK YOU HAVE WHAT IT TAKES, YOU WILL EXPERIENCE THINGS FEW EXPERIENCE. THIS TRIP WILL CONSTITUTE A LANDMARK IN YOUR LIFE AND TRANSFORM YOU FOREVER - YOU MIGHT EVEN WRITE A BOOK ABOUT IT.

I'm in. Despite the fear I am experiencing, I will always be in.

So, this theory that fear and uncertainty hold the genius of creation in their midst, positively resonated with me on this dreary morning and began to tug at my confidence. Wishing to pull myself out of the hole further, I went on to read portions of the author's book via the generosity of Amazon's "Look Inside" feature. Gradually, an interesting lot of emotions began alternating inside me: Excitement – frustration – envy – doubt – frustration – anticipation – frustration – conviction *(frustration was definitely the star of the show).* The accompanying thoughts were a mix of: "Ah Ah!", "That's it!", "Of course", "Exactly!", "Oh, but how?", "That's me!", "Why not me?", "I'm not alone", "Keep Going", "Don't let them bring you down" and "Go girl." Help, I'm actually on the right track.

What I read fit my need like a glove: I learned about the successful stories of people who dared to upset their *status quo*, abandon a good life that no longer suited them, and made the bold decision to follow their heart and passion. This was revitalizing.

After a difficult evening and morning, I am relieved to feel my resolve recuperating strength. For now, I am accepting that this space of uncertainty and fear is part of my environment but I am also determined not to let it paralyze me. I am a venturesome traveller; I will keep pursuing my dreams. It can be done.

Believe in your truth.
Have the audacity to go for what you love,
The defiance to ignore the naysayers,
The courage to face the unknown,
The tenacity to hold on through the night,
And the faith to embrace your wavering faith.

OCTOBER 6TH, 2011

THANK YOU

For a moment, I feel like being grateful. Grateful to all those who refused to help me, who made my life difficult, who did not support me, who stole from me, who turned down my projects, who did not answer, who did not want to get involved, who did not give me a job or a chance, who went off on vacation in the worst of times, and to those who told me I should give up, give in, settle, stop thinking so big, stop dreaming and believing, or at least, to believe within reason. You have played your parts to perfection.

I thank you all because you have brought me to this moment, doing this, writing my book. And I think this is what I needed to go through, the bottoms of barrels I needed to scrape, and in the end, the place where I needed to land: a place of total fearful nothingness and insecurity, and ultimately, a place of surrender. As a person who lives intensely and perhaps, at times, ventures into the extremes of human experience, I needed this. If last week the coffee shop manager had been there, if two weeks ago the investor I was relying on came through, if my lottery ticket had been a winner, I would not have come to the conclusion that this was the perfect time to write a unique book from the middle of things.

I also thank the few who supported me, as I am, with my big dreams.

I thank you.

Sometimes life pushes you to the limit, hoping you will find the opportunity that lies within adversity. If you are either lucky or wise enough, you will – and if not this time, at some other moment in your life. A missed opportunity is not fatal: a window onto what you are meant to do will open again and offer you a choice repeatedly.

OCTOBER 7TH, 2011

A NEW ERA, FREE OF MORAL PROSTITUTION

A loaded title for a small event, but this one embodies a large issue for me.

Yesterday I received a response to a claim I had submitted to the company who moved my belongings last summer. Some of my things were damaged, others lost during transport. Their answer is absurd; it is an insult. They claim zero responsibility, make no apology, and offer me a generous $ 100 in exchange for my signature agreeing to give up any rights to pursue this further.

Of course, as we now all know, I need money in a big way. But this incident brings to the surface an unfortunate history of morally prostituting myself for money. So today, I have decided that it is enough. Enough twisting and bending myself in all sorts of shapes and licking people's boots because I need something from them: it is both exhausting and unsanitary. So even though I need that $ 100, I will not sign. I have reached a limit, and I hope it pays off *(pun intended!)*.

Who knows, I may even use some of my creative juices and pissed-off energy to pen a complaint to the Better Business Bureau *(shame to waste energy on that though)*. And even if I don't, breaking this unhealthy pattern is in itself a powerful decision: enough subservience.

This new stance represents a good step towards my financial independence: I am signifying to the Universe that I will no longer compromise myself for money thus implying that it should now work on a new strategy to provide for me. "Good job girl."

By putting up a sign that a certain road is closed, you compel the Universe to find a new course. Let your intentions be known within and without; life is very resourceful and will clear a new path if it needs to.

OCTOBER 11TH, 2011

HAPPY BIRTHDAY

Today was *(still is)* my birthday. In my mind, my celebration was perfectly appropriate. It was simple and it was good. I spent a calm day, went for a leisurely afternoon ocean walk, treated myself to some take out *(I kindly asked the cashier to wish me happy birthday so I could have one person doing so "live" today: he obliged with a gracious smile)* and came home with two sushi rolls, French fries and a piece of tiramisu. I lit some candles and watched television.

Treating yourself on your birthday does not have to be extravagant. The secret is to maintain a benevolent awareness that the sun rose in your honor that day *(and that you are worth this salute)*, to indulge in something you love *(in my case, a walk on the beach or in the forest with no goal of performance, time limit or obligation does the trick)*, to move slower than usual, and not let things bother you. This should insure your state of grace and contentedness and make it a good day.

> ***Your birthday is a day celebrating that you were born. It is a day to recognize that if you were not on this Earth, the world would not be complete. Kindness of body, mind and spirit should prevail on this day. And if no one is around to pay tribute to your being, make sure to take the time to do so yourself. You are so worth it.***

OCTOBER 12TH, 2011

STILL HERE

You may have noticed that there were a few days without journaling prior to my birthday's quickie comment *(or you may not have)*. As you are just beginning to know me, I would like to clarify that I did not divert from my commitment of dedicating myself to telling my story for two weeks. Although I have shamelessly revealed that I am changing my mind rather frequently these days and I also may have given the impression of being a little bit of a flake, I have not wavered on this. The decision reflected a desire of my deepest heart, and that, I always take very seriously. On the contrary, when I choose to listen to my inner-voice, I can be a rather hardheaded woman *(proof of that would be that I am living in Vancouver!)*.

I did write daily for the first seven days, and it felt good. Having at last initiated the long-awaited process of putting down my thoughts with an intention greater than private journaling, has given me a new sense of purpose. The subsequent days, I spent polishing my text. Surely, this was a little premature but since I am toying with the idea of publishing this, the extra attention symbolized the seriousness of the endeavor.

So this is what I have been up to in recent days. I am still committed, and I like it.

One word that should never be broken is the word we give to ourselves. Beyond all others, which reflect our character to the world, this one determines the level of respect we hold for ourselves, and is vital to our existence. The amount of time it may take to fulfill our promise is an irrelevant human preoccupation; the importance is to stay true to our word.

OCTOBER 14TH, 2011

WHO'S THE BOSS

THE STRESS MANUFACTURE

Earlier this morning, I became aware of something: my stress level has somewhat gone down and I am breathing easier. Of course, it's a wonderful thing because as I said at the beginning, I had been holding my breath to the point of hardly being able to breathe. Really. Breathing was not occurring instinctively anymore; I actually had to make a conscious effort to breath fully, while repeating: "Stop being so stressed, stop being so stressed, I'm too stressed. Oh my God I'm so stressed." Obviously, being so stressed, was stressing me out even more. Bad.

As I noticed I was doing better on that front, I wondered: What changed? And the surprising reality was: Nothing. I still did not have a job, the bottom line of my bank account was the same, and my health was still being an issue. So what had happened? Why was I feeling different? The answer was that although my situation in the world had not changed, something had: inside my head.

Two weeks ago, when I nearly went off the deep end with the news that the coffee shop manager was on vacation and made the decision to chill and write, what I did was change my inner world. And that's how a shift occurred, slowly, day by day. By *deciding* to stop fretting so much and dedicating my time to something corresponding with my truth, I had changed my inner dispositions, and that's what made all the difference. Something inside me had stopped bouncing around.

So I have come to understand that I can *choose* to stay in my center *(and I believe that doing something I love has a lot to do with that)* and not to get lost in my anxieties. I understand that I really do have a choice in the matter. Whether I spend my days filled with anxiety and fear or not, will not affect my worldly situation. The facts will remain the facts in that moment; but I can *choose* to have either a miserable day or a good one.

THE MOOD FACTORY

I remember reaching a similar conclusion some time ago. I once lived with someone who could just push my buttons and ruin my days; and it happened often. One particular morning, I had been in a great mood, had meditated and aligned myself with life, and it happened again. The person came around and got me steamed.

Once I was left alone, I decided to go for a walk to cool off. I began my stroll grumbling about how my day had been wrecked and how once again, my morning efforts to get myself in better dispositions had been razed. After a while, a thought came to me: What do I want to feel today? Will I choose to feel frustration, tension, anger, or choose to enjoy a beautiful day? I realized then that even if the other person was wrong, irrational or abusive, or even if they were right about everything and I was wrong, what my day would be like was entirely MY choice. Ultimately, I would be the one who paid the price for my state of mind.

On that day, I successfully willed myself to switch my mood and it felt like a great victory. I allowed peace and wellness to settle in my heart and belly. I reappropriated my power of mood-determination by refusing to give it to someone else. It was a beautiful day and I was going to enjoy it, which I did. And if I hadn't, it would have been my loss only. Realizing that I had the ability to operate a complete mind-switch was a potent revelation. I could actually really choose what I was feeling regardless of what was being thrown at me. And even though it felt strange doing it, it also felt really good. But it boggled my mind to the point of wondering if I was just fooling myself: Could I really be pissed off one minute and will myself to feel good the next? If so, was I just playing a role? As I pondered this, I realized that no, I was not pretending; my joyful state of being was indeed authentic, and was up to me. Letting someone else's actions determine my mood was an option, not an ineluctable fact; a part of me had the power of decision. Lesson learned – I think.

OOPS, I DID IT AGAIN

Just now, I am letting my landlord above get to me. Ironically, just as I am writing about learning not to let others get to me, this one sneaks in! Typical.

The issue is about my garbage *(from my domestic living, not my head).* The raccoons and black bear love it. They even seem to enjoy undoing the bungee cords I have stretch around the bin to secure its cover – I have now had to clean up a mess three mornings in a row. Since no one else leaves garbage out because of our friendly wildlife, I have asked my landlord to store my trash in his garage, where he keeps his. His response was that this would be a problem. After ruminating on this for a while, I got myself good and riled up and really wanted to let him know he was wrong *(my ego loves doing that!)* and that, as my landlord, this was his responsibility *(perhaps I could even point my finger as I say it).*

Then I heard my inner Wise One say: "Annie, Annie, Annie. What are you doing? Are you by any chance letting someone else determine your state of mind on the very day you're preaching about it? Silly woman. Find your own solution, be self-reliant and let go. You are in charge of you."

"Yeah, I guess you're right."

In the end, I'm the one paying for negativity in my day. I'm here brooding and he is out going about his business. I will keep my organic refuse in my freezer until garbage day and stop wasting precious brain cells on this.

When someone or something is ruining your day, remind yourself, "I am the boss of my state of mind. Under my roof, I make the rules." If you don't like the party crashers intruding in your head, feel free to say, "Get out, you are not welcome." The kind of day you will have is up to you.

OCTOBER 15TH, 2011

ROADMAP FOR THE FORGETFUL

Yesterday's little irony reminds me of an important lesson for all students of the human condition. Listen up and take notes.

Over the years I have realized that we, as oh-so-complex human beings, can have a tendency to be, say, scatterbrained. Speaking for myself, not only do I forget the book I read twelve months ago *(which turns out to be very economical)*, but as well, and less valuably so, life lessons I naively thought in the moment were learned for good. *(As pointedly demonstrated yesterday, such a bright moment can literally overlap a less shiny, slightly amnesic one.)*

Has this not happened to you before? A situation occurs and you come to the same conclusion you had before, only to reproachingly tell yourself: "Why am I doing this? I know it doesn't work!" or "Oh, I remember understanding this before but I forgot" or "Darn, I had promised myself I would not do this again." It certainly happens to me a lot. Actually, sometimes I think that the more I learn, the more I forget, which reminds me of an amusing (pontificating) phrase I once heard: *"What you have not yet learned, I have already forgotten."*

Anyway. To compensate for this most common foible, I have found that we need to take notes. In order to help ourselves, we need to write down what we learn as it occurs.

When we are graced with the clear understanding of a recurring pattern – why we choose the same type of men (women), the mechanics of our eating habits, the source of a propensity for self-sabotage, the cause for over-reacting to the same emotional prodding – or with a solid conclusion after especially lucid reasoning, or with crystalline knowledge of what needs to be done or never done again, we need to take the time to record these illuminations. We need to do so because I can almost guaranty that the light will dim and the lesson will be forgotten. Mysteriously, such is our nature. How did Nietzsche put it? Human, all too human? Indeed.

> ***As human beings, we tend to travel the same roads and repeat the same patterns again and again. We take the same wrong turns, miss the same signs, and get lost the same way, only to realize after the fact, "Oops, I did it again!" By writing down our glimpses of understanding and enlightened conclusions, we draw a useful personal roadmap we can later refer to in order to avoid the same hurdles.***

OCTOBER 16TH, 2011

CREATURES OF HABIT

Yesterday I suggested that most people repeat patterns throughout their lives *(I know I do)*. When we are willing to take notice of such behavior, we might find ourselves astounded by how strongly the undercurrent generated by these patterns actually governs our existence. Consequently, and not surprisingly, we humans are often described as creatures of habit.

Indeed, when we find something or someone we like, we tend to put our hooks into it and are reluctant to let go. An apt and amusing illustration of that came up as I was chatting with an acquaintance just the other day. He was telling me how he had been wearing the same aftershave for twenty years and how on one horrible day, he had discovered the company was discontinuing the product – Oh! Panic. Who would he be without his familiar scent? He proceeded to go nuts *(his account)*, searching frantically for some balance of stock he could acquire. The internet was his salvation and he purchased a large enough quantity to secure his olfactive identity for years to come. This afforded him, as he said, sufficient time to get used to the idea that he would have to change aftershave eventually. Ludicrous, but I can definitely relate. As sorry as I am to admit, I have been known to indulge in comparable neurotic behaviors myself. Haven't we all done something similar? Whether our attachment is to a product or a person, we tend to identify to it, latch on, and hang on. Change is difficult. Nothing really new or too subversive up to now, right?

So here is my existential question of the day. If we are such creatures of habit that we naturally resist change and too often desperately try to hang on to people, things and situations, and even emotions, because they are familiar, then explain to me: Why is it so hard to keep a good habit?

HABITS DIE HARD. WELL, THE BAD ONES DO

Since we don't like change, I can understand why bad habits can be hard to break but once we have acquired good ones, why shouldn't they also be hard to break?

You know precisely what I'm talking about. You may be cruising along on your well-established lifestyle diet, optimizing your fitness with a strictly regimented exercise schedule while peacefully reaping the benefits of your daily meditation-induced-zen-zone for months, and yet a single more or less significant ripple can push you off the wagon, throw you right off the tracks or derail you completely.

There is no getting around it. Truth is: Bad habits stick, good ones don't. Whatever the psychological, chemical or evolutional reasons (learned behavior, effects of dopamine and opiates, or the idea that change is against evolution because our eco-friendly brains like to conserve energy), getting rid of them is a muscle job. We'll sometimes painstakingly need to reach for steel wool to scrape them off our life while good habits slip and slide as if over a fresh coat of Teflon. It just does not seem fair to me. I strive for a society of equal opportunity. But in this Habits Country, bad guys appear to be the stubborn rulers, in most jurisdictions anyway.

THE BRAIN'S PATHWAYS

I see no significant silver lining here. I am the doomsayer. I traffic no magic pill. Neither scientific nor metaphysical treatises on the subject have provided me with a satisfactory holistic approach or explanation to this conundrum. I have, however, come up with a helpful imagery to understand the process of creating new habits.

To introduce this metaphor, I will use one scientific precept: The brain does not know how to *not do*, it only know how *to do*. We can make our brains trace new synaptic pathways by *doing* something new, but we can't "tell it" not to do something *(worse still, just thinking about what we don't want probably stimulates the exact area we wish to avoid)*. With repetition, the brain develops new connections – practice makes perfect.

Now. Imagine a forest through which pass several of your personal trails. Long-standing habits and routine (good and bad) make you travel the same ones regularly, and by doing so, these trails have become wider and more defined. Eventually, their ground is trampled enough that it is without vegetation, thereby granting easy access and effortless use.

When we try to implement a good, new habit – whether of physical activity, thought patterns or emotional behavior – we are making the decision to go off-trail. We are agreeing to become daring explorers seeking a new route, abandoning our familiar terrain. Our first foray into the unknown may frighten us a little, and we may backtrack to the main trail for a while. If we choose to go out into the wilderness again with determination, we scout further, and begin clearing the new path we wish to travel along from then on. The more we use it, the more distinct it becomes.

In actual managed forests, some trails will be officially closed up with posted signs asking the hiker to stay away in order to allow nature to grow back. With time and usage, the newly travelled trail will become better defined while the old one slowly disappears and returns to the forest. *(Of course, every time an unruly hiker ignores the signs, the recovery process is delayed.)*

Maybe this is why, when we make a decision to change a pattern, falling off the wagon is so detrimental. It's like going back on that old trail we are trying to rejuvenate so that it becomes indiscernible. By walking on it once more, the fragile new growth is trampled, and the process set back to its beginning. In nature, it will take years for new vegetation to take over and be mature enough to withhold the passage of an occasional hiker without damaging consequences. For us humans, the necessary period of time may vary *(consult your conscience or a counselor)*. Fortunately, once we have successfully reached the goal of obliterating the old-habit-path, and once our newly created path is the only visible one remaining, occasional straying will not have dire consequences : you can always spot your new trail and get back on.

Creating a new habit is like opening a new trail: The first and most exerting stage will probably be akin to bushwhacking; subsequent clearing will entail less effort. With repetitious travel, only occasional maintenance will be required for the new path to be freely enjoyed.

OCTOBER 17TH, 2011

KINGDOM THOUGHT

Now that I have mentioned Habits Country *(not Hobbit)*, I would like to take a moment to touch upon the peculiar laws governing the inhabitants of this Middle-Earth nation *(couldn't resist)* named Thought. You see, in this somewhat screwy kingdom, not only does democracy not rule, but to boot, certain laws of physics seem not to apply; in particular, the law of gravity as we know it, or more precisely: the mass of various elements is awry. You see, in this land, a tiny morsel of negative thought behaves like some mysterious matter that weighs tons per particle, whereas a ginormous chunk of positive thought has the density of feathers. You can imagine how this would unreasonably tip off the balance of scale. *(I don't think I like this country.)*

When I hear stories about the workings of this foreign society, it is those discrepancies that always gnaw at my *(albeit limited)* comprehension of the world. These incongruities could explain why I have always been bothered with certain principles emanating from the literature of this alien land. What I am referring to is the troubling information we are fed by the plethora of self-help methods touting the absolute powers of positive thoughts and the devastating consequences of negative invaders. Since their theories do not relate to my world, I cannot abide by their blanket affirmations.

Understand, I do not wish to put down the virtues and practices of such positive citizens, but the *absolute* nature of this purported law rubs me the wrong way. The native philosophers of Kingdom Thought would have us believe that negative thoughts are dangerous heavyweight thugs who can throw off a scale just by showing up. The consensus among them appears to be that a commitment to positive thoughts must me total, absolute, unwavering and untainted. Gatherings must be uncorrupted, not even disturbed by a single rebel resident gone rogue. One such dissentive citizen can have the power of throwing a monkey wrench into the whole assembly of positive Thoughts. These authors seem to attempt to drill gravity laws into our heads that apply to matter that do not exist in our surface countries. Something is amiss.

I don't want to believe these are our rules. In this case I proclaim, "above is not as below." Up here, in our surface world of Thought, other laws have to be at play: Democracy prevails, majority rules, critical masses are reached and quantum leaps are made. I have to believe that, if not, I'm doomed. Because despite all my might and focus, I can guarantee that the totality of my conscious and subconscious thoughts will not be positive. I can only hope to tip the scale favorably with thoughts that have equal density: one negative thought equals one positive thought.

I want democracy. I want my thoughts to be represented fairly in a democratic contest. I want a ballot; I want my ruler to be determined by majority and I want to own the responsibility of having elected him, and the prerogative to change as many votes as I want whenever I want and do a recount. This is what I know: To win a game, you need one point more than your adversary; anything beyond that may cause you to celebrate with more exuberance, but regardless, the game is yours.

Let us be compassionate towards ourselves for the inevitable imperfection of our attempts at having only positive thoughts. As humans, we are fated to fail at such an endeavor. But let's always keep in mind that the scale can be tipped to one side or the other, and that we are the ones who hold the hand of Lady Justice.

OCTOBER 18TH, 2011

THE DAWN OF CHANGE

Those of us who believe in personal evolution do work hard at improving ourselves by implementing positive changes in our lives. For some, the harder the work, and the higher the degree of challenge, the more they are stimulated. For others, change comes by with less enthusiasm. But whether we are of one type or the other, we cannot refute that at our core, we are all creatures of habit: We create our groove – emotional, physical, behavioral – and grow comfortable with that which is familiar. Even for those who will argue they enjoy movement and adventure, I will point out that the mere pattern of seeking adventure is familiar – for you, it is not seeking it that would be unpleasant and challenging. Everyone has areas of life grounded in wont.

Indeed, we love the familiar. Our allegorical (or literal) scuffed slippers, frayed blue jeans and favorite tattered sweater are difficult to let go *(in the allegory, the slippers, jeans and sweater can be substituted for a house, a job or a spouse)*. Yet, surprisingly, there will be a morning when you know they have to go, or, for the more passive type, you'll wake up one morning and they'll be gone! The harsh light of this moment of clarity will reveal that life-as-you-know-it will not go on.

You may wake up one morning to realize you can't stand the sight of this beloved shabby sweater, or wonder how you could have possibly felt good wearing this once-cherished dilapidated pair of jeans, or wonder how come you had not noticed that your slippers don't even fit you right. This shocking realization may have surreptitiously crept-up and now stares you in the face. Or, you may have consciously noticed a gentle dwindling appeal over time, and reached this moment of truth. One way or the other, time has come to take action. For the passive type, at a moment you won't expect, the last thread holding your pants will finally snap, the dog will chew-up your slippers, or a guest will have used your favorite sweater as a rag. Either way, they'll be gone. Ready or not, you are in line for change.

THE WINDS OF CHANGE

The universe changes constantly. It wants to grow; it has to evolve. Inertia is an impossibility. Progress is only achieved through movement, and evolution only occurs through change; and change will inexorably take place whether by explosion, implosion, collapse, shift, transformation, mutation or transmutation. By any means necessary, the universe evolves. The *status quo* is not viable for very long, if at all.

As humans composed of the same particles and energy as this universe, we too are subject to the same irrepressible urge to evolve. Our clock ticks to the same primordial impulse. In spite of our torrid love affair with the familiar and our atavistic fear of change, an intelligent inner compulsion coaxes us that we are getting bored and prompts us to seek (or attract) change.

As I alluded earlier, change may come into our life in what could be coined a Darwinian manner: gradually transforming through incremental modifications and naturally occurring choices. Or perhaps, it will come in a more dramatic style akin to the spontaneous morphogenesis theory of his rival thinker Prigogine, who proclaims evolution occurs through sudden leaps. *(Note: this latter method will most likely throw your life helter-skelter and will probably end-up happening more often if we refused to hear the gentler nudges and whispers murmured along the way.)* But one way or the other, change will come calling. Evolution will not be ignored.

CREATURES OF PARADOX

Just to recap and make sure we are all on the same page, let me sum up a few of the paradoxes that make up our human condition:

—We are creatures of habit, yet good habits are hard to keep.

—We love the familiar, yet get bored easily.

—We are afraid of change, yet we can't escape it.

So, don't feel too bad if some days are spent in dazed confusion. Being human is no simple task. Although it may be true that we are creatures of habit, we are above all, creatures of paradox.

A BETTER FIT

Sometimes, before a full-blown wind of change blasts our way, a gentler breeze may brush against our consciousness and introduce us to the idea of things to come.

A year before I moved here, as I was preparing for my ill-fated yet oddly successful business trip to Vancouver, I wrote this premonitory reflection in my journal: *"It is time. Ditch your old shoes Paquette, dump the familiar, thank your fears and move forward!"** Even before I would hear the whisper on the pier, a part of me was already getting acquainted with the changes I did not know were coming. Unbeknownst to me, I was about to experience the critical dawn when old threads become hopelessly obsolete. Unknowingly, I was getting ready to go shopping for a better fitting wardrobe; slippers, jeans and sweater included.

As a matter of fact, the moment I stepped foot in Vancouver a year later, not only had my life changed, it instantly felt more like my life

---

* By now you have realized that I have this strange habit of giving a voice to the various aspects of me. As far as I know, there are two main characters: my ego and my wiser, inner-self. Certainly, this supports the idea that I may be a little zany, but I maintain that I am not exactly crazy. These conversations work for me, as they allow a friendly observer to debate with my bustling mind.

than, I believe, at any other time before then. Regardless of the fears and health difficulties I was experiencing, and despite the unfamiliarity of everything and everyone surrounding me, the extreme makeover felt right and reflected my true nature.

Though we love the comforts of the familiar, change will inevitably come knocking at our door. Whether we open it welcomingly or allow a gust of wind to blow it open, this agent will be let in. It is up to us to set the tone of the visit.

OCTOBER 19TH, 2011

THE FREEDOM TO LIVE AS ME

Throughout my life, I have been a seeker of coherence, an explorer of boundaries, and an emissary of beauty.

For as long as I can remember, I have yearned for my life to be congruent with my being. Despite the elusiveness of such a lofty aspiration, I have refused to believe it to be chimeric. This ideal state of being where the fullness of who I am would be manifested in life has been at the core of my perennial quest.

As I write this, I am reminded of a symbolic anecdote that took place on a White Mountains' road of New Hampshire just a few weeks before my predestined first trip to Vancouver a year and half ago. I would like to say that road trips have always had a magical appeal to me, and usually provide me with my clearest and most inspired thinking. When I get on the open road with everything I need alongside me, I am swept by an almost sensual feeling of exquisite freedom and endless possibilities.

On that particular day, I stopped by a pristine creek running through Franconia Notch. As my life was in its normal state of dissatisfaction and inner turmoil, I needed to connect with the power of nature, and so opted to take off my sandals and walk ankle-deep in the cold flowing waters. The air was rich, the water energizing. The wind roared through the deep woods until it reached the stream, blowing through me its healing gust. Fatefully, nature reached inside me. Instantaneously, it calmed me down and returned me to my essence. I heard the wind telling me to relax, to have faith, that I was loved, that I belonged. I asked for each of my steps to be gently guided and for help in aligning my actions with my soul and spirit.

With my body and faith revitalized, I walked onto the sandy shore, sat on a sun-warmed rock and allowed my feet to dry. I then strapped on my sandals *(brand new fabulous hiking Merrells)*, and as I took my first steps, I had a joyous vivid feeling that my sandals were a natural part of my feet! Still entranced and fresh out of my nature-induced spiritual experience, I mused that this was how my soul needed to feel about my spirit. Holding two fingers together as a sign of a tight-knit relationship, I uttered, "Oh yeah, my soul and spirit, they're like that!"

Yes, I have longed my entire life for such a feeling of correlation and compatibility. I have longed for my life to mirror my aspirations; for my greatest aspirations to be expressed through my actions; for my actions to harness my full potential; for my potential to serve my purpose, and for my soul to be aligned with my Spirit. And this unattained state of being has resulted in a persistent, deep-seated condition of unease.

Up until my daring recent move across the continent *(and even that came with doubts)*, I have always felt I was supposed to be doing something other than whatever I was doing, or be somewhere else than where I was. With few momentary exceptions, I have never felt at peace with life, long enough to truly live from my center. Something has been off forever and I have been searching ever since. Frustration and impatience have been mounting as I hold a profound knowing that I am much bigger than the life I have been living. I have much more to offer than what I have been showing.

For a number of legitimate reasons *(excuses)*, I have been projecting a censored voice into the world. When I think of it, throughout my life, I have oddly either felt as an underachiever – because I was not being all I could be – or as an imposter – because I was not showing up with the full version of me. Professionally, praises and accolades that came with some of my successes were uncomfortable to soak up, even though I craved the recognition. *

Bits and pieces of me have always left a bitter taste in my mouth; I need the full courses to enjoy the feast and feel satiated. I will not rest until I reach this state of fulfillment.

So this is what I am doing here in Vancouver: Ending an era of censorship. This is the ultimate gift I have given myself: the freedom to finally live as me. Having removed the external hindrances from my life, I am giving myself the opportunity to blossom into my full potential. Even though some obstacles are still in place *(some I am*

---

* I remember the house I designed being selected for a Society's House Tour and 800 people visiting in one day, many of them expressing their admiration to me. Their comments delighted me as they were shared but the evening found me perplexed, overwhelmed and crying. I felt the adulation was misplaced or undeserved because I was receiving it for stuff I had done – not even actually done by me: the creation had passed though me and I had simply brought it to life. I wished to be praised for who I was, not what I did. Since I can acknowledge that one of my gifts is creativity, it turned out to be a very confusing night.

conjuring up myself, but I am working on that), I recognize this as the most propitious moment of my existence.

For the first time, my life feels like *my* life.
For the first time, I am living in my truth and that is exalting.

If you feel you should be doing something other than what you are doing, if the impression that your life doesn't reflect your aspirations is gnawing at your core, if you suspect you are not serving the purpose of your soul: chances are that you are right. These feelings cannot be ignored; frustration will inevitably mount and become a destructive force. Pay attention and slowly find a way to express your true self and eliminate censorship. Your life depends on it.

OCTOBER 20TH, 2011

THE BIG REVEAL

It has now been three weeks since my inspired, ballsy, and necessary decision to pretend writing was my job, for two weeks. As I mentioned, the initial and intentional first fourteen days dedicated to pursuing a dream actually did yield some of the intended results: My frenzied mind *(somewhat)* stopped being the tail wagging this poor dog; or if you prefer, this dog stopped chasing its own tail for a while. The reprieve was short lived though. The moment the grace period had elapsed, my mind's hooliganisms came back with a vengeance.

So if my last week's log is actually intelligible, it will definitely be because somewhere down the line, I chose to sort it out and work it over. As it stands today, it is the irrefutable brainchild of my current state of mind: a fine mess and hodgepodge of promising thoughts.

I did stop by the coffee shop after the two-week period, in a half-hearted, feeble attempt at working there. The manager was absent *(I had not called ahead, which shows how serious I was)*, and it was just as well. I really only went there to follow through with the promise I had made myself. I had not been doing well physically and doubted I was actually capable of working at all.

This is a tough one. I don't like talking about this. But in order to paint an honest picture of my life, I am going to have to explain what is behind such statements as *"my health has not been something I have able to rely on for thirty years" (to be exact, more like thirty-six)*. So, I guess I will, reluctantly, sketch my health portrait and then we can move on.

At the age of eleven, I was introduced to a digestive system illness that would be at the center of pretty much my entire life. *(What I mean is the center of my functioning-physical life – although often fueled and spurred by this challenge, my spiritual quest absolutely supersedes this particularity.)* Please forgive me, but I don't feel like naming the thing. It is absolutely selfish, but I fear that doing so would hyphen my own name: Annie Paquette-Illness and I don't want that. Not that I have not embraced my condition – it is a part of who I am and it has come with many gifts – but for now, I don't want to be married to it, and I like my name as it stands. Throughout my life, this illness has certainly been an omnipresent and determinant factor with which I have had to contend. It has, indeed, dictated many of my choices by limiting some options. But all in all, it is merely a fact in my story, which, other than the point of view and growth opportunities it has granted me, is irrelevant. Furthermore, and despite the central role it has played in my personal life, I have not allowed it to determine who I am in either my professional or leisure activities. In the eye of the general public, I am a vibrant individual *(which I really am)* and the picture of health *(which I am not)*. My crashes have been kept behind closed doors.

BARE NAKED LADY

Here is the story.

At eleven, I started experiencing abdominal pain and symptoms I kept hidden for two years *(I was embarrassed, go figure)*. At thirteen, I biked my way to the specialist's office and had the invasive necessary exam *(a short colonoscopy done in his office without a nurse present – nothing like how it is done nowadays)*. When the family doctor called to give my mother the diagnosis *(which was normal procedure since I was thirteen)*, I spied on the conversation and was furious *(something I kept to myself)* that he would talk to her without asking my permission. I was also outraged by the fact that he told her I would just have to learn to live with it because it would never go away – How dare he!

For the next seven or eight years, the painful symptoms appeared on and off. By the time I could drive, I began making appointments with a multitude of holistic therapists in search of a natural remedy *(and I am still on it)*. Before the age of twenty, it began to conflict with my ability to attend classes, which brought on a great deal of anxiety.

Through this decade, I was told more than once, that without surgery I would die. But I vehemently refused to be operated on, claiming I would rather such a finality than have pieces of me taken out. I survived. During those years, I continued to refuse to share with my family the seriousness of my condition and asked for little help other than financial from my father. I isolated myself. A part of me felt I was a failure and that I was being less than what I should have been. What I secretly dreamed of was to escape to a Tibetan monastery for six months. Despite the doctor's gloomy prognosis of permanence of my disease, I intuitively knew that peace within me would heal me. But the dream remained unarticulated and unfunded. Retreats were not so trendy in those years.

At twenty-eight, once more on the verge of death in a hospital bed, the grace of God descended upon me one night, as I lay awake. In the morning, I told the doctors I accepted the procedure. I was choosing to live.

The reconstructive surgery was successful, the feared subsequent pathology results showed no trace of cancer. The experience was the most frightful event of my life. Physically, awful things happened; emotionally, I remained in a place where I mostly refused visitors or help, afraid that sympathy would undermine my resolve – I also probably had a martyr streak in me for the longest time. Psychologically and spiritually, I was broken and at a loss. Up until then, I had identified with my pain and disease – as if they were jealously *mine* – and when I awoke, I was filled with dread at the realization that, all my life, I had been processing my emotions through my gut – which was not longer there. As a result, I woke up not knowing who I was, and unable to feel anything. Scary. But magical. I was reborn with a blank canvas and I was aware of the privilege. This is when I really began the journey to the center of my self. Within weeks, still carried by morphine, I began making drastic changes in my life.

The following years were physically and emotionally very taxing. I had several complications from my surgery, which kept me moored for weeks at a time. I presume my ego still identified with being sick and was taking his sweet time to catch up to my soul's decision to live. Somewhere in my mid-thirties, I remember amazingly catching glimpses of a possible older me in the future; until then, I had never appeared in my own mind's projections as someone older than about forty.

Around the same time, I discovered the gifts that lay beyond the threshold of accepting help. During one of my health crises, I asked my mother if she would come and take care of me. She showed up in a matter of hours, prepared to stay for as long as needed. It was a great healing act of surrender and humility for myself but almost above that, it was an act of decency and kindness towards my mother. I believe I had denied her the right to care for her child. The thought of this remains very moving to me. This event marked the beginning of an ever-precious relationship that has not stopped growing to this day.

In 2009, when I was again seriously ill and was once more unwilling to go back home to let my mother care for me *(faithful to my old habit, I did not want her to witness the seriousness of my condition and feared worrying her too much and also, I anticipated her pity would make me break down)*, a friend told me: "Annie, go home. Let your mother worry, it is what mothers do." That time, I instantaneously got it.

In various forms and degrees, the necessity to dedicate time to my health remains part of my life. Although I have not yet experienced an unimpeded full year, I remain convinced that it will come.

I am not blind to the correlation between my health and my lifelong soul's "dis-ease"; I have little doubt that my perpetual off-centeredness, frustration, and sense of unfulfillment, birthed my condition. Even with the small stuff, my body is a most sensitive barometer. And that's a blessing and a curse. The blessing is that feelings of physical uneasiness frequently appear as reliable signs guiding my steps: if someone is not well intended towards me, if I choose a wrong trail when I'm hiking, if I'm in the wrong place, if danger is lurking, I feel ill. Of course, there are times when I wish my body did speak but it doesn't: like when I want to know if I should work at a coffee shop or not, but that's besides the point. The point is that my health is my truth compass. And since, at some level, I have been living a lie for nearly my whole life, well, I have been sick for just as long; that's where it's been a little bit of a curse. In view of this, I hold great hopes for my future. Since I am finally living as myself, health can only follow.

ONWARD

Health wise, the novelty of the past ten years is a serious case of tinnitus, which has unfortunately further cramped my style. In the months prior to moving here, I also began suffering from constant nausea that appears to stem from mild (occasionally severe) vertigo or dizziness. This had occurred before, but last spring, it became debilitating and lasting (24/7). You can imagine how this diminished state upped the ante of my decision to start a new life across the continent. At the time of booking my flight, getting through my days required colossal effort, but my faith and resolve were greater than my malaise.

During my first weeks here, I saw gradual improvement and was able to network tirelessly to find employment. I firmly believed in the intrinsic healing power that laid within the positive changes I had dared to make in my life. I assumed that at long last, aligning my self with my life would override my health's shortcomings and boost my weakened stamina. Also, and just as importantly, I figured that trying out a new lifestyle that included a paycheck would go a long way in alleviating the stress that certainly had a pretty big hand in my condition.

This "logic" *(and much existential vagaries)* remained the driving force behind looking for a job as a barista that is, until my latest lackluster effort. Since then, my unwellness has overridden my willpower. For this reason, my job searching endeavors are currently tepid and it is also why I am still writing, three weeks later.

Done. What a relief. You have now officially been brought up to speed.

Our body's responses can serve as reliable indicators of the soundness or disruptiveness of what is going on around us as well as inside us. Our physical state can be read as a dipstick measuring the level of authenticity or falseness in our lives. It can accurately reveal whether we are living in a manner that is consistent with who we truly are, or not.

OCTOBER 21ST, 2011

FEAR & CO.

I am crying right now. I have been online watching short videos and reading book excerpts and articles from various inspirational contemporaries, and I'm thinking that despite all my acquired wisdom, faith, courage and illuminations, I have gone off track. Way off track. Again.

My situation is scaring the living daylights out of me. The vertigo and nausea have whirled me into dysfunction. I am petrified. How the hell is my life going to turn out?

Among those pieces I am scanning over, I read about financial health: *"How to be responsible for your finances and free yourself from overspending."* Sarcastically, I give the article an emphatic "Suuure. I agree with all of it! Very judicious and valuable info!" But how exactly do you navigate these waters when you don't have a penny to your name, are too sick to work, have no one to rely on financially, live alone, won't admit defeat, and still want to thrive? Damn it. What is my support system? When can I rest a little? Where is my shoulder to lean on? Jeez. I am feeling so sorry for myself: it's pathetic. I am even wallowing in the regret that I have never focused on one career, or got a degree, and that at 47, I am in this crappy situation *(even though I am clued in to the fact that I have always given my all and done what I thought was best).* And the cruncher is that I *know* this kind of energy does not generate openness, love, abundance or health. This sucks.

THE ENERGY COLLECTIVE

This might be what is getting at me the most this morning: knowing that the energy I am putting out does not serve anyone and is counterproductive to my own goals.

Right now, all I am doing is fight life, resist circumstances, and fear the future. I am living, thinking and exuding fear. Sure, in the overall scheme of things, my courage and quest *(which I think is pretty honorable)* counterbalance some of it, but it's nothing to write home about.

Since I believe we all participate in the global energy of the planet, then I must own-up to the poor quality of my current contribution. Let's face it, in the here and now, I am responsible for putting out crap in the universe. I am one of the grains of dirt in the engine. I am not a good member of the collective.

Even though I still think and talk faith, if I were to monitor the brain-time spent on love-and-faith and fear-and-resistance *(we need an app for that)*, fear-and-resistance would win out, hands down.

I can do better than that. I am better than that. And given that I know that, this is not acceptable behavior.

NO EXCUSES

As I watch previews from the *Wake-up* documentary online – a film by Jonas Elrod about a man who begins to physically see energies around him – I am reminded that I too, have "seen" the energy at times; I have sensed it, worked with it, been affected by it. I know there is more to life than what my eyes can see. I am cognizant of the fact that there are countless unnamed crews working behind the scenes.

As a somewhat awakened sentient being, I should know better than to take life at face value. I should not be getting completely lost in the scenario. I know better than to allow fear to take the helm. So why am I letting my circumstances demoralize and squash me? Why am I sitting here, scared, alone and unhealthy?

This is not what I want.

WDGW?* (WHAT DOES GOD WANT?)

This is not what *I* want, but what if it's what God wants? He might have his particular reasons for me to be experiencing all these hardships. Wait a minute; can it really be that God "wants" me to suffer?

Let's be honest here, shit does happen; bad things do happen to good people. So what gives?

GOD WANTS US TO SUFFER: HE DOES NOT, DOES TOO, DOES NOT, DOES TOO

Let's put God's intention aside for the moment and presume he has nothing to do with our suffering and that we are responsible for everything in our lives; we do hear that often, don't we? That whatever is in our life we have either attracted or created? So this would mean that if we were projecting only good energies into the world, life would be a walk in the park wearing rosy colored glasses? No exception? Therefore, according to this line of thinking, if we are not walking in the park barefoot on frosted pink grass, it's our own fault and we should bear the guilt, right? *(I am particularly good at this practice of self-flagellation – it must be my Catholic descent.)* So what about a sick child or a cancer ridden peace-emanating Lama?

Hmm.

If it's true that we bring all bad things onto ourselves, then God "doesn't want" us to suffer; it's our own doing! Since I have a problem

---

* Just had a novel idea: there could be a bracelet for that! *(I'm kidding right? It's been done with WWJD.)*

with that – that each of us is responsible for anything bad happening in our lives – then am I saying that God "wants" me to suffer? I don't like this absolutism either.

BRAINTEASER

We may be encroaching on one of today's scientific conundrums. Research has shown that the laws of cause and effect seem to breakdown in the world of the very small, that is, at the subatomic level where events seem to be governed by probabilities. The ensuing principle of Uncertainty has established that there is no such thing as absolute certainty. The observation of quantum mechanics has given rise to the possible need of developing a new form of logic. At the quantum level – where particles alter their behavior depending on whether or not they are being observed – saying that something is either true or false no longer suffices. The third option of this new logic –which is now necessary to introduce in order to assess situations of this hitherto hidden reality – is the "neither nor" or "undecided" option.

That being said, if I ask which of these affirmations is true: "God wants us to suffer" or "God does not want us to suffer", the answer is "neither nor". This is the new quantum era; get used to it.

SERIOUSLY

(WELL, I WAS BEING SERIOUS, BUT YOU KNOW WHAT I MEAN)

But really, I mean really, is suffering all bad? I have learned so much through my difficulties that I can't honestly say that it is. Yes, it has been way too hard for way too long, but the gifts are undeniably here. And by the way, what is suffering? Is it what we don't want? What we don't like? What we disagree with? What we don't understand? Did not expect? What is unpleasant?

First of all, I think our initial problem is that we give two thumbs up to joy and peace but try to avoid pain and chaos like the plague because they are unpleasant. By simply recognizing them as part of the deal, as part of the possible spectrum of experiences, we would already be ahead of the suffering game.

If we could objectively consider sadness and sickness as different locations on the gradients of mood and health, it would be possible to simply say, "Today, I'm sick!" or "Today, I'm going to have a really good sad-day", and simply let it be so, or heaven forbid, embrace it. The proviso is we can't allow ourselves to get too familiar with those states and let them become bad habits that will be hard to kick.

Problem number two lies in the dangers of invoking what we *want*. *(I know, I know, if we don't ask for what we want then we probably won't be getting much – perhaps what comes next will nuance this.)* Let me explain. We, as egoistic beings, tend to pray (or focus on, or visualize) for our "wants" rather than "what is best for us" *(we should all strive to become a person for whom those two things blend into each other)*. And that's where we start getting into trouble. Not only because what is best for us *(what God "intends"?)* will always remain a mystery, but also because not getting what you want – although it may constitute a personally objectionable setback – may actually be perfect for either your own growth, or be the best thing for someone else. We are, after all, interconnected.

Since we won't always get what we want, we may be wise to realize that life may not be about getting what we want but rather about what we become while we experience what we get.

In my opinion, the best we can do is to ask for what we want (to set goals) and not get mad if we don't get it. Once we throw it out there, we should differ to the Higher Wisdom as far as the end result is concerned. It's the old adage: Work hard for what you want but let go of the outcome.

'DON'T TAKE IT PERSONAL'

So when bad things do happen, what's it all about and what should we do? *(I'm talking about when bad things happen to "good" people of course – if not, it's called karma. Just kidding, I know karma is an energy and thus doesn't differentiate. But this is not my expertise and I will not tackle the principle.)* One thing we should understand is that there is a chance that it's not personal. Let me tell you about one of the silent cartoons my sisters and I used to watch *(over and over and over)* on my father's old Super 8 projector *(which I was allowed to operate alone before I was five – thanks Dad!)* in the basement of the house. I only recall enough of the story to illustrate my point, and although I do not recall the title, it could have been :

THE COLONY

The movie opens showing bug-like denizens of a forest busying themselves in their little colony. "Men" are chopping wood and building log cabins ; "women" are stirring dinner in large cauldrons over a burning fire. Kids are canoeing down a little river having a blast. We even witness fights between the members of the colony and some rival feather-wearing-Indian-like inhabitants *(sorry, it's an old movie)* living in the same forest. Seasons go by : a heat wave is followed by freezing weather to which succeeds a flood swelling the rivers. Through it all, our colony weathers the harsh elements and lives through the tribulations. Suddenly, all hell breaks loose : the ground shakes, the cabins crumble. It's an earthquake ! Panic sets in and mayhem ensues.

Cut to the next shot. Slowly, the camera pulls back up, high into the sky, and we see that the colony is actually a bunch of fleas living on a dog, and we realize – through the dog's mind flashbacks – that the heat wave was a fever, the deep freeze was a winter walk, the flooding was a bath, and the earthquake was the dog sneezing and vigorously scratching himself.

The moral of the story is that sometimes, the dog you live on needs to care for itself : And whatever the impact, it has nothing to do with you.

THE DYNAMIC COSMOS

Since we know the universe is in constant flux, it implies that balance always needs to be re-established. Perpetually seeking a new harmony from an arising chaos is in the universe's nature; adjustments are forever necessary. An adjustment of the universe may extinguish a few million stars and create a few million more; just as the sneeze of a dog may destroy a colony, and taking a dip may flush out hundreds of fleas.

The Earth, "living on" the universe, is thrown off balance by the sneezes of the universe and must itself seek its own new equilibrium by adjusting: tectonic plates will shift and volcanoes will erupt. An adjustment – a natural disaster – may extinguish a few thousand lives and create and environment that will welcome a few thousand births.

And this logic can be extended to our physical and emotional bodies who, governed by the same laws and subject to constant and countless inputs (not only from electro-magnetic fields but from food, body lotions, cleaning products and emotions), need to adjust constantly – always subtly and sometimes more obviously. An adjustment may result in fever, cancer, unexplained sadness or irritability. Even diseases are signs of the body's wisdom: It's just trying to find its equilibrium. Fighting it may not be productive; assisting in seeking a new harmony may be a better course of action.

We too, are living organisms living on a living organism. Sometimes the earth shakes and the ground we stand on gives out (literally or figuratively), and as hard as it may be for us to comprehend, it's not always personal.

Perhaps when the earth shakes we misconstrue God's intention or misinterpret it as an intention in the first place.

In the movie *Avatar*, the Na'Vi people of Pandora shared great wisdom about this: *"Our Great Mother Awa doesn't take sides, she only protects the balance of Life."*

SUMMING UP (TO THE BEST OF MY CURRENT ABILITIES)

Let me attempt to answer some of the questions and address some of the issues I brought up today. I don't actually have the answers to all of the above, but I can offer partial ones *(which makes sense, because the partial brain I am using as a human being cannot fathom God's mysterious ways).*

1 WDGW?

If we choose to believe in a greater design and call it God (and give it human-like emotions, judgment and desires), I don't believe there is a divine will for suffering. In my opinion, if anything – and in the image of the universe – God wants us to evolve. He might throw us a few curve balls, but it is the lessons that he intends, not the suffering. I cannot imagine him relishing in our anguish as he witnesses our misery while at the bottom of a deep dark hole, but I am pretty sure that he rejoices at the cleverness and resourcefulness we draw from within, as we dig ourselves out and bring our knowledge to the world. Now that sounds more like one of his plans for our soul. The injuries we sustain while at the bottom of our hole, and the time we take to get out, now that's our business. God does not get off on suffering.

2 What is suffering?

Suffering is really just a challenge we don't accept. Until we oppose resistance to a situation, it is but a fact. Once we incorporate excessive amounts of fear to the mix, then it becomes toxic; then we really know the meaning of suffering.

3 Life is all: the good, the bad and the ugly.

Because, as humans, we have a mind of our own and experience emotions, we are pretty much bound to resist and destined to suffer *(I don't think the universe suffers because it doesn't like what's happening).* Whether we suffer a little or a lot depends on us *(and let's face it; humans seem to understand more when they experience pain).*

4 Divine gratification.
Asking, praying and acting for what we want is not the problem; complaining about what we get is. Even though we are often *(usually)* clueless of why things happen the way they do, a little blind faith that there is a master plan can alleviate some anguish. Whether we invoke Life, the Universe or God, if we believe in something greater, then exercising simple trust is sometimes called for.

5 When bad things happen, what's it all about?
First, it may not be personal; it could just be Life seeking harmony. Second, it could be karma *(come to think of it, that's kind of like life seeking harmony on a smaller scale: your personal past and present leveling off)*: the energy you once put out might be coming back to bite you. Third, it may be your destiny: some circumstances may be written in the stars or divinely prescribed. And finally, there may be the possibility of random occurrences. Who knows?

6 When bad things happen, what can we do about it?
Life guarantees disruptions will occur; we can minimize our pain by opposing less resistance. Going with the flow is certainly less exhausting that fighting the current and it *will* inevitably carry us somewhere.

Part of the resistance is attaching a painful stigma to what we qualify as "negative" feelings. A sad day is not the end of the world.

Overall, bad things will happen; what is up to us is how we react. The quality of our own life depends on it, as well as that of the energy we contribute to the whole – our family, environment, the world, the universe. We have the power to determine our response to a situation. We decide how much resistance we offer and for how long; we choose to learn to control our fears or not. We are the ones who decide if our performance will be graceful or erratic. In the end, only *we* are responsible for what we become through what life serves us, whether what showed up on our plate appeared randomly or through divine intention.

Don't take every tremor that shakes your life personally. It could just be the dog you're living on scratching an itch.

Trials and challenges are not necessarily meant to hurt us but rather to sculpt our character and shape our lives.

Sometimes, shit happens. Graciously deal with it.

PART II

After all the mind-boggling reflections that followed my unpleasant morning, I had to make a plan for my day. Here is what I came up with:

—Relax into what is.
—Take time to breathe away the resistances in your body.
—Go to your appointment for financial aid *(yes, welfare!)*.

REALITY CHECK

Well, well, well. I'm just back from my welfare appointment... can I just say it's not for me, and I don't belong there? I'm not even eligible because I have access to credit! It certainly was an interesting experience though.

The lady who was my caseworker *(so funny to say I had a "caseworker")* was absolutely kind. Since I was applying for Disability benefits, I had to share my story with her, starting from my early illness to my current vertigo, chronic fatigue and debilitating tinnitus. I can usually tell this part of my story without getting emotional; it is a story I own and choose to share matter-of-factly only to explain how it has shaped me, and to convey the wisdom it has brought me. But today, I got teary eyed and I think its because I was "using" it to ask for help – something I have avoided doing most of my life.

Despite the seriousness of my situation, the appointment ended up being quite jovial: we laughed at the idea that faith would have to carry me further, and laughed about the fact that I thought I gotten to the point of going on welfare. I told her how I was writing a book, that I had all kinds of projects, and that I had actually accomplished quite a lot in my life. She took a look at my résumé and was rather impressed. I looked at her incredulously and said, "I know!" concurring with the irony and absurdity of the situation. She looked at me and said, "Everything will be fine for you, it will work out. I can feel it." She also told me that, if nothing else, this meeting had made me realize that I was not so bad off. Indeed. My problems are definitely not solved but this meeting actually gave me strength and a bit more confidence. Instead of depressing me, it has uplifted me a little.

One thing is clear: I have to make a shift on the scale of my thoughts: the positive must outweigh the negative. This has to be priority number one. Nothing good will happen until I accomplish this first step.

Also, I have to figure out how to bring my health to a functioning level. I am still certain that it is possible. I can remember last February having a full two weeks feeling absolutely fine, when I was full of energy, and the mere idea of lying down during the day felt ridiculous. Which means, my body can do it! My cells know what to do to create a state of health. It's in me. I just need to prompt the memory of my body, or at least stop blocking what it wants to do. I am certain that it would prefer to be healthy than sick and it is probably thinking: "Come on girl, give me a chance to be all I can be! You're the pain, you're always putting a stick through my wheels!"

And finally, I have to get to the business of earning, finding or receiving money. When I decided to move to Vancouver I had written in bold letters in my journal that my first order of business was to achieve my (financial) independence. With this accomplished, I felt I would be and feel liberated.

Sounds like a plan to me.

Boy! I can't wait until the day I am able tell these stories in retrospective. "I remember when I was so down, so scared, didn't have a penny, even had an appointment at the Welfare Office. Oh my God, if I had known what was ahead, I would have relaxed a little. What a ride!"

Our bodies will rebuild if our minds will allow it.

OCTOBER 22ND, 2011

IS ANYBODY OHM?

A BALANCING ACT

On behalf of yesterday's concluding goals of shifting my thoughts and achieving health, I decide this morning that I have to commit to some kind of wellness practice to promote calmness, slow down my mind, find silence and restore my... balance! Oh my! I just realized... my vertigo... I am off balance! My balance system is off! Of course it is! It's a simple meta-medicine diagnosis. My ego-versus-self equilibrium is off kilter. My mind is "ego-tistically" using a disproportionate amount of my time and energy, and therefore, cleverly, my physical body is manifesting this in vertigo: a problem with your center of equilibrium. Now that's a light bulb.

My choice is to get back to meditating. I used to have a deep and regular practice of it, years ago, even in the midst of troubled times. I have always known how beneficial it was but somehow, little by little, my ego artfully took over: "Not this morning, I really need to make these phone calls early." or "Not this morning, I'm really inspired to write this proposal." or "Not this morning, I did some yoga and it is an equitable trade." or "Not this morning, I am in such a crappy mood, I'll get back to it tomorrow." or "Damn, I was just starting and this person came and disturbed me." Or, I would start meditating and the phone would ring with some emergency or another. And so it is that some time ago, my ego gained some ground to the detriment of my center.

The beginning of this first meditation is a little ridiculous. All the noise of my thoughts: restless. You probably know how it goes right? Your ego is talking to you incessantly about whatever it can come up with. You then interject in its monologue and turn it into an active dialogue:

"Come on, that's enough, where do you get this stuff. Give me a break Ego, go on vacation, go for a hike, smell the roses, just shut up will you?"

Realizing you might have offended him you try to smooth things out:

"I'll give you back your spotlight after I'm done with this meditation. I'm not going to take away your job, will not deny you your value, just step aside for a moment and let me stop thinking."

"I hear you. But did you make a note that you're out of dish soap? You should probably just get a pen and write this down. Then I'll leave you alone for a while, promise. Oh, and while you have your pen handy, make a note that next year, when your Mom visits, she should bring her passport because you will probably take a trip to the San Juan Islands across the border; well certainly you will go to Mount Baker, you can think again about the San Juan Islands, depending on the cost of the ferry." says Ego with a devilish look in his eye!

But I persevere and after a long while *(half an hour or an hour?)* I finally get glimpses of my ego occasionally releasing his grip. Then the glimpses become moments.

My meditation is far from perfect, let me tell you. Negotiations are tough, and what I manage to accomplish is far from what I used to be able to achieve. But, I am proud of my new beginning and trust that if I keep at it, my ego will stop fearing it and understand that I am simply granting him a momentary leave of absence and that he can come back afterwards to take me through my day.

MY OWN ONENESS

So after easing up on the debating, inspiration is released and offers insightful impressions. What comes up is that it is time for me to gently, kindly, harmoniously integrate all the pieces of me. All those pieces that have been part of my journey at one point or another, are requesting to be unified into one, big, tall, glorious, complete Me. I feel myself collecting all those pieces, identifying them one by one: the struggles, the illuminations, the challenges, the pain, the leader, inspirer, discoverer of my self; the pieces of when I gave up, believed, forged ahead, abdicated, gained insight, did energy work, got limber, healthy, sick, was small, big, frivolous, deep, alone, godly.

Now is the time for oneness, for I am greater than the sum of those pieces. Enough of my ego running the show, running amok, running scared and running my life. My ego may be the General, but I am the

Commander in Chief. It is time for me to gather my "selves" into one, whole Me.

With this awareness, I begin breathing in my body and remember when, through meditation, I would breathe into all my bodies, inflating the energy field surrounding my physical body. I used to do that all the time, years ago. "Okay Annie, the know-how is in your memory, access it, you can do it. It is time."

Slowly, my breath expands beyond me, until I reach another familiar sensation : my body becoming shapeless until I lose reference. Where are my hands ? Do my legs start up from my shoulders ? I melt into the ground. It is as if my body collapses into two dimensions, my consciousness floating above. The experience is fleeting, but I am reassured that it is still within my reach.

From this state of abandon emerges yet another known sensory experience. Out of the stillness of my body, I sense a subtle pull – in one direction or another – an intuitive call to twist my spine, or tilt my head to one side, or lift a shoulder ; as if a inner force is moving my body a certain way *(for healing purposes ?)* and all I need to do is let it. My body leads me into the movement it "wants" in order to... harmonize ? Release kinks ? I get into weird shapes, so slowly. At times, when I either fear that my will has taken over or that I have lost the feeling, I shush my mind and allow my body a pause until I feel it again and I am brought back to center.

Thank you.

Thank me.

It appears our ego is a bit of a control freak and power-monger. The more he gets, the more he wants. It is up to us to draft a mutually beneficial and amicable agreement and to keep a watchful eye on its implementation.

OCTOBER 23RD, 2011

GUILT & SHAME

Meditation takes me a long time again today. I almost give up. It's just not happening. My ego is coming at it with a vengeance. But a phrase I heard on *The Biggest Loser (yes, a lot of television-watching going on here – fortunately, inspiration can come from anywhere)* makes me persist: *"I will always take care of me, from now on, no matter what."* And I am rewarded. Once I give up trying to replicate what happened in yesterday's meditation *(a hopelessly vain effort because as soon as you do this, you are trying to meditate with your mind and that just won't work)*, words rather than movement arise from within: Guilt and Shame. Whoa, that's a surprise! I look at them; consider them.

I do remember their mention a couple of days ago in an inspiring webcast *(wouldn't want to add guilt about watching too much TV)*. I had actually written them down, probably instinctively knowing they were important to me, but did not give them further thought. But this morning, they come in loaded with meaning. In an uninterrupted stream, memories of guilt and shame rush through my mind – no, not quite my mind, more like my consciousness. One by one, they line-up and make themselves known. I am showed a string of events only related by one thing: the emotion they generated.

Factually, chronologically, they take a step forward and tell their story: Three years old *(I think it's my first memory)*, something about being put in a crib-like bed by a nurse and forced to wear a diaper during a hospital stay *(I was way beyond that and deeply insulted)*, and getting caught climbing out of the bed in the middle of the night to go to the bathroom. Four years old: probably in protest of starting pre-school, I put on a lot of weight *(I began being self-conscious about it soon thereafter)*. Then they continue: seven years old, nine, thirteen, fourteen, sixteen, eighteen, twenty...

Oh my God, these two emotions *(other than feeling misunderstood and out of place)* are the main themes of my life! On some level, and for the longest time, I have dwelled in, and lived out of guilt and shame! And because I got acquainted with those feelings from such a young age, I now realize that I created and invited a multitude of situations where I either legitimately should have felt guilty or ashamed, or inappropriately ascribed these emotions to some innocuous and forgettable event. Whether guilt and shame were befitting, these are the emotions I chose to feel as responses to things I did, or that happened to me.

In retrospect, I see numerous either deliberate or subconscious, "wrong" choices made to ensure I would maintain myself in these familiar states of being. I cheated in exams and skipped school *(even though I was first in my school)*, was afflicted by *(created?)* an embarrassing chronic illness, and kissed men I shouldn't have *(in later years, slept with them)*. The interesting part is that I made sure to get caught at least once in most deeds. This ensured that I could legitimately feel guilty and ashamed. In other instances, I just carried the fear of being eventually found out, even of trivial acts, for years.

Guilt and shame. They are key. They have been at the root of my *modus operandi* and have manifested themselves throughout my life. In this light, I can also see that by denying myself financial independence, I have set myself up to be abused and/or controlled in relationships; all to perpetuate what was familiar to me: a general feeling of being diminished. Aware that this undercurrent is strong, I shall remain vigilant at keeping it at bay from now on.

The fact that I have now finally liberated myself from the fears of being found out, left out, or kicked out *(the financial aspect is not resolved, but I'm working on it)*, and that I have given myself the freedom to live as me, is unquestionably contributing to my new wonderful feeling of living in my truth for the first time.

I feel the need to harmonize these discoveries through sound and so decide to chant and "ohm" peace into my being. Mentally I state, "I am releasing all guilt and shame from each cell and memory in my body." And I feel it run deep. I am unemotional about it. I just witness the fact that they are in me, that they have prevailed in my life. Then I replace the space they occupied with Light and Love.

Again, thank you.

Yet another key to birthing myself fully into this world.

By paying attention to the general picture of our emotional experience, it is possible to detect a connecting thread that repeats a pattern over and over. The predominance of this motif ultimately determines the global impression of the tapestry of our lives. Once identified, we can pull on the end of this thread and the entire shadowing weave will come undone, revealing the radiant image of our unblemished essence.

OCTOBER 24TH, 2011

DAY BY DAY

Day by day, my recent insights are sinking in. It appears crystal clear to me now that the chief culprits blocking the way to experiencing my best life are Resistance and Fear *(they are probably the heads of their family and use their cousins, Guilt and Shame, to cause trouble – chances are, a bloody horse's head in a bed is not beneath them).* I can feel it in my body: when I give into them, I suppress my true self. When I let them rule me, I deviate from God's plan. Resistance and Fear cause suffering and exhaustion.

Those scoundrels have insinuated themselves in my life and have gathered too much leadership. Their voices may be loud but back when I decided to move here, my inner voice was louder. That's when I fearlessly took the leap of faith. As I said on the first day of this story, I've jumped already. So what is the point of allowing resistance and fear in, after the fact? It is fortunately a little too late for them.

I'm getting a visual here: I'm in mid-air, just off a cliff. After much vacillation and hesitation, I made the decision to jump. With a deep breath, I ran to the edge of the precipice and leaped. My arms are spread wide; I'm smiling, enjoying the freeing sensation of open space rushing against me. Here, I have a choice in what follows.

Choice #1: I realize the stupidity and dangers of what I have done. I begin screaming, frantically flailing my arms, fighting gravity, scrambling to grab onto thin air. All I can imagine is my untimely *(and messy)* demise at the bottom of the abyss. In my panic, I lose all presence of mind and miss the extended life-saving leafy branch sticking out the side of the cliff, and scare off some mythical creature swooping by and offering me a ride.

Choice #2: I rapturously continue to enjoy the liberating feeling of the free-fall. I am exalted by the blissful feeling of being unchained, unrestrained, unshackled. I marvel at the view and revel in the satisfaction of knowing I have defeated my fears. Lucidity prevails as I realize panicking would now be pointless. I rest in my faith, confident that either the ground will be a bed of thick moss, or that I will resourcefully come up with a solution, or that one will serendipitously present itself. From the corner of my eye, I catch a glimpse of a brightly colored bird.

This reminds me of a reflection of movie mogul James Cameron who said that many people jump off a plane with a chute, but not many jump with a chute not yet sown together, knowing they will have to do it as they fall.* I can surmise I am on of them.

AMENDMENT

On the 21st, I concluded my crazy day by stating that my priority consisted of modifying the balance of my thought. I said that my primary issue was to work at making my positive thoughts outweigh the negatives ones, that second, I needed to bring my health back to a functioning level and thirdly, get to the business of money.

I feel the need to amend the order of this plan: number two should be number one. If I make my health number one, it means I am accepting my physical condition and the fact that it is indeed, the primary issue. By accepting what *is* and no longer fighting it, my thoughts will necessarily improve. As for the money, it is pretty much a non-issue until my health is better, so it shall remain at number three.

---

* Seen on *Master Class*, a program featuring visionaries on OWN television.

Sometimes you have to step into the void and have faith that the landing will be soft, that a colorful bird will providentially swoop you up, or that you will actually have time to sow up a chute while enjoying the free fall.

Once we take a leap of faith, we have a choice to enjoy the thrill or give into panic.

OCTOBER 25TH, 2011

OKAY, SO I CAN'T WORK

I feel like grabbing my own shoulders and shaking myself: "What have you been thinking, trying to bypass the central issue? You can't pretend, not even to yourself, that you have the stamina to work. As smart as you are, you can't fake your wellbeing. You've been working yourself up into a tizzy feeling guilty about not doing something you can't do!" But then, I realize that having done so, is also understandable. I don't have to be so hard on myself. I know what I've been thinking. I've been thinking that I need to earn a living *(what a terrible expression – as if we need to do something to earn the right to live)*: having money is, after all, essential in this society. From one point of view, given my situation, not working might make sense but it's a really hard sense to come to.

But I can no longer avoid reality. Even though I am used to barreling through with diminished physical fitness, right now, I have no choice *(well, I do, but I just find this one smarter)*; I need to give myself time to get better.

NEWSFLASH

If I am unable to look for work, then I can't work! Duh!

As much as I worry about living on credit, nothing is going to change for the moment because I can't work! "Do you get it girl? You. Can't. Work. At. The. Moment!"

So what's left for me to do? Take care of number one *(just as I concluded last night)* because without that, nothing else can be done; it's the bottom of the pyramid, the first stone, the pivot, the center of my universe. I can do nothing until I find health (balance) again.

Yes, get better and stop worrying *(this is a seriously recurring theme. How many times do I have to come to the conclusion that worrying is self-defeating before it is a lesson permanently learned?)*. Worrying is not only detrimental to my health, both physical and mental, but if I persist in doing so, I will continue to give out an off-centered vibe. In truth, in spite of all my wisdom, I have been running like a chicken with its head cut off, because I have been scared and desperate. And desperate is not a quality that is sought after. So, if I want to attract the right job, if I want to manifest the fullest expression of myself, if I want to attract my perfect man, then I must have a stable center of gravity. What I mean is: If we attract people, things and event of like frequencies, do I really want what I have been attracting of late? Definitely not.

THE VIRTUOUS CIRCLE

My meditations of the past few days have begun slowing down my breathing and mind, and somehow, a (relatively) relaxed mind has been making me feel like preparing better food, snacking on an apple, spending time in nature and feeling grateful. It's a virtuous circle. My calmer demeanor is also allowing the wisdom of my recent epiphanies *(realizing that not being able to work right now is a fact and that resisting and worrying about it is useless)* to sink in even further.

Even though I have known in the past that taking care of myself (physically and mentally) had to be a priority, it feels different this time. I have now begun the task of sorting myself out, and because of my new choice of living in my truth, I feel I have a better grasp of its significance. Although I know this to be a significant endeavor, and that it will require my full attention, commitment, and dedication, I also feel like it is not such a big deal. I just need to put in the time; I've already done the work.

It feels like I'm at the end of a twenty-five year study, during which I have gathered information, researched, performed trials, had failures and successes, and now, all that is left to do is bring it all together; simply organize the data into a nicely bound book. I just need to take a deep breath and start assembling. It occurs to me the exact same conclusion echoed in my meditation the other day wherein I sensed it was time for me to collect to various pieces of my self into one.

On that day, I felt my oneness, and as I begin taking care of myself, I am feeling my wholeness.

It is important to be able to recognize when the time has come to turn our attention to our own wellbeing. A healthy "me" provides a solid and level base to any pyramid. Any construct built on a wobbly foundation cannot sustain shocks and is bound to crumble eventually.

OCTOBER 26TH, 2011

BLAME IT ON THE MOON

A crucial part of my return-to-self and health-rescue program must consist of spending time in nature. Ideally, coupling nature and adventure. I am a nature lover. Just yesterday, while walking in the tall luscious forest, I could not stop myself from declaring my affection to the woodland out loud, and shouted, "I love you!" to the green collective. Few things move me like nature; and I like nature wild. Hilly mountains, arboretums, built-up beaches don't do it for me; I need soaring peaks, untamed deserts and windswept shores. The unleashed power of a storm ignites life within me. I relish being ravished by the wind on an open ridge. Nature wow's me, energizes me, centers me, and inspires me. This is why hiking is my favorite thing to do. Understandably, along with the whisper of my inner voice, the allure of British Columbia's wilderness drew me here.

The need for adventure is in my own nature. It's in my blood, in my stars: I cannot escape it. My type of adventure does not have to be dangerous *(okay, maybe I like to spice it up with a dash of risk once in a while)*, I am not a thrill seeker; I am an unknown seeker. It has more to do with uncharted territory than danger. I guess I would have been a great explorer. That's why road trips suit me, as well as hiking new trails. If I'm driving to a known destination, I'll map a new route; if I'm on a known trail, I'll go off trail – there are many tricks to temporarily quench my unquenchable thirst for newness.

If I go more than a few weeks without such an outing, I feel my energies festering and I get antsy. Even though I know this about myself *(actually put my finger on it relatively recently)*, it still occasionally comes as a surprise: "Oh yeah, right, that's why I'm impatient; it's been a while since my last outing *(or last storm – it can have a comparable fulfilling effect)!* Must go out."

What I have learned is that it is not just a caprice: the need for opened gates and open spaces is engrained in me, and demands to be heard and respected. Whether I choose to look at it as something I was born with or something I was raised with, the fact remains: enclosure and routine are toxic substances to this nature-loving freedom warrior. I was born a Libra (characterized by freedom and liberty) with a "Sagittarian Moon" (freedom is necessary for breathing)*, a Dragon in the Chinese zodiac (the ultimate free spirit), and with numerology numbers that conquer with identical notions, and I was raised with liberty as a companion. There is no escaping it. In my case, it is not nature versus nurture; it is nature *and* nurture.

THE MAKING OF

If I look to my youth, I don't need to dig too deep to explain this indisputable need for freedom, love of nature and taste for adventure.

First I must pay homage to my mother. She was a stay-at-home Mom by choice and wholeheartedly, and serenely, dedicated herself to raising her children. In our younger days, we were allowed to watch half an hour of television in the morning, and the rest of the day was composed of books and creative toys, arts and crafts *(weekly neighborhood sessions occurred in our basement)*, and the ineluctable time spent outdoors. Rain, snow or shine, we went outside every single day *(with our mother at first and later by ourselves)*. Every type of weather was reason to celebrate and enjoy: puddles were meant to stamp on,

* I took my first astrology classes while living in Sedona. I was fortunate to find a knowledgeable and kind-hearted teacher in Gavin Carruthers. He has dedicated his life to assisting individuals on their quest to align themselves with the purpose of their spirit and offers consultations and classes locally as well as real-time online. He can be found at: www.astropotential.com.

trickling roadside water to build dams, snow was for forts and snowmen, and sun, well, for anything else including building teepees and concocting picnics. We had the proper attire for all weather so that every experience was enjoyable. For cold days, we were equipped with snowmobile suits and boots, wool socks, and a long scarf expertly wrapped three time around our heads: once around the neck, then around the forehead and finally over the mouth and nose, until there was only a slit left for our eyes to peep from. We would often ring the doorbell for our mother to blow our noses, readjust our scarves *(since mittens rendered our hands as dexterous as lobster claws)*, or slip on a warm fresh pair of mittens over our hands and sleeves when they got too wet *(or fresh socks or a change of boots)*. However often we showed up at the door, we were always greeted with love and consideration, and we never came back inside because we were too cold, too hot, or too wet.

Over the weekends, when I was a toddler, my parents would venture off in the woods for hours. In order to comfortably carry me along, they had punched out two holes at the bottom of an old Scout's canvas backpack, allowing my legs to dangle freely while looking blissfully above their shoulders *(this then-innovative contraption predates any of today's fabulous child carrying backpacks – how I wish they had patented their idea!)*. I actually remember the feeling as well as some blazing autumn colors from this vantage point.

From the age of three, I grew up spending summers at my parents' cottage built on the shore of a pristine lake (drinkable water!), up in a remote forest of Quebec. When my father bought the land in 1963 *(I think)*, there was no road to the property *(he also had quite an explorer's streak – see, it's also in my genes)*. Each year, the day after classes ended in June, the car and trailer would be packed up with luggage, supplies, dog, cats, fishes *(sometimes)* and pajama-clad kids; only to return a day or two prior to the new school year. While my father traveled back to the city for the workweek (except for his two weeks vacation), my mother would remain at the lake with the four kids. Once we were old enough *(which, when I think of it was really early – I was probably nine or ten)*, my mother would travel with him, and us three girls (and later with our young brother too) would regularly be left to themselves with this great big world, plenty of food, and a list of chores to complete before their return on Friday night *(yes, it sounds idyllic – much of it was – but there were also growing pains of sibling relationships, which I am leaving out)*.

For months on end, the lake and woods were our playground. We, the kids, would be gone all day, left to ourselves, barefoot in the forest, out on boats – canoe, row boat, fishing boat, speedboat – captains of our time, exploring the world. As early as five years old, I would awake at dawn, quietly collect my fishing gear, swoosh the boat onto the mirror-like waters, and head off into the morning fog. Among the myriad instructions involved in raising resourceful children, my father had taught us how to start a boat motor with a piece of rope in case the pull-handle broke off and how to deal with a fire. We were, of course, also strong paddlers and swimmers.

We played hard but worked hard as well. As I said, chores and house maintenance were part of the deal. My father had three capable daughters (our brother being younger), so it was up to us to do the work: shoveling sand at the sand pit, clearing the forest of fallen trees, painting the dock and decks, mixing concrete, pargeting the foundation walls, etc.

Since we were usually out of sight during our free time, my father had cleverly come up with an efficient way to call us in for dinner: he bought a French horn. We could hear it for miles. All the neighbors knew that when the sometimes-dreaded French horn sounded *(pretending not to have heard it was a poor excuse)*, the Paquettes were being called home.

Even the indoors was a playground. The chalet was designed as a glass façade two-story building with cathedral ceilings *(beams of which were made out of* BC *fir – perhaps my first taste of British Columbia!).* The first level was one huge room, half kitchen, half living area, and the mezzanine was an open space with maybe a dozen mattresses permanently laying on the floor *(a private gymnasium it was).* To give you an idea of the dimensions, the kitchen table was a sturdy homemade ping-pong table with wooden benches along its sides. For the purpose of practicality, my mother had sown a twenty-five feet net that could be pulled from wall to wall – dividing the space – in order to contain the ping-pong balls to one side of the great room when we played. Two tall closets of maybe six feet by three stood in the great room, abutting the bedroom walls. Their top surfaces were on the same level as the mezzanine floor and could be accessed by climbing over the railing. These eagle's nests were a favorite place for us kids. I even have a picture of my cousin and I playing table hockey nine feet above ground.

When I was eleven, I got a 50cc Honda minitrail motorcycle *(my two sisters had gotten one the previous hear).* As for any luxury item, the cost, $ 500 in this case, was half-paid by my father while the other half had to be covered by our own earnings – which keenly developed our entrepreneurship abilities. Indeed, at eight years old, I was a prolific Regal representative – home shopping by catalogue – administering hundreds of orders per year *(by myself, I must proudly say).* Anyhow, these blessed mini-bikes opened up an even wider world.

I was so free: gone for hours, discovering and blazing trails through the woods of the national park that stretched behind the property, pushing up to the last fumes of gas and risking getting stranded. This was adventure. Fear did not play a part *(admittedly, some mishaps did test the limits)*; we had been taught to handle the unforeseen and emergencies.

We were encouraged to seek predicaments for the fun of it. One of our uncles *(one of many: my mother had twelve siblings and my father seven – you can imagine the lot of cousins!)* enjoyed taking us along in his 4x4 Blazer into the forest with the expressed goal of getting stuck in the mud, or otherwise. If we got stuck but could get unstuck in a reasonable amount of time (digging, filling holes with rocks, bridging a gap in the road with logs and branches, using the wench), then we had not been stuck enough and he would push on until we got really stuck. This constituted an afternoon's activity *(feeding bears from the roof of the truck at the dump also was)*.

One summer day, I distinctly remember this same uncle inviting my sister along (with other cousins) on a trip in Quebec's Great North, and my mother asking her brother when she could expect them back. His answer was, "In 4, 5, 6, 7, 8, 9, or 10 days." No kidding. With those dependable words, he left and came back 10 days later. Since there were no cell phones or answering machines back then, and since long distances were pretty expensive too, the established code to convey that everything was all right was for him to call collect, and ask for Bob Dumouchel (a fictitious name). My mother would answer the operator *(live people back then)* that there was no one by that name at this end. They would then both hang up: message received, my daughter is fine, no charge.

My parents really did embrace sharing unique experiences with their children. When a worthy storm would erupt in the middle of the night, they would actually get us out of bed and bring us out onto the screened porch where, all bundled up in our sleeping bags, we would watch nature's outburst as awed spectators letting out a series of "Ahhh. Ohhh. Wow!" with each exploding flash of lightening. Once the show slowed down, we were carried back into our beds.

In this spirit of the taming of darkness *(not that I am now 100% immune to the occasional uneasiness of being alone at night. Television and society have had their effect on me. Although I have noticed that my fear of the dark is indirectly proportional to my own empowerment)*, they would also organize occasional night games, which implied we had to be woken up after the night had completely shrouded the forest with blackness. In this game *(called "branche-et-branche" I think!)*, there were two opposing teams. The objective was for one team's members to catch and make prisoner each adversary until the opposing team was decimated. Interestingly, prisoners were not to be brought back to camp, but rather, they were to be neutralized, which meant tying them to trees, gagged, so they could not warn their teammates of their whereabouts and be freed.

On several occasions during those summers at the lake, and for the sheer adventure and feeling of liberty, my sisters and I would spend the night inside the anchored-down speedboat *(a modest 14 footer)* in the quiet cove of an uninhabited area of the lake. We would bring our sleeping bags, deck of cards, some munchies, flashlights, and return in the morning.

One time, during an overnight camping trip on an island *(where we were dropped off in the afternoon)*, a storm broke out; and I mean a storm. The thunder was deafening, the tent was taking water, branches and trees were falling down; it was a long night. After the sheer power of the storm had rendered vain their attempt at rescuing us during the night, my parents finally reached us in the morning. When they arrived, we had a fire going, breakfast was over, makeshift clothesline were drying all our belongings, and we kind of wondered why they had come earlier than what we had agreed on the day before. Of course we were all right!

My goodness, no wonder I seek adventure and shun restrictions today. No wonder urban adventures are not my style and that I'll take the splendor of an unmanned forest over any city when travelling *(unless the city is ancient and sits amidst an unmanned forest, a desert or at the bottom of the ocean!)*.

I realize today how privileged this aspect of my childhood has been; how my father's audacious allowances shaped me and how I was taught to forever make room in my heart for beauty and wonder, and learned to always show up awake, aware, and with all my wits available at a second's notice. Above all, it instilled in me this irrefutable need for adventure, for pushing the boundaries, and for freedom.

Oddly enough, in adult years, my father would often reprove the fact that his children refused to be herded into society's mainstream and snubbed conventionality, and lamented that having to do things their own way was just making their lives that much more difficult. I remember one day telling him "Huh..., well duh, Dad! Where do you think it comes from? You did this! You raised a bunch of cowboys! Don't you remember? You brought us to our first rodeo! You can't really disown your own doing!"

This streak of nonconformity prominently transpired in the résumé I had concocted while searching for a job in Vancouver. This process of self-discovery had begun by writing a few self-determining and clarifying questions on separate pieces of paper: *What I am, What I am not, What I like, What I do,* and *Where I am at my strongest.* Faithful to my unconventionality, these titles actually remained in the final version. In my then-budding spirit of full disclosure, this is what I wrote under two of the headings. *What I Am:* "A believer in boundless possibilities, a non-conformist who can play by the rules, a person who takes 'no' for an answer only as motivation." *What I Am Not:* "Designed to play in a fenced backyard."

THE FENCE TEST

There are those for whom a fence is an obstacle on a steeplechase and there are those for whom a fence provides a comforting perimeter of security.

I asked one of my boyfriends one day, what he would do if he found himself in a fenced schoolyard? I told him that if it were me, and there was an enclosing fence around the playground, one of the first things I would do would be to walk over to it in order to see what I was being denied. I would appraise, and if what I found interested me, I would start devising my plan to get over, around or under, or to simply remove it. He calmly replied that he would be perfectly content to play with his friends and would not even give a single thought to the fence. We were not compatible.

Maybe Match.com should have the following as a defining question by way of determining your level of compatibility with a prospective mate: *What kind of person are you: A fence jumper or a fence abider?* *

People who do not need to jump fences make the world go round and are good playmates. People who must jump every fence make the world move forward, are not restful friends, and have eventful (sometimes exhausting) lives.

---

* I am definitely not the fence abider kind. I have been known (more than once), when coming across a mountain road sign stating: *Road Closed, do not go beyond this point,* to get out of my car, move the barrier, drive through, get out of the car, and put back the barriers behind me for the "others", who should really not go beyond this point.

OCTOBER 27TH, 2011

HERE I AM

Today I went to meet Count Baker, I mean Mount Baker, in the state of Washington. It's the eternal snowy peak that teases me in the distance from my balcony on clear days. Actually, not on every clear day. It was invisible for many sunny days when I arrived here – something to do with particles in the air – then was suddenly in my face, dominating the horizon like a ghostly apparition. My introduction to this great giant (10,778ft) was so solemn that a proper title, Count Baker, seemed appropriate. Its majestic presence inspired deep reverence and filled me with awe and admiration.

I drove across the border and up to the end of Glacier road at about 5,000ft, the three-hour drive assuaging my thirst for exploration, then strolled in the deeply colored surrounding meadows, and hiked through snow under a beaming sun. I gorged myself on beauty, purity and open views. I swallowed the mountain air gluttonously, satiating my appetite for nature and adventure.

The outing was very taxing physically *(I think I went beyond my limits)*; the return trip required my last drop of energy *(nausea still toying with me)* but it was worth the exhaustion.

Tonight, as I watch television *(supine, immobile and trying to recuperate)*, I see the advertisement for Shania Twain's *Why Not* series. I have been seeing it for months, but this time, a phrase resonates deeply within me. In the voice-over, Shania says, *"All right life, if this is my moment, here I am!"*

And I feel this is *my* moment as well, and I wish to enter it as *I*, a fully authentic, empowered *I*. Feeling the power of the moment, I say,

"Hello Life! Here I am!"

There are moments when life taps on our shoulder and says, "You're it!" Our turn has come. We are given the opportunity to take the lead of our destiny, and our willingness to embrace the nomination is the only prerequisite.

OCTOBER 28TH, 2011

ANCHORS AWEIGH

Although I have slightly up and pretty down days, little by little and overall, I am getting healthier emotionally, spiritually and physically.

I am breaking the chains holding me back.
I am releasing my past and its attachments.
I am coming fully into myself.
I am reaching my state of wholeness.
I am closer to manifesting my fullest expression in the world.
I feel the change within me, a gentle euphoria is stirring, and I contain a knowing smile, in anticipation of some great thing on the verge of happening.

Looking into the sun, new horizons are rising.
I am getting ready to soar, as Annie, free.

"Hurihia to aroaro ki te ra tukuna to atarangi kia taka ki muri i a koe."

(Turn your face to the sun and shadows fall behind you.)

Maori Proverb

NOVEMBER

MEADOW REPAIR

NOVEMBER 1ST, 2011

SHOCKS MAY BE OPTIONAL

Yesterday I drove to the Seawall for a walk. It was an absolutely energizing scene. The winds were blowing harder than I have ever seen since I moved here, the waves were tall and powerful, and the sky a crisp autumn blue. As soon as I stepped out of my car, I heard the ocean roar and felt the wind blasting against my body. By the time I got close enough to see this magnificence, I was grinning from ear to ear. After walking a hundred steps or so, I saw a woman standing there, with a smile similar to mine; we glanced at each other, obviously sharing the same delight. I said, "Isn't this incredible?" and we started to talk.

We quickly swapped our stories. She told me she used to live here but was currently living somewhere in the boondocks after a bad divorce had left her with nothing; she was working on her comeback. I shared that I had just moved this summer after hearing the "Welcome Home" whisper last year, that I had done it on faith. She looked at me wide-eyed, and confided that hearing my story was her confirmation that what she was doing was the right thing – that she would indeed find her way back here – that my story showed her it was possible. She thanked me for being the messenger of what she needed to hear.

As I was listening, I was thinking that nearly every time I share my story, someone is inspired. And not only this story, others as well, on other occasions. Apparently, there is indeed something in the way I experience my life that can be of inspiration to others, and I must keep this in mind. Today, by thanking me, this woman was a messenger for me as well: My story should be told, I must continue writing, even as I remain in the dark as to the exact message my conclusion will provide.

As we were enthusiastically chatting, I mentioned that I had experienced some health problems, which had recently prevented me from working. She said she could relate, because she was just coming out of a bad bout of bronchitis – a regular occurrence in her life. She explained that she was a Type A personality, and that it was simply in her nature to keep going full speed ahead until she inevitably gets sick, which forces her to stop and lie in bed for several days. She described, as a matter of fact, that this was simply the way her life went: Running around full tilt until "The Big Guy" intervened by saying, "We need to do something to slow this one down." And for her, this translated into being struck down by one divinely ordered physical ailment or another. It puzzled me; sounded quite absurd actually *(also embarrassingly familiar)*. If she *knew* that what she was doing would indubitably result in sickness, if she could *predict* that illness would stop her, then why not slow down before it happened and do it of her own accord – and avoid the shock, distress and suffering?

I must confess that I have not been immune to this kind of passive, unreasonable reasoning. Heaven knows I have done more than my fair share of ignoring good sense and making a stubbornly poor show of sensibility, and in so doing, giving ample opportunity for "The Big Guy" to vigorously pull the reins and command an unambiguous "Whoa, Girl!" in order to veer me in the right direction. What follows is where my mind went after listening to her story:

As I mentioned earlier, I had been living out of long-term suitcases for many years before moving here. And although I love adventure, not having my own home is definitely not an adventure I would willingly choose. Honestly *(because I will keep being candid)*, the sole reason for this was a dry well of *moola*, an *arroyo seco de dineiro* or a famine of dough *(pick your choice)*, caused by a series of unrelated financially crushing events. Mind you, throughout the journey, I was most generously hosted in beautiful (exquisite) dwellings. So my vagabondage has been an upscale one, but the cost was my expansion, joyfulness, peace of mind, and sense of belonging. Although no anchor weighed me down, I felt trapped. And for a freedom-warrior-barrier-braking lover of open spaces, this cage was causing deep gashes in my flesh and drained me of precious life-blood. I cried for roots *and* an unrestrained wide pair of wings.

Admittedly, my years of wandering began willingly. In 2002 *(a lifetime ago)*, after a personal bankruptcy caused by unsustainable costs of medications and treatments, and inability to work a regular job, I decided to cut my losses and vamoose. I was in need of new air: my lungs were shrinking and I was choking. So I proceeded to close down my company and consign its significant inventory in an international barter network *(big mistake – despite having done my due diligence, I was taken to the cleaners. The guy was a professional crook who had repeatedly defrauded the government, banks and a sorry group of individuals – who were all suing him – and I was one of his casualties. I refused to play dead, got my day in court six years later, won my case, but the authorities could not find a way to make him pay up: he was indeed a pro)*. In order to be more mobile, I disposed of all my furnishings and "stuff", except for effects I deemed useful or personal, which added up to an impressive number of carefully labeled boxes and plastic bins. Officially, I moved back in with my parents. Semi-officially, I accepted an open-ended invitation to stay at the Massachusetts friend's house I mentioned earlier, where I shipped a truckload of said boxes. Since this once temporary home turned out to be repeatedly temporary and for extended stays over the following years, it will be mentioned time and again in this book. And so from now on, will be referred to as FriHo, MA. (**Fri**end's **Ho**use, yes?).

In 2006, after completing a long, demanding and submerging project, I took a life-assessing, health-restoring summer hiatus in Sedona, Arizona. It felt like home. I met Richard. I decided I would find a way to live there. Until I could legally do so permanently, I was to take as many trips as my wallet and immigration laws would permit. And this meant more suitcases.

Throughout those border-crossing years I was an itinerant: first sharing my time between my parents' house and FriHo, and later including Sedona in the circuit. I was constantly packing and unpacking and, being a nester, I would set-up each of my new dwellings as if it were a permanent home. I was seeking, at least, the illusion of roots.

Early in 2008, after a year-and-a-half long process of preparing my application, I was granted a two-year coveted USA residency visa for "Person of Extraordinary Ability" *(nice for the ego)*, with Sedona as my new artistic headquarters. Unfortunately, and for various reasons, I was unable to take full advantage of this status: money, health, family and Richard issues combined in preventing me from taking more than a few trips (of up to three months at a time) during those two years.

Forward to April 2010: Crossing the border on my way to FriHo after a few weeks spent with my mother, I was denied entrance to the USA. Noooooo! Yes. I was getting my own divine intervention. The "Big Guy" had spoken.

At the time, my visa's renewal was pending, awaiting some final paperwork. What I had been unaware of was my requirement to inform the powers that be of this interim, temporary change of status from "resident" to "visitor". I learned that ignorance was not a defense. I was nearly barred from the USA for five years. Any infringement of the law can have such dramatic results, and the sentence, or grace, is entirely to the discretion of the officer assigned to your case. Thank God mine was in sunny dispositions that morning and kindly informed me of the steps to take to be uneventfully granted passage in the future. Even though I was told things would be fine, I realized with horror that I would have to ease-up on my travelling for some time in order to avoid any possible troubles *(this was later confirmed by a lawyer)*. And let me tell you, I was not going to risk being disowned by a country I loved.

I did manage to keep my cool and semi-carefree attitude during the one-and-a-half hour interrogation. Internally though, I was an utter mess, in a state of panic and disbelief.

Getting back in my car, I could not even properly surrender to my feelings of despair because I had a demanding *(sleet and snow were involved)* nearly four-hour drive back to my mother's place. And this required imposed focus. I did make it safely back, and although I really wanted to give into a dramatic scene, I could not: My mother was already in enough grief over my situation without having to witness her daughter completely falling apart at the seams. In my head, I kept repeating: How much can a woman take? What am I supposed to prove, and to whom? Enough already!

That was the day when the world as I knew it (and wanted it) came crashing down. All my plans for the future were being dismantled in front of my very eyes: "Down went the pail of milk crashing to the ground, and with it my imaginary eggs, chickens and dreams"*. Reality was that despite my dissatisfaction with my situation in general, I did consider FriHo (and the USA in general) as my home, and I was in desperate need of this space to collect myself, reassess my situation *(things had unequivocally ended with Richard in February)*, heal my wounds, and get back on my feet. Ironically, only a month earlier, I had done some intense inner work to finally come to a place of peace, appreciation and gratitude for the security and beauty that I could enjoy in FriHo. I had emailed a friend saying:

---

* From the fable *The Milkmaid and Her Pail*, by Jean de La Fontaine. (Please note that there are many variations on this title.)

I am back in FriHo and my goal is to focus on the only things I can focus on : being here, working on my yoga products, stop fighting my life, appreciating my environment, choosing my daily dispositions. I really don't have the luxury of wallowing anymore, and it is not helping anyway. I hope to keep a positive attitude and not slip into discouragement.

Although the days following the stint at the now infamous "border barracks" were very dark and difficult, something inside me was whispering that this would turn out for the best *(I did wonder though, whether I was being resilient or stupid)*. Twenty-four hours after the incident, I remember tearfully telling my sister : "I can't wait for the day when I will trace back my happiness to the moment my world fell apart and be able to say, 'That's why it all happened ! If it hadn't, I would not have done x, y, z and never ended up here'."

A part of me understood this drastic event was not meant to destroy me but to guide me. As the wise manager in the movie *Maid in Manhattan* says : *"Sometimes we are forced in directions we ought to have found ourselves."*

In fact, in between the tremors of the aftershocks, I began to feel a sense of relief. So much time spent in another country had taken its toll. Although I had never broken any laws, my extended stays had created a baseline of stress and uncertainty that had insidiously eroded my energy. Being an expat definitely did not equate peace of mind : not in these times. Now, reluctantly picturing my life in my own country began to feel like a bit of fresh air. I could anticipate finally inhaling *and* exhaling. "Can you imagine Annie ?" my inner voice softly spoke. "Yes I can. And that's what I want. I am tired of my complicated choices. I am tired of fighting my circumstances."

Yes, clearly this incident had not been a random one. It was a personal message. Quite frankly *(still committed to honesty)*, over the past years,

I had had a growing feeling that something was amiss. Everything was just so hard *(those were signs!)*. I was being relentless in my efforts to build a life South of the border; I worked hard, persevered, focused, visualized, prayed and believed, and yet, was ultimately striking out across the board. Business or relationship wise, nothing flowed. Money wasn't coming, health was not being achieved, projects I dedicated myself to *(brilliantly)* were not materializing, and of course, love, well, we know the story.

Here is what I wrote at the time:

> *So I am living with my mother, taking it day by day as best I can, in her beautiful but small condo (my office is in her bedroom – my room is too small for a chair and desk – not easy for a woman who is used to and needs space). Even though I am getting cabin fever and I am having a difficult time dealing with my general situation – 45 years old, no money, no diploma, no proper job history, no job prospect, no partner, no home, iffy health – and still living out of my suitcases, I believe that something good will come out of this. Of course, if I allow myself to go inward to dwell on my current situation and fear for my future, it is easy to fall apart. But I am pretty successful at not doing it and at keeping my head above the waters of depression. I try not to look too far ahead, and work at my fitness products, still hopping and dreaming to receive the phone call telling me, "Yes, we want your products. Let's work together."*
>
> *The not-so-obvious but clear idea emerging of this whole thing is that "someone" is making me get back to Canada. I have been forced to do something I did not want to do but which makes sense.*
>
> *Perhaps I was not where I was supposed to be in order to live my best life. Perhaps, I was not meant to settle in the USA, despite my will and desires. I did not see myself remaining in Canada at all. But maybe the truth is that Canada is where my energies are. Maybe now that I have accepted my Canadian self, and am*

beginning to embrace it, maybe, just maybe, my energies will be better aligned and allow for a flowing and abundant future to be created and unfold. I am hoping that all my feverish pedaling will finally get traction on the Canadian ground, and bring me to my just destination. Frankly, if all it took were hard work, dedication, faith and vision in order to create, I would have created something good by now. It has not happened in spite of my greatest intentions, actions and prayers. So I guess I have to believe in geography, cosmic and telluric energies, karma, and many other variables that have input in our realizations.

There it is, as of this morning, I have no clue where this is leading me or what invitations will come out of this. I try to live today for what it brings, not only living it to pass the time until something good happens. I remain alert; I listen; I am receptive to unexpected (and expected) opportunities. Of course, I have many scenarios written up in my head: the phone call from the president of a certain company inviting me to work with him, "my man" noticing me somewhere and getting on that wave, or someone calling me to purchase the bulk of my artwork. I can even imagine my sense of relief from having won the lottery... Jeez! Despite all these scenarios, I pretty much know life will surprise me with its own, as usual. *

As a result of being thrown back onto Canadian soil, I have decided to refocus my attention on a Canadian yoga company to market my products. Coincidentally (is there such a thing?), this

---

* Although life's surprises are not always that surprising: Just a few days before being turned back at the border, I had been sitting on the porch with my mother, reading a book in which a man's world was turned upside down by being denied entrance to the USA. I looked up and related to her what I had just read, and commented that I should be ready because this could happen to me at any time. The same type of thing also occurred two days before my visa's renewal was eventually denied. That time, I had had conversation with a friend in which I philosophized that if were to lose my visa I would accept it as a sign that it was time for me to make new choices. So it seems I do get glimpses of the future, which means my silly scenarios may not be so silly all the time.

company was my first choice for a partner when I began my fitness inventions journey two years ago. Funny how things go.

I am planning on calling them today. I have great hopes, which scares me.

We know now how all of this played out and where it eventually led me: Here, exactly where I ought to be. The company I was referring to and contacted that day was the one that first brought me to Vancouver to hear *the whisper.* Although the road that got me here was evidently not designed with the expediency of the shortest route in mind, it certainly allowed me to see a lot of scenery along the way!

The point of this long story is that, just as the woman I met by the ocean yesterday, I too had then allowed "something" other then myself to intervene in my fate because I had not modified its course of my own volition *(which can make anyone spiral down into a state of "acute victimitis").* I had not heeded the warnings, read the signs, listened to the whispers: not all of them anyway. But of course, vision after the fact is usually pretty good. The real strain on the eyes occurs in the midst of the action, when things are not so black and white, and when that line between stubbornness and perseverance (stupidity and tenacity) is blurred. As you know, I am definitely not one to turn a blind eye to signs or a deaf ear to whispers; at the time, my intentions had been honorable and justifiable. I mean, wanting to be united with my Love and working on products that were dear to my heart and good for the world did not seem too disrespectful of life. But sometimes, the next level of challenge is the subscript of the signs; the subtle warning informing you that you are now crossing the border between "anything worth having is worth working for" and "this is not for you".

Thinking back, even though I had successfully talked myself into gratefully accepting living in FriHo a little while longer just before the border incident, I had had that sense that something around the corner would stop me in my current, probably misguided, tracks. As I said, my exhaustion and the endlessness of hardships were telltale indications this experience had run its course, and probably fulfilled its purpose.

But in good conscience, I cannot slip into self-blame on this one *(or any other really; self-condemnation is an utterly useless exercise)*: I did my best with my best intentions at the time, within the choices I thought I had – but I am willing to learn.

Difficulties and challenges are one thing, but a gut feeling telling you something might be off must be given thorough and utmost consideration, If not, an external force my shove you into readjusting your aim.

Targets are important to focus our intentions, but once in a while, we need to walk up to the front of the shooting gallery and make sure the bullseye we are aiming at still has our name on it.

THE SELECT CLUB

A great new prerogative has showed up since I moved to Vancouver. I have had the pleasure, really, of hand picking the people, events, and energies I am letting into my life. I am like a traffic cop standing at a critical intersection telling incoming traffic which way to go, or like a bouncer at the door of a select club granting access only to the best candidates: "Looking good, I like your vibe: You're in. You're not, don't like your attire: Step away."

Starting over in a new town has led me to discover the privilege of such an empowering luxury and it's a wonderful feeling. It also makes me realize how much I have denied myself the right to choose in my prior life. I wonder how many of us consider selecting to whom and what we grant passage into our lives as a legitimate entitlement rather than as an indulgence we can't afford. In actuality, as I reflect upon this, we should be taught as children that being selective is not a luxury but an expression of self-worth. Oh, this is so true... The only explanation as to why I have allowed and hung on to bad energies (people) in my life is because I believed I did not have a choice. I believed that I had to put up with it in order to get what I needed and that I could not find better, which can sadly be translated into: I did not believe I *deserved* better.

I do understand that in a regular life, as opposed to landing in a new city, exercising this right will require a little more finesse and artistry *(there are obligations, families to consider)*, but nonetheless, I am certain that most of us have forgotten, or even never knew, that selectivity is indeed our right to claim. It is a demonstration of the love and respect we hold for ourselves. Certainly, we can all keep it a little more present in our minds as we go about our lives.

Last month, when I did not accept the $ 100 settlement from the moving company, I was drawing from this well of self-worth.* I had felt disrespected but this time, would not submissively bow with my hand out. Today, my resolve was tested again, with higher stakes at play, and I can proudly say I did not fold *(or to be exact, I opted to fold and it was the right thing to do)*. I chose to refuse a loan from someone who was injecting bad energy into my life.

As I was considering accepting, it became evident that doing so would go counter-current to my current outpour of efforts towards cleaning-house of all things negative. A surge of inner-moxie arose and I told myself, "No more. I will not do this again."

---

* Update: I wrote a letter to the company clearly laying out why their position was unethical and concluded by saying I was refusing their offer. They replied (still without apologies) with a $200 settlement, which I accepted. I did so not because I was compromising my beliefs but because I was choosing my battles; getting into a legal round with them would bring me down at the level of their energy. I had said my piece, had stood my ground and was now okay with signing off.

I replied in an email consisting of a polite "Thanks, but no thanks." As soon as I did, I felt a wave of joy rushing through me. It felt as good as if I had just completed some great feat, confirming I had done the right thing. Good job.

On a roll now. I have just made another small but meaningful decision. For the past several months, I have been gathering store-credit cards from different shops – like a squirrel preparing for cold winter days – with the thought that when the time came that I would run out of resources, I would have this meager stash to get me through. But it occurs to me that by doing this, I am living with the anticipation of even leaner days ahead; in other words, I am planning that things will not work out!

Building a contingency reserve may be construed as wise but it also implies accepting the possibility of failure. My brain always gets into a quandary in these situations. Having a Plan B may be smart but it also seems to taint the whole concept of visualizing, thus creating, the future you want. It's a little bit of a metaphysical and quantum mechanics dilemma: as soon as you consider a Plan B, you create the space for it to exist. I can offer no wisdom on that.

But today, I choose to stick with the exclusive certainty of Plan A *(actually, no need to assign it an A since there is no B – it really is simply "The Plan")*: I have decided to use-up all my accumulated store-credit and to move forward with the belief that all things will work out. Failure is not an option.

Just as we select the ingredients we use to create a good dish, we should carefully choose the energies we select to create a good life: bad ingredients will not make for an enjoyable meal.

Be the guardian at the gate of your life. Remember that turning people away is your prerogative – a reflection of self-worth – and not an unaffordable luxury or whimsical indulgence. The cost of not exercising this right is your life.

NOVEMBER 3RD, 2011

MEADOW REPAIR

Here I go, entertaining Guilt this morning. After being properly dismissed just a while ago, this old buddy has knocked at my door and let himself in, unbidden. How did it happen? Easily. Old habits do indeed die hard. It's been about ten days since I figured I had to give myself time to restore my health and it has actually borne fruits, albeit not ripe ones, but for sure, visible nascent ones. I have been doing somewhat better in the past few days: taking care of myself has sufficiently alleviated my nausea, making it possible to enjoy some outings. It all sounds good except that there is now justification for feeling guilty about doing activities unrelated to finding work. I mean, if I have the strength to go outdoors and enjoy myself, then I have the strength to look for work, and that's what I should be doing. There is just no peace with this brain of mine: damned if I do and damned if I don't. It is, however, the way my *faulty* logic has always worked, and in retrospect, I can now qualify it as faulty because thinking this way has resulted in never giving myself enough time to really heal. Fortunately this morning, I have new material to ponder.

Yesterday, I returned to the heart of Mount Kulshan (Mount Baker's original Indian name). I think I am in love with this mountain. The hike was glorious. I woke up three hours before dawn, drove down to the mountain and hiked along icy lakes gazing at glaciers amidst strong winds, rolling clouds and occasional sunbursts. I was alone on the mountain, apparently the only human soul for a few miles around. Imagine. This was definitely custom-tailored for this Dragon's free spirit to soar and for a rapturous sense of freedom.

As I was hiking, I saw small wooden signs here and there planted low amidst the groundcover and displaying the simple words "Meadow Repair". Certainly, they had been there on my previous visit to the mountain but I must have only distractedly noticed them then. On this trip though, the words took on a fullness of meaning and resonated with my heart's healing aspirations. Each time I came across one of them, I benevolently gazed upon the area it was aiming to protect, smiling empathetically, imagining the tiny plants breathing freely, unimpeded in their photosynthesis, stretching out their burgeoning leaves. There they were, existing without the fear of being stepped on, simply concentrating on growing and reinforcing their root systems: grateful of having been granted the time to do so.

Without imposition or demands, and with only two words, these unpretentious little signs related compelling stories of injuries and overuse. This lexical duo eloquently spoke of the tale of someone having mercifully noticed damage; of someone recognizing wounds that needed tending to and who cared enough to take compassionate steps to assist, and allow healing to take place.

With only two words, these signs appealed to my respect in the process, understatedly suggesting I stay out of the way. The message conveyed to me was: "Something is happening here, I'm taking care of myself, rejuvenating. Give me a little time and my glory will be restored for you to enjoy."

So this morning, as I grapple with my guilt for feeling better and not being fully functioning and productive at trying to earn money, I bring forth to my awareness the image of yesterday's Meadow Repair sign. I ponder the message of healing it spoke of, and the feelings of similitude it had awaken in me. As I do so, I am filled with the knowing that this is precisely what I am doing now in my life: I am in Meadow Repair mode so that I can eventually reveal my full potential in all its glory for the world to enjoy.

I feel I was just given a key to a lost secret. This is a pivotal moment in my journey, a cornerstone onto which I can rest. I solicitously remind myself that it is not because I am declaring myself in a state of Meadow Repair that the repair will happen instantaneously. It will take time, and I must kindly, patiently and lovingly grant it to myself. More than a few days of feeling better will be necessary for my root system to strengthen and for my wounds to heal. I have years of damage to repair.

Guilt, my morning visitor, is no longer an acceptable guest and I unaffectedly show him the door. I calmly go to my desk, pull out a pretty pink piece of cover stock and a fern-green felt pen and make myself a Meadow Repair sign, which I post very visibly on the wall.

All is well, my sign is up: Regeneration is in progress.*

Declaring a personal state of Meadow Repair can sometimes be the wisest step to take. This healing pause allows for a delicate and critical regeneration to occur. Once the process is complete, the world will once again be able to enjoy this revival in all its glory.

---

* Note: I have seen similar signs elsewhere when hiking. In Vermont's Mount Mansfield National Park, they read: "Regeneration Area" and appropriately, in the Coconino National Forest surrounding the spiritual mecca of Sedona, the signs state: "Healing in Progress."

NOVEMBER 4TH, 2011

'GET WELL SOON'

Just to confirm yesterday's realization that it's going to take time and patience to achieve rehabilitation, I have spent last night and today experiencing severe feelings of nausea and exhaustion. All I have been able to do is lay down, be still, and focus on breathing delicately.

So I guess I can really lay off the guilt about not looking for work just yet, because I really can't. I presume this stubborn one needed this very concrete, in your face, not-so-subtle reminder that she is not cured yet, and that a day of feeling reinvigorated does not a healing make. I am still undergoing Meadow Repair.

Mother Nature has a pace of her own. Let us remember that one cannot pull on a seedling to hasten its maturity. Under the benevolent gaze of a greater wisdom it will do so in its own, perfect time.

NOVEMBER 5TH, 2011

RESISTANCE IS FUTILE

As I continue contemplating my life from a new Meadow Repair standpoint, the lessons that have emerged, as I tread water in this journey, are becoming clearer. The fear of being swallowed-up is subsiding, as I understand that if I stop fighting the surrounding sea of "isness", it can actually carry me. I am learning how to swim.

The fact is, most themes of my ruminations can be grouped under a single heading: Resisting "what is" is futile. And not only is it futile, it causes pain, fogs the mind, clouds judgment, and devourers energy. Worrying, stressing, refusing, fighting, being disappointed or disillusioned: it all comes down to not accepting what is.

Each time I have found momentary peace, it was because I stopped arguing with reality. Right now, I'm alone in a foreign city, I live on credit, I am sick, and I can't work. It is my reality today; I can state it or fight it. I can also choose to see a different reality because this same situation is also that I live in beautiful Vancouver, with mountains and ocean within reach, that I finally have my own home, that I can enjoy a fresh start, that I am making leaps and bounds towards my true self, and that I am writing the book I have dreamt of writing. What comes into focus is what we turn our attention to.

Regardless, resistance *is* futile. Every time I push back on life I feel the struggle, the tug of war, and the strain. Every time I resist, it hurts. I realize that willing too hard is also a form of resistance: when I seek, search, push, yearn, question ceaselessly to the point of exhaustion, I am unaccepting of the natural rhythm of my life – and most likely hindering its natural course as well.

I wish for my will to subside in order to give way to the flow of my destiny.

I must, absolutely, learn to go *with* my life and relax *into* it rather than stand it its way. As I think of relaxing into my life, the following metaphorical image appears in my mind:

THE COMFORT ZONE

Visualize your life as a wooden sculpted chaise longue *(I know, it's a stretch, but just go with it)*. For the sake of this exercise, it sits in a meadow *(keeping with the Meadow Repair theme)* east to west. Imagine coming upon it, looking at the surroundings, and deciding to lie on your right side – head to the East because you feel your preferred view is to the North. As time goes by, you begin thinking that this is a hell of an ill-matched life-chair because it causes you to wake-up stiff-limbed every morning, and to suffer through agonizing days. This goes on until one particularly sore morning, you decide to stand up and take a few steps back in order to contemplate this contraption of torture from some distance. Reluctantly, you consider that insisting on lying on your right side with your head east, may not be the best posture to adopt given the shape of the chair. Perhaps readjusting your position may relieve the kinks caused by those awkward bumps and moody depressions. Certainly, you think, it's worth a try. Resolutely, or timidly, you seat yourself again, this time reclining on your back, head west, and now facing east. Incredibly, you discover that the previously oddly-angled-cramp-causing-sinuous shapes, knotty hollows and mounds, are actually a spine-supporting-reclining back, a derrière-conforming-scalloped seat, and cleverly-placed-arm-resting swells. Now comfortably resting, you contemplate that although you may miss the occasional Northern lights, this better-fitted position offers you the pleasure of daily sunrises and may even, once in a while, treat you to some spectacular ones.

Eventually, you realize that espousing rather than objecting to the shape of your chair alleviates pain, which in turn allows for clearer thinking. Surprisingly, molding yourself to your chair-cum-life structure also results in more freedom of movement rather than less. And I would venture to think that waking up rested every new day, rather than weary from restless combat, might even make you feel like setting out, and thoughtfully begin designing a brand new chair for yourself.

That's what I imagined when I said I must relax into my life *(a fertile imagination I have)*. I must accept its form (today), lean back and exhale lest I suffer the kinks from bending myself out of shape.

SHOULD HAVES

Within and beyond the land of Meadow Repair, "should haves" should be banned. They too fall under the same heading of useless resistance. Accepting "what is" implies not regretting what is not, whatever that is *(a little mind-bender here)*. If you are anything like me, this means taking an honest look at your ongoing inner monologue. At a time, earlier in my life, when I was becoming particularly well versed in the discipline of second-guessing and doubting myself, I did just that and I must say I was quite offended by the contents of my mind. My spontaneous silent comments sounded like this: "I should have taken a different road, I should have worn more comfortable shoes, I should have brought an extra sweater, or my camera, I should have made this call, I should have written this letter today, I should have ordered three instead of two of this stuff, I should have gone to bed earlier, I should not have eaten this, I should be more active, be more open, be more centered, be less reactive, less impatient, less critical, etc." Wow. Really?

It was obvious I needed to remedy this and so I decided to play a psychological game with myself. I intentionally began practicing flipping every such statement in my head, and they became: "This is the right road, there is probably an accident on the other. These shoes make me feel like I'm walking barefoot, nice. This little chill is quite refreshing. Good thing I did not bring my camera, I might have broken it today. Good choice not making this call, the person was probably in a crappy mood. Good thing I did not write this letter today, I will write something better tomorrow, etc." I even practiced when I got served the wrong thing at the restaurant: "Grapefruit juice? Why didn't I think of that? It's exactly what I want."

The exercise revealed how much of my misery depended merely on what I said about any given situation. This is a lesson I have gone back to often, and I think now would be a good time to review the contents of my inner monologue once more.

Instead of filling our heads with "should haves", let's tell ourselves that we are doing exactly what we should be doing, that our choices are the right ones, and that what we are managing to do in our situation is commendable. Let's implement another uplifting mantra: My decisions are great; what I am doing or not doing is great; my thoughts are great, I'm great!

Resistance** is **futile. Pushing back on life is always a struggle and the scuffle will leave painful marks. Arguing with reality is pointless and leads to exhaustion. Better to try fitting into our life until we can change it, if we wish to.

NOVEMBER 6TH, 2011

VULCAN: THE UNSUSPECTED CRADLE OF YOGA

In case I am being too obscure with this title *(which is probable)*, *Star Trek*'s Mr. Spock used to say, *"resistance is futile" (yesterday's title)* while performing his famous mind-meld. Since he came from the planet Vulcan, and yoga teaches about non-resistance, well, that's where my mind went.

The reason I invented yoga products was to fill needs that arose during my own practice. Although what I do consists more of mindful movements than proper yoga – because I am more of an intuitive than a learned enthusiast – I have a profound appreciation for yoga's wide-ranging benefits.

THE ART OF LIVING

As we learn to breath through demanding poses, so we learn to breath through demanding times.

As we increase our physical flexibility, so we become more flexible in stressful situations.

As we develop fluidity in the transitions from one pose to the other, so adapting to life's inevitable turn of events becomes more effortless.

As we learn to stretch to a manageable level of discomfort and satisfactory reward, so we learn to determine and respect our limits in life.

As we recognize the progress we achieve through the commitment of regular practice, so we integrate the concept that dedication yields results.

As we learn to relax muscles unrequired for a particular pose, so we learn to be more focused on the essence of events, and be less wasteful with our energy in peripheral useless tensions.

As we sit within our inner stillness, we remember the path to a quiet mind.

As we develop the ability to move with grace, our life becomes more graceful.

> ***A mindful practice of yoga can assist in preparing for the business of everyday life. It allows us to experience new behaviors applicable to life's circumstances. It can teach the preciousness and fullness of each moment.***

NOVEMBER 7TH, 2011

THE WINDMILLS OF MY MIND

My mind is spinning.

Just as I am learning to accept "what is" and to relax into my Meadow Repair mode, just as I have decided to put job searching on the back burner until I am healthier, just as I have stopped worrying about the future and am able to smile from within at my situation, I am offered a job: an unsolicited job at that.

It is not my type of job, not a job I want, but it is a job: the first

---

Note: Being an enthusiast doesn't mean I have the discipline to maintain a steadfast commitment. I am seriously flawed in this department; my practice can certainly be characterized as sporadic and is sadly near the top of my list of "should haves".

offer since I've been here. It does have some positive aspects to it, but it is definitely not in the realm of where I see myself. It's mostly a paper pusher's job, with few on-site visits, filling out numbers in long forms to award green-building accreditation to constructors. It would require I study a large volume of data in order to become accredited as an inspector myself.

My head is spilling dilemmas.

My initial reaction, after attending a brief and pleasant meeting with the president a few days ago, was that the timing was off and the job was, for obvious reasons, not for me. *Thank you for thinking of me, I'll get back to you* type of thing. The next day – to keep my mind at ease and not close the door entirely too hastily – I sent an email asking if I could meet the person who would be my mentor, in order to get a better feel of this job I was planning on peacefully turning down. I felt secure in concluding that the offer itself was but a wink from the Universe : a cosmic acknowledgment that I had been heard, signifying to me that my new attitude of unclenching my fists and "letting go" was the right strategy to adopt.

To me, this job offer represented a sneak peak into how things would work in my life from now on, as a result of the Meadow Repair makeover: "You won't have to try so hard anymore; things will come to you with ease. Enjoy this preview." I felt confident I was getting the message and knowingly winked back at the Universe, "10-4, Roger that!"

This was nothing to write about – and I didn't, which is why you are just now hearing about it.

GUILT : BACK BY POPULAR DEMAND

But today, my mind is overwhelmed with unbridled doubt and indulges in confidence-withering self-doubt. I should have known, relaxing had been too easy.

Apparently, Mr. Guilt – prime to remind me that taking care of myself is not a worthy occupation and certainly not willing to let me off the hook so easily – has been lurking back stage, eager to jump right into the scene regardless of the storyline, invited or not. This seems to be a major, though unattractive, trait of his character. Unabashed, he took the floor and is now making his forceful, mind-numbing – but unfortunately eloquent – voice heard. Unrepentant, he liberally shoots at what I thought was my newly acquired bulletproof armor of wisdom, and shreds it to pieces. My ego jumps on the ban-wagon:

> "What do you think you're doing? This job is just about custom-made for you. It is part-time, can mostly be done from home, which will allow you to adjust your schedule to your health. You need money and it is double the pay of a coffee shop job. It corresponds to your aspirations of joining a business with some level of social consciousness; it's about protecting the planet. The people you will meet will indubitably have an environmental awareness and desire for sustainability, and you like that. It is not a dead-end job: there is a possibility of advancement within the company.
>
> "And by the way, since you are always looking for signs as confirmation, this one comes with half a truckload. This job offer comes on the heels of you working hard (your claim) at transforming your negative inner dialogue with the belief that it would attract the right events and opportunities into your life.
>
> "The offer also happens to correspond with your new state of Meadow Repair in which you have released and accepted "what is" without residual anxiety. Just as you stop resisting, this offer shows up.
>
> "Furthermore, when you met with the president, you actually listened with a neutral mind, not wondering "what can he do for me?" and you have been looking forward to such a day for a long time.

"Also, you have an interesting history with the guy. Ten years ago, when you met as you were working as an architectural designer, his supplies company bore the same name as yours. Six years later, when you needed him as an ally for a lawsuit in your barter debacle, you found out he had moved to Vancouver, contacted him and he graciously offered his help. On top of that, last year, he is was the Vancouver contact who informed you that Vancouver was a 1st and 2nd degree city, and prompted you to move even before you secured employment.

"Coincidences? I think not.

"And finally, you've been saying that you would be receptive and opened to invitations. Was it just rhetoric and you can't live up to it? Are you just talking the talk and not walking the walk?

"How can you possibly justify refusing this job?"

Oh my God. Good thing my follow-up email was non-committal and I kept my options open. What *was* I thinking? Here I am, praying to God to help me out and I'm about to dismiss His offer. I feel I'm the guy in the flood joke. Have you heard it? It goes like this:

THE FLOOD GUY

As a terrible flood strikes a village, a man stands on the roof of his house watching the menacing waters surge around him. Being a man of faith, his hands are raised in a prayer for his God to save him. As the water reaches the eaves of the roof, a giant piece of timber drifts about and he calmly watches it float by. Some time later, neighbors row towards him in a boat and invite him on board. He declines the ride, undisturbed. As the evening falls, the man is precariously perched on the ridge of the roof, for this is all that remains un-submerged. In their last ditch effort of recovery, a search-team helicopter is deployed

> and hovers over him dangling a cable, urging the man to grab on. Unwavering in his faith, the man refuses the help shouting that his God would save him. (You see where that's going right?) Well, not much later, the man perishes in the unforgiving floodwaters. As he gets to Heaven he earnestly asks God, "My Lord, I waited for you, why didn't you save me?" and God to reply, "I sent you a log, a boat and an helicopter, what more do you want from me?"

Am I being such a fool? Am I refusing to recognize God's helping hand? Am I standing on a symbolic roof – amidst my own torrents – awaiting an offer that I claim should be more aligned with my expectations of what God's hand should provide? Does this job constitute an unexpected door ajar and it is up to me to see the light and push it open? By refusing the job, would I too, be edging towards my demise?

Perhaps this could be my steppingstone into a world unforeseen? If I choose to, I am capable of creating promising scenarios *(I am very talented at this)* such as having my architectural design talents recognized by a developer and being asked to join in humanitarian housing projects, or going to an environmental convention and being discovered as an individual of vision and invited to partner up with a company eager to market innovative green yoga products. I *can* imagine ways this job could allow me to meet people who "see me" and offer more fitting opportunities.

So, is this my log, my boat, my helicopter? Am I supposed to take this job?

KISS (KEEP IT SIMPLE SWEETHEART)

I must admit, I was expecting something more obvious *(a helicopter would fit the bill for me)*, an irresistible invitation to create or join a project that fueled my fire from the get go. Although, is this a realistic expectation?

But then, am I supposed to be realistic in my dreams and aspirations? *God has plans much bigger than you can dream for yourself,* I do believe that, and that statement certainly doesn't sound like a hymn endorsing being realistic, sensible or reasonable.

So am I supposed to stick with my Meadow Repair program *(I sure am using "supposed to" a whole lot lately)*, keep writing this book, and allow life to surprise me from its generous folds? Is *this* offer from a generous fold? It sure doesn't feel like it at the moment; but I am willing to consider that my perception may be biased and muddled right now, and I am even willing to concede that given my situation, it may be time for me to inject myself with a healthy dose of realism.

I am making this waaay too complicated. I am building this up to an impossible equation when I should bring this data to its simplest expression: 98,638,748 / 49,319,374 = 2. This is a job I can do from home, right now, for twenty dollars an hour. Period. I think that's it. Reality is that I am living on credit and I need money.

Okay. Now that I have allowed myself to wallow in ambivalence, I conclude that I would be hard pressed to say no. Refusing this opportunity would be really difficult to justify to myself and to those around me who are aware of my financial situation.

When I get a reply to my email, I will go forward and take the job.

YES WOMAN

Have you seen the Jim Carrey movie *Yes Man*? It's about a guy who decides to say yes to everything that presents itself to him, and who discovers what life brings if you say "yes" to whatever it offers. Maybe I should just become a "Yes Woman" and stop worrying where this small choice will lead me. How would I know? How foolish of me to presume I can imagine where this turn of the road would lead.

Yes! Keep it simple sweetheart. No projections, no cause and effect, no analysis...

BUT...

But I wish this were a better-suited job. I wish it did not imply memorizing so much material by rote. I am simply not designed to be a technician; I know it is not my role in this world. I live my life "by heart" but it is far removed from *learning* by heart. And actually, I even doubt I would be able to memorize a book of numbers and criteria if they do not relate to my inner purpose or to human nature. *(I could however, see myself memorizing a book of yoga poses – names, benefits, origin – if I had to.)*

I wish this could be a job where I would meet more people rather than mostly work from home, isolated again. But then at this moment, my health is not strong enough for me to commit to an outside job. If I do accept, the president is understandably asking for an honorable commitment on my part since they would be investing time and resources on my training. Which means that changing my mind in a few weeks or months would be unfair and disrespectful, and this gnaws at my sense of integrity.

And what about my health? Am I not just fresh out of realizing it did not allow me to work right now? So why am I giving this so much thought?

Should I be exercising more discernment or do I take the first thing life throws my way?

Is the Universe trying to make it easy for me or am I being hasty?

Should I recognize the opportunity or stick to my recently acquired guns?

Is this recognizing opportunity, or selling out?

Is 47 the time to compromise and become a paper pusher or is it exactly the time to hold on a little longer and persevere?

But then, if this is my opening, why am I so stressed about it?

Why is this sitting so wrongly inside me? Is it simply because I am afraid of a regular job? Or is it my inner voice telling me this is not right?

(I am driving myself crazy... and you too probably.)

I am also afraid that this is not a big enough development in my life for me to write about. It seems that my book will suffer from making this choice. Up to now, the material for the book has been about my bold and gutsy choices, and my *(faulty)* faith in finding my true voice. And just the idea of accepting this job feels like I am folding, giving in, compromising, accepting less than what I know I am meant to be: it feels like it is diminishing my light. By accepting this job, am I killing my muse? Am I dousing my fire? Am I giving up a future better aligned with my aspirations for the immediacy of a few bucks because I lack the strength to hang in there? Am I selling out?

As I consider what I am now equating giving up on my dreams, I feel as if I am loosing my identity. That's what it is: I feel that the prospect of taking this job is messing with my identity. Oh dear, could it be that I am identifying with not having a job and not being a conformist? Am I identifying with my lifelong quest of being on the quest, struggling, fighting, believing against all odds but not getting out of it? Am I identifying with my state of crisis? Most likely, on some level I am; but is this identification strong enough to make me sabotage opportunities that would pull me out of my struggle? Or is my quest worthy and be pursued until I have unearthed my truth?

Oh, can I please stop thinking.

As the morning hours wear down, I wander through a demoralizing battlefield strewn with the carcasses of my army of thoughts. I am weary, dispirited, confused, exhausted, unshowered. I spend the rest of the day doing nothing, sprawled on my couch, watching television. I am treated to such fittingly depressing programming as Dr. Murray's trial conviction (the Michael Jackson case), Herman Cane's sexual harassment accusations, and what should be an uplifting contrast, *Oprah's* "Joy Rising" show where she makes people's wildest dreams come true, allowing them to live their best life – which only leaves me feeling more dejected.

For some reason, my decision to accept this job makes me feel like I have thrown in the towel and no longer have a need for my feisty determination, which is what ignites my spark. I am on my way to submission; I have capitulated, like most people in this world. I feel I am giving up on the fact that life can, and should be, more than succumbing to the demands and conventions of this world. My sacred fire is extinguished.

I SURRENDER

By the end of the night, as I get to the messy business of disposing of the vestiges of the slaughter, and slowly decant disquieting images of the day's events, I realize that my ego's attempts at presenting a reasoned front, have miserably failed. The intel and strategy of this commander were ineffectual in this situation. I conclude that I must fall back on a more primitive, but perhaps more reliable competence: What did the eyes on the ground witness today?

They observed that I was left depleted of life vigor, that I wasted my day, lost my inner smile, did not eat well, and that my tinnitus went up a couple notches. This job prospect is bringing me no peace, nor joy, or anticipation. And despite my faulty health causing a fear of performance, I can surmise that the prospect of a better-fitted job would be cause for some excitement. This job prospect is stressing me out and derailing me from the path of wellness I was tracing with my recent steps. *That* is the truth.

Now whether accepting this job would be sensible or not – and I think it would be, in more ways than one – my reality is that I am not ready for it. Perhaps my nerves are currently too frazzled. Perhaps once I repair them, the idea of this exact same job would not throw me in such a downward spiral, feeling disconnected from my essence.

It is decided, when I get a reply to my email, I will go forward and refuse the job.

Tomorrow, I am getting back on track with my Meadow Repair, confident that I am doing the right thing: putting down the first building block of a healthy and fulfilling life. It appears my ego was momentarily able to set another of his notorious "spin cycles" in motion today. Fortunately, I eventually heard the intensifying rattling noise and successfully pulled the dial.

I can breathe. I am at peace.

When our logic and mind are unable to provide us with guidance, we must remember that we hold within ourselves the ultimate navigation tool. Our inner compass faithfully relays data in the form of emotions, physical sensations and psychological states. When we can't think straight and are in need of finding our magnetic North, the best thing to do is to stand still and get back to basics by asking ourselves: How does this* feel*?

NOVEMBER 8TH, 2011

THE MORNING AFTER

With a peaceful heart and a pacified mind, I slept better last night. I realize now that yesterday's bewilderment resulted from a hat trick of wrong-for-now aspects. Mentally, emotionally and physically, I could not handle the prospect of getting on board with this job; this was at once conviction-crushing, hope-annihilating and nerve-grating.

This morning, just to support my belief that if at least one of those three negative aspects was removed from the equation I could muster the stamina to handle a job, I sent an email to the CEO of a yoga company – with whom I have had previous dealings – and offered my services. I doubt it will yield anything immediate but I suspect that in the event of an affirmative response, it will not send me into total panic.

Now, is it a trick of my ego in an attempt to justify yesterday's refusal, or is it a sound knowing? Regardless, all I can do is believe in myself. I have been proven time and time again that my instinctual responses and inner voice can be relied upon. Generally, confusion only arises *after* they have made themselves heard, which is when I unfortunately too often choose to defer to my ego and mind to debate the validity of those intuitive responses.

Stay connected within, believe in your choices, and trust life to unfold as it should.

NOVEMBER 9TH, 2011

THE FIELD OF DREAMS

This morning may be a good time for one of those couch-sessions where I will expand on the origins of the deep misunderstanding and disappointment in humanity that have plagued my life until my late thirties. The turn of the millennium is when I finally opened my heart to loving humans, flawed as they were, and accepted to be one amongst them. I have even developed a genuine appreciation for these fascinating earthly creatures. We are all endearing little case studies – granted, some more endearing than others.

As I mentioned, I have stood as a hypersensitive observer of perplexing human behaviors from my earliest days. At home and at school, I was confused and dismayed by the cluelessness and affects of my fellow humans. Temper tantrums were puzzling, feuds and hostilities devastating, lack of empathy and goodwill pained and disconcerted me, raised voices shook my core, and anger filled me with fright. Through the years, I cried more from my broken heart and disillusioned soul than from any emotional or physical pain I endured.

This separation I created between myself and "the others" certainly explains why I grew up without ever having a true confident, a best buddy, a BFF. I never found anyone I could trust with my deepest thoughts, that is, until I met Richard *(which is one of the reasons he was so hard to let go)*. Each beginning of a new school year came with the hope and burden of finding a friend, and with an encouraging pep talk from my parents telling me this could be the year – sadly, it never was. This sense of distantiation and isolation, of course, contributed to turning me into the perfect target for bullying.

BULLSEYE FOR BULLIES

I do have some legitimate justification for my grievances. First of all, being the third girl in my family implies that I have two older sisters. Growing up, the general picture was that, naturally, I wanted to follow them around and I would even at times plead for it; and, I guess understandably too, they would devise plans to literally run away from me. My parents would now and again force them to take me along, and they would usually comply although with a lot of resentment. Once alone, they made sure I knew how much they despised their assigned duty of babysitting.

In other situations, the bullying was a shared experience. For instance, when walking to and from school as children, two neighborhood brothers regularly pelted my sister and I with rotten crabapples. We always approached the infamous street corner – where they usually stood – with caution, and dreaded their presence.

In elementary school I was a very successful student: always the first kid in my class. In fact, I skipped 4th grade after the principal had urged my parents to make me skip 1st, 2nd and 3rd grade. Teachers liked me; I guess being mature made me stand out. I was pretty good in sports and had lots of boyfriends – no BFF, but lots of boyfriends. Unfortunately, this "success" was turned against me in my first year of high school. Mid year, this girl, who really disliked me, decided to create a gang: the GCAP (French acronym for: *Gang Contre* [against] *Annie Paquette*). At first members where limited to her closest companions, but in a short amount of time, membership increased to unsettling proportions. In order to identify their allegiance, individuals who joined actually wore badges she had designed. This girl began threatening kids who did not enlist, and eventually – I don't remember how, she was anything but a popular girl – she got to my closest friends. They came to me with apologies, and contritely explained they had no choice but to join the group. I told them I understood, which I empathetically did, and off they went, no longer allowed to associate or even talk to me. *(Heartbreaking isn't it?)*

As a result, you can imagine what kind of equation was imprinted in my brain: success = being hated + rejection + isolation. Nice. No wonder that later in life, all my endeavors miscarried on the brink on success: I was programmed to avoid it.

The following school year, I convinced myself I was not smart enough to understand some of the curriculum, and fell behind. I was no longer the first student of the school.

Finally, throughout high school, I was privy to the age-old clash between French and English – this is part of the history of Quebec. The building was divided in two sections, one French one English, and the passage between the two was guarded by dutiful security guards whose job was to prevent any student from crossing the boundary – which, of course, some did, and vandalized the other side. At some point, if I remember correctly, bus stop fights and bus ride bullying became such a problem that new schooling hours were implemented so that French and English would not share the same ride.

Sports matches between the two factions were, to say the least, intense encounters.

So my disenchantment with humans was fueled by two sources: one acquired from being bullied and misunderstood, and the other, innate to my soul's incarnation, and manifested in my hyper-perceptivity and precocious empathy for humans.

To give you an idea of the precociousness, and as crazy has it sounds now, I can recall a conversation with my 6th grade teacher. Even as a ten year old, I felt a deep affinity with this vivacious, thoughtful man; he had a light in his eyes I adored. At the time of that conversation, he was expecting (or had just had) his second child and, sensing his anxieties, I explained to him how this addition would change the dynamic of his family, and that it would require some time and adjustments. I reassured him that his apprehensions were legitimate. Really, I told him that.

I kept in touch with him, and the story goes that for several years, I occasionally visited my old teacher at his house. What happened next, was a heartbreak of sorts: On the occasion of one of my visits, while we were chatting and he was playfully entertaining his very cute youngest girl, I remember his slightly overweight oldest daughter coming into the living room. She wanted to show him a collage she had just completed. He looked at her impatiently, told her she had made a mess with the glue and bits of paper, and that she was supposed to have been cleaning up; she was sent to her room. The little girl was devastated and so was I. I did not return for several years until one day, I visited with him once more. As I arrived, I rang the doorbell; his wife greeted me, informed me he was in the basement, and invited me to go see him. I walked down the stairs and was shocked: He was sitting on a large leather sofa-chair – which I presumed was his well-worn personal throne – he was fat, and sipping on a two-liter bottle of Pepsi. He did not get up as I walked in and greeted me with little enthusiasm, and I immediately noticed the light was gone from his eyes. We chatted a little about nothing important and I left, heartbroken, never to have a conversation with him again.

This is how my story played right into the hands of my raw sensitivities *(which figures – our life-paths usually take us through the darkest and most uncertain areas of our beings in order to give us the opportunity to turn them into bright and safe neighborhoods).*

I feel certain that countless people have worse stories to tell than mine, and that they went on to thrive in the world without being too affected. They were probably better equipped to put up walls of protection around themselves, or even had the spunk to flip anyone who would give them a hard time. As far as I am concerned, I was always better at absorbing hurt rather than flushing it. Not the best way to deal with things.

Plaguing as it was, my disappointment in humanity was also the wellspring of my heightened consciousness. And I would not want my awareness to be anywhere other than where it is right now.

WHAT DREAMS ARE MADE OF

Well, I am not quite referring to the romantic notion of dreams but rather as a breeding ground where the story of a wounded soul is free to flourish. The oneiric tapestry that is woven in my sleep by the uninhibited hands of my psyche is a powerful reminder that I still carry resentment for affronts and dismissals of younger days. Although it paints a surrealist picture where characters and events blur the lines between past and present, real and fabled, possible and implausible, the feelings that linger in my awaken state are vividly familiar and well grounded in my reality.

Such were last night's wanderings of my mind and I awoke, yet again, with feelings of being unvalued, unrecognized, inadequate and unseen.

I really want to clean up those feelings. Rancor and bitterness, conscious or subconscious, past or present *(admittedly, I still have a few contemporary hiccups to sort out)*, have no place in the life I am building now; I wish to transcend them. I know they are hindering my expansion. Every time my body is twinged by one of these feelings, or whenever I allow a judgmental thought to invade my mind, I feel my inner smile retracting, my body contracting and my possibilities diminishing.

I understand today that what I then perceived as mean-spirited, dismissive or contemptuous behaviors, was not personal. And as true as this was then, so too it is now. When I feel someone's action is hurtful to me, I must remind myself that it is about them, and not actually about me. They are simply being who they are, on their own path in this life, playing their own roles perfectly. And in doing so, past and present antagonists have participated in my process of becoming the greatest version of me.

I don't have to like everything everyone does, or has done, but I want to love everything they are. I wish for love to move in and dissolve all of my hurts, blame, sadness, and desire for things to be different than what they were, or are, for this only brings me suffering.

I will go out of my comfort zone here and make this heartfelt statement: "Thank you brothers and sisters of my life for participating in making me the greatest me, and playing your roles so well. I love you!" How's that! *(And I really do mean it. I am feeling it in my core.)*

Forgiveness is the answer to everything. *

---

* Principle of life set forth in *A Course in Miracles.*

NOVEMBER 10TH, 2011

THE CLIMB

THE GROUSE GRIND

Today I went for a strenuous hike. Strenuous for me anyway. People in great shape passed me easily, breathing hard but unstoppable. This particular trail is a popular training circuit here in North Vancouver. This hike is the reference point of the sport community and consensus is that you should make this hike in under one and a half hour if you want to participate in many other fitness groups' activities; it took me two and a quarter hours. This made me realize I still had a long way to go before I am even close to being in-shape, and it also made me feel mighty proud that I was able to climb the trail all the way to the top (2,800ft in 2.2 miles). The last time I hiked 2,800ft was nearly ten years ago when I was the self-proclaimed Queen of Mount Mansfield of Stowe, Vermont; and that was over 3.3 miles of trail, not 2.2.

ALL THINGS ARE NOT CREATED EQUAL, OR ARE THEY?

Did I mention I love hiking? I do. I do. I do. But all hikes are not created equal. They can just as well propel me in the upper sphere of spiritual holistic experiences, as exclusively ground me in the mental and physical realms. In the later instance, and to put is simply, my mind just won't shut up: As I walk and climb I get this annoying inner monologue where I project myself into an imaginary conversation where I am telling someone what I saw, what happened, how steep, how tired, and beautiful it was. I make copious mental notes of the story I am going to tell, and instantly miss out on being present for the sake of the moment. This unpleasant practice inevitably makes me slip into the undesirable world of "should haves": "I should be feeling happier being in nature, I should be more in the moment, I should stop thinking, I should do more yoga, which would help to stop thinking so that I could be more in the moment."

When this happens, as it did today, I try to be tolerant: instead of condemning my less-then-ideal state, I repeatedly congratulate myself – until I believe it – for being on the mountain regardless of whatever almost stopped me from going. I recognize that I am filling up with its energy regardless of the fact that I don't have a quiet mind. I remind myself that I am still ahead just for doing it.

When my forays into the heart of nature are not the pure and spirit-lifting meditations I hoped for, I consider them as one more opportunity to practice the ubiquitous teachings of "accepting what is". When I have in mind to train for this demanding discipline [of "accepting what is"], occasions to do so really do abound: Some days my writing flows unabated; others its a commitment. Sometimes my meditations take me to faraway places; sometimes it's just about the grinding discipline of getting it done. Some days I eat exactly the way I wish I did all the time; others, I have to be satisfied by telling myself it could have been worse. Some days I radiate light for miles around me; others, my glow is neutral *(or even less)* and I have to be okay with that too.

Life is not only about sunny days, it is also about dreary ones; it is not only about blossoming flowers, it is also about destructive fires; it is not only about happy feelings, it is about the gambit of possible emotions.

Life is not always about a perfect hike, it's about hiking, period. *

* Let's also keep in mind that rain nurtures life and forest fires enrich the soil and breed new life.

NOVEMBER 11TH, 2011

11-11-11

This is my day: I was born on the 11th, and today is a once in a lifetime trifecta of my favorite number. I must stay alert and aware, on the lookout throughout this day: take notes, take notice.

Let me go out there in the world and see what happens. Right now, I am writing this on page 11 of my current Word document! Very auspicious.

I was out in the world and although the day was event-wise unremarkable, what happened inside me was life changing. Here is what this magical day gifted me.

BEFRIENDING ISAAC

A few days ago, I watched *Oprah's Lifeclass* online *(yes, I am a fan)*, which was about Newton's 3rd law of physics: For every action there is an equal and opposite reaction. Applying this law to the realm of consciousness, this 3rd law becomes: Your life is reflecting back to you exactly what you put out; it is a reflection of what you think. Your life is the mirror of the energy you exude.

I have been aware of this law for many *(many)* years and quite frankly, I have always detested it. Kind of silly to detest a law of physics, I know. To be more specific, I have had no problem recognizing the core principle as true *(I have actually studied physics)*, but honestly, I could never believe that it was as absolute as it was made out to be; it just couldn't be so black and white. There had to be some caveat, some exceptions written in the fine print, some time line that our human mind could not grasp. There had to, simply because my life has not reflected the content of my thoughts, and so evidently, defies this law. Obviously, Newton forgot something. Unfortunately, I wasn't around when he wrote his 3rd law so that my very existence could challenge the veracity of his findings.

For years, my search for an explanation that would justify the discrepancy in my *(very unique)* case, has been fruitless. Perhaps the causes and effects are not immediate? Perhaps some effects get lost in the universe and affect something else? Perhaps God has a plan for me that bypasses those earthly laws, and consists of me struggling despite my beautiful mind? I guess I'm still juggling with the multi-facets of WDGW (What Does God Want): the internal debate I attempted to convey in October.

Anyway, in spite of my greatest efforts and willingness to sort this out, for my own benefit, I have failed at solving this riddle and my incongruous situation has remained a brain-teasing and discouraging enigma.

I mean really, I have lived in awareness almost all my life, I have always been a good person, I have always strived to understand others and to better myself in my personality and as a conscious being. I have healed any resentment about being sick and gratefully gleaned wisdom from it. And although I may lack a little self-confidence, I have a rather high self-esteem.

So, what's the deal? Why do I continue to be unwell, why does my financial picture look like a satirical caricature, why don't I have a darling man by my side, why have I not found my place under the sun, been seen and recognized? Why is all this eluding me? Why doesn't a proven law of physics apply to *me*? *(I know I'm special but I don't really wish to be that special.)* This mystery has tormented me for decades.

But today, alas, I get my long awaited aha! moment; the light bulb comes on in a blaze. My mind is blinded, allowing my soul to see.

If I extract the salient points of my life's story from the sole perspective of the essence of my inner-truth, and gather them into one over-exposed snap-shot, here is what I get. It's a rather bleak picture, but truthful:

As I have established a couple days ago, I was a wounded outsider as a child and I also became a people-pleaser in an attempt to be liked. As a teenager, I was outcast for being smart, and learned to deny my intelligence. Here is what followed. When it came time to choose my major in school, science was deemed a respectable field and so I studied science, even though it did not correspond to who I was. My twenties were a decade dedicated to a relationship with a married man with children *(who eventually divorced, but still, not too proud of that – I adored these children and our separation was unfair and traumatic)* and culminated in the event of my surgery. I eventually had a couple better years with a good-paying job but ended up having to bend my values in order to keep it, and ultimately got dismissed *(okay, fired)*. Later, I got involved in a relationship where self-compromise was the price of the roof over my head. Then, I had my relationship with my alcoholic beloved one *(and we all have an idea how unhealthy that can be)*. And lastly, I remained in a situation that clipped my wings because I believed I had no choices.

Over the years I did, however, have a few spurts of lucidity when the wrongness of my life came to light. I can recall two instances right now: On the first day of my fourth semester in a science program in university, I entered a class... and walked out. The certainty of being in the wrong place had unequivocally spoken inside me. I collected myself and went on to teach arts and crafts to children in elementary schools – though only for a while, until this wasn't right either. In the second instance, the glaring truth came from a creative director I was working with in advertising. He held me, and my talents, in high esteem but was somehow frustrated about the finer points of how I lived my life. He saw I was not really living as *me*, and one evening, as we were strolling the sidewalk of a trendy street in Montreal – after a fancy dinner accompanied with good wines *(okay, we were drunk)* – he stopped dead in his tracks, faced me and shouted: "Why the fuck don't you just be what you are, damn it!" Unsettling it was, but also easier said than done.

THE TRUTH, THE WHOLE TRUTH, AND NOTHING BUT THE TRUTH

Back to today's glorious revelation. *(I'm almost there; I needed the build up.)* All and all, I realize I have muffled my voice, compromised my beliefs and censored my "self" pretty much all my life *(I did come to this conclusion earlier but did not quite understand the full implications).* Just to recap: in the early days it was in order to be accepted, and from my twenties on, one way or the other, it was to buy the security I could not provide for myself.

And here is the clincher: *Beyond all my positive thoughts, aspirations, actions and prayers,* this *is the energy I have been putting out: an energy of non-truth and censorship.* This *is the discording sound I have been emitting as my frequency.* This *is what life's mirror has been reflecting back to me all these years.*

It has only been months since I have finally extracted myself from a life of untruths and unchained my gasping self; only weeks since I decided to take care of *me* and ditch my fears; merely weeks since I named and released deep seated guilt and shame; and only days since being able to love my past and present detractors, and release the hurt.

Truth be told: My purified output of energy is a brand new thing. I am putting out a harmonious sound for the first time in my life.

OMG, THE UNIVERSE *IS* GOOD!

This is the game-changing gift I received on this special day: The understanding that the Universe loves me and has loved me all along.

I have just finally realized that THE UNIVERSE DID NOT BETRAY ME NOR CONSPIRE AGAINST ME. I was the one who did not live in my truth and was its hindrance! It has not been plotting against me. It has not singled me out to give me a hard time. It has not transgressed its own laws just to make my life difficult: It did not betray me. I no longer need to harbor resentment or anger towards it. The Universe is fair, it is good, it loves me as a valuable constituent. What a revelation, what a relief.*

> ***If you find that your life is not reflecting what you put out, question again what you put out. Look beyond your thoughts, prayers, intentions, willingness and even actions and service. You may be a good person but are you being* you*? Are you living your life according to the truth of who you are and what you were put on this Earth to be? Are you living away from your center, muffling your voice, compromising your beliefs, or censoring your "self"? It could be that this is what your life is reflecting back to you.***

---

* Note: I believe achieving one's truth does not have to be so challenging for everybody. Every stone doesn't have to be unturned in every case. But this kind of thoroughness corresponds with who I am and thus, became my experience.

NOVEMBER 12TH, 2011

LIFE IS GOOD

Today was a good day. It began by successfully turning around a dream in which a woman was bullying me, thereby reactivating my childhood wounds. As I half awoke in the middle of that dream my first thought was, "I love you just as you are sister. I hold no resentment." And I went back to sleep, pleased with myself. I was so grateful that, even in a semi-conscious state, I was choosing to alter my thought-pattern, thus rewriting my story and alleviating the hurt I have been carrying. Simply by shifting my point of view, I am freeing myself from the pain of my past. Fascinating.

Okay, so today's title is *Life is Good.* Why? Because I felt it in my gut, and as a result, had a wonderful day. I did my meditation-stretch-yoga thing in the morning, followed by a pleasant Skype-chat with my Mom. Then I went out in the pouring rain – this *is* November on the West coast – to purchase micro-spikes for my winter hiking, and got on a local gondola to the top of a mountain to treat myself to the viewing of a selection of Artists for Conservation Festival movies. There, I met with two Squamish Indians, an exceptional sculptor (Xwalacktun) * and a shaman (Huuyaah) **, and shared a life-full moment with them, as well as with some volunteers of the festival. There was beautiful live folk music, and I believe it was the first time since I moved here that a few men "saw" me and smiled.

When I walked-in where Xwalacktun was demonstrating his craft,

---

* Aka Rick Harry: www.xwalacktun.ca . Creative Journey Studio.

** Aka T.R. Baker.

he looked at me with a huge smile and said, "Well, well, you look like you're having a great day!" I told him that indeed I was, that I was standing on top of a mountain and that this was good. He taught me a Squamish expression: *Sna7mmn Smanit*, "the strong Spirit of the mountain", and told me I was wearing the color of protection, my sienna-red sweater, which seemed very appropriate since I am in Meadow Repair mode: a self-declared protection area.

A few hours later, I rode down the gondola amid the darkness of this autumn evening magically glistening with falling snow, grateful and inwardly bubbling with joy, feeling this was the beginning of a bright new path. Once I got home, I actually broke into a few dance moves in the mirror, cheering myself on. I could hardly contain my joy. I felt this day was the result of my inner shift of point of view, of the release of my resentment and its replacement with genuine love. An unexpected thought rose within me: I am loving my life right now – a rare occurrence in my forty-seven years of existence. I felt a little seed of euphoria stirring in my belly: a sense of being on the edge of deliverance.

The best way to stand in life is:
Centered within yourself
Inspired from above
Connected to Earth's energy

NOVEMBER 13TH, 2011

TWO BALD EAGLES SITTING IN A TREE

I went for a walk by the ocean this afternoon and there was a couple of bald eagles sitting side by side atop a hundred foot spruce, just watching the world go by. I am sure my new Squamish friends could share with me the spiritual significance and symbolism of such a vision. Here are few Eagle interpretations and key notions I have gleaned from various sources. *

Keywords: Spiritual protection, Freedom, Rising above, Honor, Bravery, Strength, Illumination, Courage, Balance between Earth and Spirit.
Teachings: Ability to see the highest truth *(how à-propos)* and reach great heights.
Spiritual Energy: Freedom is our birthright *(I like this too).*
Elements: Air and Water *(I am Air, I should look for a Water man!).*

To the Native Americans, the eagle represents a state of grace that is achieved through inner work. It symbolizes the reclaiming of personal power, the passing of initiation, the gift of clear vision, the permission to be free and reach the joy of the heart's desire, and an increased understanding of spirituality and overall patterns. They also believe that aligning oneself with the eagle comes with great responsibility as the repercussion on one's actions promise to be strong and quick.

I choose to heed the sign and endeavor to honor its gifts.

---

* The above ideas about Eagle's symbolism appear on several websites. Therefore, I was unable to assign them a single source.

Nature enriches our souls, speaks to our minds, and breathes life into our bodies. It can be a messenger, a teacher, and a paragon. With an open mind and open heart, and with awareness, we can always glean wisdom, guidance, or solace from within its folds.

NOVEMBER 16TH, 2011

THE TRUTH OF THE MATTER MATTERS

This morning I woke up before dawn. I had a good night. A few dreams about how things used to be in my life, about some of the abrasions that have occurred, but as I woke up, I simply decided that my memory was releasing more of the old clutter in order to make room for my new wardrobe. I am maintaining my readiness and availability for new habits of bright colors and perfect fit.

As I was lingering in bed, enjoying the delightful feeling of a good night sleep, I began formulating a new affirmation : *My body is healthy, lean, limber and strong.*

In the midst of this serene moment, I somehow felt that my newly acquired dispositions of truthfulness – and better understanding of a friendly Universe – would at last support the fulfillment of such want-to-be prophecies. I say "at last" because positive affirmations are not a new tool for me. Years of usage have nearly sullied the name and relinquished it to mere slang in my vocabulary. Nonetheless, I have always maintained a soft spot for them ; always believing in their potential power of transformation and manifestation, except : they have never worked for me. *(Just in case though, I made myself a little poster-card for this one and placed it on the bathroom mirror.)*

Not only have I (unsuccessfully) worked with affirmations over the years, I have also worked with the slew of tools and schemes that have crossed my path. Through the meanderings of my quest for life-improvement and self-betterment, I have looked high and low, left and right, and into every nook and cranny within me. I have stood on my head, changed my patterns, the ones I could think of, and those I could not even fathom. I have even tried not to look, unclenching my will then aligning my will to my intentions. I have written affirmations thirty time a day for thirty days, set goals on paper, practiced laser focusing, visualized, petitioned God, prayed with my hands full and with my hands empty, worked on accepting my life, on letting go, on surrendering*. I have practiced forgiveness and gratitude, and flirted with the somewhat obscure principles of Ho'oponopono.

I have participated in numerous workshops, analyzed my psychological make-up, contemplated my youth, named and released countless wounds, gone through several rebirth processes. I have consulted with healers of all kinds, travelled through my inner world and all the way to the underworlds of the souls guided by a shaman, underwent soul retrievals, participated in rituals, and attended sweatlodges. I have spent privileged time with a Tibetan Tulku Lama *(a magical story to tell one day)*, I have prayed to the Moon and the Sun, and connected myself with the powers of nature.

I have labored relentlessly, all in the name of purifying my heart and allowing my soul to shine through. Amidst the foundering myriad attempts, I was from time to time blessed with true illuminations, divine graces, and shepherded intuitions.

All these experiences have provided me with a richness of life, great insights and healings, and have opened my heart. But I have never,

---

* I must concede though that when I did *accept my life*, it was usually more in defeat than in peaceful surrender, and I would consider myself somewhat of a victim of my circumstances.

despite it all, been able to manifest health, abundance, a good partner, or a life of less struggles.

Over the years, I have annoyingly *(please understand my position)* heard all the trite comments such as: "It's all inside you." "You have it all within." "You hold the key to your future." "You are the creator of your life." "Your thoughts create." "Just let go and let God." "Surrender." Oh, gag me with a spoon. As far as I have been concerned, these phrases became disembodied parroted lines from *Awareness 101* – a drop of truth in a vile of snake oil.

My years of earnest (though vain) efforts, have led me to the conclusion that the nowadays popular notion asserting that *"hard work, perseverance, faith, and willingness to grow from lessons learned will necessarily result in your goals being achieved"*, was erroneous and far too simplistic and linear to be true. If these were truly the only elements involved in finding the key to a successful life, I assure you that the human race would count many more winners and happy campers. There is an abundance of good, dedicated, on-the-path-of-consciousness people in this world who don't get a break and who do not get the results they seek.

I need to break the news to the growing number of motivational public (and private) speakers who proclaim this partial truth [that hard work, blah-blah-blah, success] as the panacea for searching souls *(making all of us folks feel either guilty or inadequate for not following the plan properly when we thought we were)* that they are missing something. Ladies and Gents, there is something more at play.

LUCK, ACCIDENTS AND TWISTS OF FATE

Here I would like to open a parenthesis to address a kindred source of vexation, which I feel trickles in the same pond:

Does luck exist? I have heard different responses from various successful people, spiritual or not. I must admit I am a little taken aback when someone states, with seeming authority, that it does not – implying that any good fortune that has come their way was their own masterful doing.

My personal answer is: I'm not sure, but.... Here is a roundabout way to approach the question: Does chaos exist in the cosmos? Now this, I can answer *(scientists can anyway, so I'll take their word for it)*: Yes. And what happens inside chaos? Fields of energy, particles enormous and tiny, randomly fly all over the place: exploding, colliding, crashing onto one another and occasionally (if the conditions are propitious) creating new worlds. All in all, pretty much haphazard behaviors and occurrences take place: good, bad, flukish, ... lucky?

For eons, the universe appears to have demonstrated that chance encounters (more like collisions) do happen. Since we are "multi-particle beings" of said universe, logic dictates that we may, at some point in our life, find ourselves in the trajectory of an erratic cluster of particles, thereby making us involuntary participants in an accidental collision. That being said, if you ask me again if I believe in luck (good and bad) I have to deduce, more or less reluctantly, that yes, I do; perhaps at a blue-moon frequency *(which is coming up in August)*, but nonetheless.

I concede that certain conditions must exist in order for a chance encounter to produce a viable creation: In the universe, we are talking about gases, temperatures and water; in humans, a state of preparedness, alertness and willingness to run with it, probably plays the same role.

In any case, I must suggest we consider that luck does exist. Something to think about.

End of parenthesis.

EAGLE'S EYE VIEW

Now back to my statement that something is missing in the recipes to success we are encouraged to follow.

The problem is that people willing and caring enough to teach us how to achieve success – whether personal or professional – teach from experience. I know this shouldn't be presented as a problem: teachers are better and more credible if they have tested what they speak of themselves. Obviously, how they got to where they are has worked for them. And for most, success has indeed come with a good measure of hard work, perseverance, picking themselves up, faith, intention, and vision. Any omission on their part is quite unintentional.

Understand that I do not refute the validity of their processes and that I will not contradict the once secret notion that intention, emotion, and action must be aligned in order to yield results. It all makes sense.

But I think that many such teachers and proponents have missed the forest for standing by the tree of their own success. The fact that the heaps of fertilizer I have concocted during the course of my life have grown no such tree for me, ultimately spurred me to take off *(with a hint of defeat in my heart)* and fly over the forest with an eagle's eye focus on what was going on. How did their trees grow and what's different with my dwarfed seedling.

T.H.E. M.I.S.S.I.N.G. L.I.N.K. !

What I have discovered, the epiphany that struck me in mid-flight, the missing piece to the puzzle responsible for the demoralizing failures of countless people *(including me)* is that unless you are living in your truth, any and all efforts will most likely yield nothing you want and leave you panting and disheartened!

What has been missed in the shuffle is that all these people who generously transmit to us their blueprint for success are already doing in life exactly what they were meant to do; which is to say: They have been proceeding from their truth. And because this is part of their natural state (like a beating heart), they never thought to notice or mention the existence of this vital prerequisite ("By the way guys... you have to have a beating heart first.").

Because they have been proceeding from their truth, their hard work, perseverance, learned lessons, and dedication, were stacking up on solid ground. The ones who failed have been attempting to build without first standing in their truth and that is like attempting to build on quicksands. Architects from both groups may be as talented, hardworking and driven by faith, but efforts of the latter will never yield anything grand or enduring. The successful architects did not think they needed to mention: *location, location, location.*

RECIPES FOR SUCCESS

It's kind of like a chef giving all the ingredients and instructions for an exquisite recipe but forgetting to say that you need to start with a pot – too obvious to even mention. Except that when the pot is the essence of who you are, it must be mentioned, specified, described, explained, emphasized, belabored, stressed, written in bold letters, and highlighted. Without it, pupils are left baffled, defeated and sobbing.

So here is the gold-leafed illuminated page I am adding to this culinary book of life:

Before you even consider cooking any of the brilliantly authored recipes contained in this book, you must first – unless you aspire to fail – make certain you stand in your Truth.

From experience, I really believe this. It appears clear-as-day to me now that the reason I have failed to manifest success is that I have not been living in accordance with the truth of who I am. And it is not that my goals were not lofty and honorable *(the three years I have spent attempting to market products I loved and that would enhance mindful practices all over the world, were virtuous, proficient and creative)*, the problem has been: not proceeding from a place of truth – and most likely not doing what I was meant to do *(something one probably figures out once they live in their truth)*.

For decades, I have hoped that success would result from my ceaseless efforts and that the ensuing financial latitude would afford me the "luxury" to then pursue and live in my truth: I was hoping success would free me and propel me into my truth. What I know now is that I had it backwards: FIRST YOUR TRUTH, THEN SUCCESS. And by "your truth" I mean no censorship of your voice, no denial of your gifts, no sacrifice of your values.

Once you stand in that place, I wholeheartedly believe success is achievable – and you can then follow one of the recipes. And if, once this is done, success still doesn't come, then we must consider that something beyond this "missing link" is at play, and that it may be called luck, karma, kismet, fate, destiny, the stars, or God's plans (and I will not meddle with those). * But I would bet that once you reside in your truth, you *are* congruent with your destiny, in flow with the Universe, following God's design, aligned with your stars; and you can then finally ride your chariot with brio.

The choices I have made recently are putting this theory to the test and I am confident the outcome will prove the premise. I shall keep you abreast of my findings.

So this is what emerged from my rested state this morning *(perhaps I should rest more often)*. This is why I sense the possibility of redemption for positive affirmations *(and prayers, actions, dedication, efforts, vision)*, why I feel that once released, their utterance will no longer reach deaf ears. This place of truthfulness, authenticity, self-respect,

---

* And if success comes to someone who appears not to be aligned with their truth, then it may also be called luck, karma, kismet, fate, destiny, the stars, or God's plans.

and integrity is the fertile soil from which my greatest potential can finally grow into a remarkable tree, thus enhancing the world, and perhaps one day sheltering younger seedlings under its canopy.

And this is where my recent feeling of a quivering seed of euphoria is stemming from: I think I am ripe for an unimpeded growth spurt.

FIRST, YOUR TRUTH: THEN SUCCESS

We must know our truth
We must choose our truth
We must say our truth
We must act our truth
We must live our truth

Anything less will not create what we hope for.

NOVEMBER 18TH, 2011

AMNESIA: A TWO TRICK PONY

THE 28-DAY PROGRAM

This morning I realize it is hard for me to remember how it was that I was so stressed, panicked, and depressed. My new attitude is beginning to fit me; it is turning into a very well adjusted bodysuit. There is some science out there that says it takes 28 days to create new pathways for behaviors: 28 days to detoxify a nebulous system, 28 days to wean yourself of unproductive or destructive practices, 28 days to rectify a course you no longer wish to follow. For me,

11-11-11 was the day I entered my own sobriety program: a program that consists of freeing myself of toxic thought patterns, behaviors, fears and doubt. It is my Ego Sobriety Program. 18 days in: I'm on my way.

I do occasionally wonder if I am living in Lalaland *(as an ostrich to boot)* for not being worried anymore about not working and accumulating debt everyday. But somehow, my positivity is self-contagious – a kind of reversed autoimmune reaction in which the good guys win: when a happy cell gets in contact with an unhappy one, it infects it! *(Now* that *would be a worthy vaccine to develop.)*

Right now, I cannot foresee how I could possibly go back to the way I was dealing with things before. I even feel as though, if something in the future did not go my way, I would be okay *(note to God: I am not asking for more challenges, okay?).*

I would be okay because I feel a sense of steadiness from standing on the solid ground of my truth; as if whatever may happen around me could no longer move me from my center. Allowing the winds of change to sway your opinions may be perfectly fine at times, but life is definitely easier when your faith is steady.

However, experience has taught me that enlightened states and insights do fade away and that, as inconceivable as it seems today, I may even have to learn this all over again. *(No, not this time, this one is gonna stick.)*

Unfortunately, amnesia goes both ways: One day you can't remember what it takes to be miserable and the next you can't remember the road to feeling good.

THE WHEELS OF THE BUS GO ROUND AND ROUND

The good news is that each moment of enlightenment and insightfulness, even when temporary, is cumulative. We may be relearning the same lessons several times over or come to the same conclusion as to what we need to do to improve our life, but let's not fool ourselves in thinking that we start back on square one each time. Somewhere in the ether each experience is compounded until one day, a critical mass is reached and the scales are tilted. And that is the day when a lesson is permanently learned, the day when you find the courage to finally take the step you were afraid to take to change your life, or the day you decide to throw away your scuffed old slippers.

The earlier image whereby clearing a new path was a metaphor for creating a new habit in our life is fitting here as well; the idea in both cases being that it takes repetition in order for humans to establish new grounds.

As we believe we are caroling the same ditty, endlessly telling the tale of the circular motion of the wheels of a bus, we are in fact inching towards our destination.

On numerous occasions in my life, the veils of confusion were lifted for me, revealing insights I thought I could never possibly forget. These were moments of such clear vision that I believed they were forever etched in my awareness and that they would either guide my steps from then on or had dissolved old negative patterns for good. The feeling of certainty that accompanies these moments can be likened to that which you have when you awake from a dream where you had figured out the answer to an existential, mathematical or whatever type of question, and thought there was no way you would forget by morning. Of course, when you wake up, what was so obvious then, now only shows up in teasing fragmented pieces.

As I said earlier, even a clear vision of what needs to be done in order for you to move forward with your life may zoom in and out of focus several times before you take action. It just so happens that I have a blatant example of such a thing right at the tip of my fingers.

In the last few days, I have been cleaning up an old email account in order to close it, and in the process, I have perused a number of lengthy letters, which I am glad I had the foresight to save. In my usual style, they detailed my various states of mind, insights and conclusions of the day. It has been baffling to read that what I described then, all those years ago, was almost identical to the reflections that prompted me to come here. These emails talked about the need to choose my self beyond financial security, about finding the courage to change my situation, about not being all that I could be, and about having the audacity to push beyond my fears and taking a leap of faith. The only difference between then and now is that then, I was unable to act upon my call for action, and this year, I did. *(Out of respect for the people involved, I choose not to give details of the complicated situation I am referring to. Please forgive me this rare exclusion. The lesson though, remains.)*

Now, the fact that I have held the same discourse for so many years may come across as discouraging *(in a way, it kind of is – how I wish it hadn't taken so long)* but the better way to look at this is to recognize that some life-altering choices need time to mature.

Sometimes, an aspiration or a calling is just a seed that needs to gather life-energy before it can sprout, grow and bare fruit. So let's not beat ourselves up when we can't seem to take the actions we feel we should take, or when we are relearning a lesson we thought we had already learned. Let us love ourselves through the process, as long as it takes, knowing that every experience is a deposit in our bank of awareness; and that one day, we will cash out.

The wheels of the bus may go round and round but in the meantime, you are covering ground.

NOVEMBER 19TH, 2011

COMIC RELIEF

After all this heavy-duty mind-bending material, I figure you can probably use a laugh or two. I am gladly volunteering for this to be done at my expense – being the cause of said mind-bending and all. A little self-derision never killed anybody.

As a French speaking Canadian I have unintentionally, over the years, created what I now learn (bit by bit) was my own lexicon of expressions. Unbeknownst to me, I have wrongly interpreted phrases phonetically, and incorrectly mentally spelled words through the dazzling workings of my own, very solid, logic. Becoming aware of these mistakes has provided bellyaching laughter on more than one occasion, particularly with a couple of friends in whose company I have no shame.

'He goated her'

Yes, this is what I thought in my misguided mind. I was correct in the meaning of the word; I understood it meant to provoke, annoy or push someone's buttons but when I would hear (or use) this word, it conjured up images of a goat ramming into someone repeatedly. Well, these images are now gone from my mind's eye *(or maybe not)* as I have learned the word is "goad" and that it sadly evokes no image at all.

'Say your peace'

I have always thought the expression was "say your peace" simply because it made sense to me. But a while ago, I realized it is "say your piece." You know what? I actually prefer my spelling. I mean what about "peace of mind", don't tell me it's "piece of mind"! So I guess you say: "Let me give you a piece of my mind" but "It gave me peace of mind" and "You can say your piece."

'Wet your appetite'

I'm on a roll, last night I stumbled upon a startling one: "It whetted his appetite." What? I always thought the expression was along the line of "mouth watering" and consequently, the expression was to "wet your appetite"! So now, instead of imagining my mouth watering, I will have to picture a blade being sharpened.

'Road Scholar'

Okay, this one is so funny I'm a little embarrassed. I always thought a "road scholar" was a highly educated individual who had studied extensively while traveling *(on the road! gulp!)* and attending various prestigious institutions. Okay, I'm cringing. When I saw "Rhodes Scholar" in my book last night as well, I shut my eyes swiftly, mouth gaping, as I thought, "No way..." Never in a million years would I have guessed it referred to an Oxford scholarship.

'Airbrained'

In this case, I actually prefer the real reference to the brain of a hare. Now when I think "harebrained" I can see little carefree bunnies frolicking in the meadow. Education is good.

'Teatoddler'

Oh Jeez! I pictured someone who liked nursing a cup of tea rather than drink alcohol. "Teetotaler" was apparently first used in 1833 by Richard Turner – a worker in Preston, England. I bet the journalist who wrote about it couldn't spell properly, and that Dick actually did mean "tea-totaller" as he was preaching *total* abstinence from alcohol and *totally* drinking *tea* instead!

'Mother load'

I pictured a big bag of loot, a jackpot. But in this case as well, I like the intended reference to lode: a vein of metal ore in the earth, a rich source of something.

Bated breath (proper spelling)

Actually, this is just for your edification. Using "baited breath" is a common mistake. This idiom even appears incorrectly in Harry Potter *(so I hear)*!

Just deserts (proper spelling)

FYI also. Apparently, the phrase is often wrongly spelled "just desserts." The real meaning relates to "what you justly deserve", hence "deserts".

I am certain my colorful vocabulary still contains many more erroneous and intuitive meaning of the English vocabulary. And I hope they cause me to laugh for a long time to come.

Laughter is great medicine. If the world around you can't provide any, look at yourself, you may find reason for a good laugh.

NOVEMBER 20TH, 2011

CHECKING, DOUBLE-CHECKING AND CHECKING AGAIN

This morning, as if the Universe wants me to stand behind my choice, I am being required, once again, to deal with that job that sent my head into a dizzying spin more than two weeks ago. Having heard nothing back from them since, I thought the matter was closed. But I am now in receipt of the reply to the email I had sent, and I am invited to make contact and arrange a meeting. If you recall, the painstaking decision to turn down the job had been reached after sending an email by which I was keeping my options open. Well, here's the option knocking at my door once more.

So I am forced to check-in with myself again: Does my initial resolve still stand? This time, it doesn't take long: The answer is yes. My first and last impressions of the incident have stuck with me: at this time in my life, this job is just not for me. My Meadow Repair is the wisest choice and it is not yet completed.

I will reply with an email that will clinch the non-deal definitely.

It is now a few hours later and although the email is composed, it has not been sent. I really want to decline but I find myself hesitating. Now, where is that coming from? Is it my usual guilt speaking, "You need money, you should be working", or my inner voice whispering, "Perhaps this is an opportunity for you to reconsider your decision?"

I take a few deep breaths, find my center once more, and gently remind myself that my intuition is trustworthy and that it had initially told me "no".

I push the send button. The matter is now closed.

When we make a significant choice in our life – something that defines an inner position – the Universe often asks for confirmation: "Are you* absolutely *sure that's what you want to do?" This test of our resolve may take the shape of temptation or offer the allure of sound logic; both of which ego is keen on. The fastest way to evolve and the best way to avoid repetitive patterns is to steadfastly abide by a decision previously made from our core, no matter what.

NOVEMBER 21ST, 2011

IF ALL HAD GONE ACCORDING TO PLAN

■ ■ ■ I would not be here today, writing my book.

As I move along with my writing, I can't help but ponder *(again)* the circumstances enabling me to do this. Even in the wake of my recent multi-pronged epiphanies I remain somewhat mesmerized by the level of orchestration that was necessary to get me to this point. It is quite astonishing that so many events I deemed unwelcomed in my life, and fought vigorously, were actually joining together in unrolling the red carpet onto which I was to step to undertake the redaction of this book; a book I feel in my soul and bones I was meant to write.

Without the soul searching and endless prayers this chaplet of unpopular circumstances prompted, I would not have learned the invaluable life-changing lessons that are opening my heart today. Beyond this convergence of unwanted conditions, I am thankful to have been granted the presence of mind to *(eventually)* seize the opportunity, as well as been provided with an environment conducive to the creative process of writing.

If all had gone according to plan, I would not have lived my life as I did and I would not have the material to write this book, which I believe is the doorway into the purpose of my life.

IF ALL DID GO ACCORDING TO MY PLAN TOMORROW

... what would happen to this book?

I can't help but wonder: If my current wishes for winning the megabucks jackpot and finding my perfect man were granted now, would I really keep on writing?

Okay, maybe. But in the least, my book's content would change dramatically. I would be writing from the other side of the tunnel, where the light is, and it would become one of many stories of individuals who write from the comfort and security *(good for them)* of after-the-fact.

On the other hand, I know that whatever this book will be will be and that that's okay too *(notice how I practice "accepting what is" even in my projections – I am making some real progress)*. But again, maybe this book is meant-to-be-written from the middle of things *(not to belabor the idea, but I still need to remind myself in order to embrace my circumstances)*. Perhaps it will be of service to more people if I continue writing from this challenging place of uncertainty*, as a greater number of individuals can relate to being stuck than to having emerged *(although stories of success are most inspiring; I am a fan myself. I love happy endings)*.

So perhaps there is after all a reason for my financial predicament and solitary life. Perhaps it is the example I need to be in order for others to benefit from my life.

---

* Note to self and God: Just another reminder that eventually, in the not to distant future, I wish to grow and evolve from less challenging situations. I have demonstrated extensively that I am a courageous person and I'm okay with life becoming easier so that I can explore other beautiful human qualities.

IF ALL HAD GONE ACCORDING TO PLAN

...I would not have ended up in Sedona in 2006 where a key chapter of my life was to unfold.

Derailed plans are nothing new in my life. Obviously, I am not always the conductor of this locomotive: I did not start out planning to travel to Arizona.

The story goes that months before my departure, arrangements had been made for me to spend the summer renting the house of a friend's daughter in Colorado. It was the most affordable destination for my much needed hiatus *(I was burnt-out)*. My tickets were booked, a car rented, boxes packed-up, shipping labels affixed and ready to go.

But then ten days before my departure, I received a call informing me the situation had changed and that the house would no longer be available to me. I was devastated, in total disbelief, feeling my curative escape was being unfairly taken away from me. As I hung up the phone, I collapsed and cried bitterly for fifteen minutes, and then asked myself: Okay, what is this telling you; where did you really want to go this summer? My answer was: Sedona. I had been bewitched by pictures of those mystical red rocks and yearned to walk upon the red dirt. I immediately got online to look for rental properties, found a magnificent house perched on the red rocks with windows from floor to ceiling. – Although it seemed way out of my league, I decided to give it a shot. It turned out the owner was just finishing some repairs and had listed the house only hours ago without holding too much hope, since the high season was already well underway. I made an offer for the entire summer, he accepted, took my Visa payment, and it was done. Just like that.

I kept my non-refundable ticket to Colorado where I picked-up my low-cost rental car and drove down to Sedona. Once there, I could not imagine what I would have done in Nowhere, Colorado for an entire summer. If things had gone according to my plans, I would have missed-out on an encounter that needed to happen *(Richard)* and perhaps been bored out of my mind.

IF ALL HAD GONE ACCORDING TO PLAN

...I would not have received the various gifts Vancouver has bestowed upon me.

Incredibly, a similar situation occurred just a few months ago as I was preparing to move – apparently, travelling is one of my teachers. Once again, my quest for a dwelling was driving my plans: I had to find a place to live before booking my tickets – a hotel suite being financially not doable. Among scores of others, I was put in contact with the daughter of an old departed friend of my aunt and uncle *(I was grasping at straws)* who graciously offered to host me in her house for two weeks upon my upcoming arrival. Figuring this was a good solution and that it would afford me enough time to find a more permanent place to stay, I booked my flight.

Pushing the "book it" button for that flight was an emotional experience. It was the ultimate commitment to this great leap of faith I was about to take. After filling out the required booking information online, I just stared at the screen, shaking, then crying, then not being able to breath for over half an hour. Time and again, the question "Do you need more time?" popped up on the screen, to which I answered, "Yes", repeatedly. Eventually, after a long hug from my Mom, I took a deep breath and solemnly pressed the key. I then sent my host an email informing her of the exact date and time of my arrival. Within hours, she replied her plans had changed and there was no room in the house for me. She concluded her email saying, "I am sorry you booked your flight. Good luck to you." I could not believe it. Not again?

It did occur to me right then that this was a repetition of Colorado, but why did things have to be so dramatic all the time? My sister, who was in the vicinity, offered an interesting insight. She pointed out that this move of mine was about independence and about no longer being beholden to anyone. Beginning my journey as the recipient of a "favor" was perpetuating an old pattern. It clicked instantly; a bright light bulb came on in my head. How insidious was this little ego of mine. As on guard and deliberate as I had been about the choices I was making, the little bugger had slipped one passed me. In a repeat performance of Colorado, I went online, confident the right opportunity would present itself, and eventually – four days before my flight! – I "stumbled" upon an available furnished basement to rent. I paid the full price, and so both parties stood on equal ground. The timing was perfect too, as the owners were leaving on vacation the day of my arrival. I ended-up staying longer then I had hoped (17 days) and learned two important things: One, if people were to live above me, the floors would have to be concrete. Two: I could not survive in a basement.

Having my own space and not living in someone else's home upon my arrival was a godsend. As it turns out I needed time to integrate my move and live through the emotions it stirred up – which was mostly panic for the first twelve hours: What the hell did I do? I was also thankful for the privacy so that I could lie down, without explanations, in order to deal with my nausea.

I serendipitously found my current spacious, concrete floors, window-clad, furnished suite, and signed a lease. Incredibly, five days before move-in day *(as if I needed more practice at dealing with last minute plans-that-don't-go-my-way)*, the suite became a non-furnished suite! Really! This time, I did not panic *(much)* and decided that acquiring my own furnishings and necessities was in fact very nicely aligned with my plan for reclaiming my life. In accordance with my means, I spent the following days going to garage sales, and pored over Craigslist ads. I created a delightful home for myself, all my own.

If all had gone according to my plans, I would have been miserable with people around me for the first two weeks, I would not have experienced independence, and I would not be writing on my own desk, watching my own TV, sitting on my own couch, or sleeping in my own bed *(I even have my own vacuum cleaner!)* – things I am grateful for every single day.

IF

... life always followed our script, if friends and foes behaved the way we wanted them to, or faithfully followed through with their commitments, or even always treated us kindly and fairly, we just may miss out on surprising opportunities for growth and joy. Of course, it doesn't mean we should seek disruptions or accept wrong doings – in some cases, it may be a sign that a relationship has run its course, for example – but when confronted with events-that-don't-go-our-way, we would be wise to follow our dramatic "What the hell!" with "Okay, not cool, but I wonder where this will lead me?" This perspective of openness will de-escalate mounting tensions and allow to navigate the situation with less pain and more grace. It is just another application of "accepting what is".

When aggravations are caused by what I consider to be insensitive, unkind or mean-spirited behavior, I try to remind myself that the offenders are also being exactly who they are supposed to be, experiencing exactly what they are meant to experience for their own soul's expansion, and getting exactly what they have come to get out of their human experience. They too are on their path. And possibly, they are unknowingly helping me get to where I ought to be.

Parable: The Bird & the Cow Pie

In the mountains of northern Italy stood a small monastery. Every day a monk would wind his way down a path to say mass in a village church. One cold fall day, he noticed a bird lying by the path, nearly dead from the cold. Without hesitation he put it inside his cloak, next to his warm body. Soon, the bird began to wiggle. As he entered the village, the monk knew he could not take the bird into church with him. Pondering what to do, he noticed a fresh steaming cow pie by the side of the road. Gently, he put the bird into the warm mixture and went into the church. The bird was so revived by the surrounding warmth that he began chirping and singing merrily. An old fox happened to be strolling about and saw the bird. In a flash, he snapped the bird out of the cow pie and ate it swiftly.

There are three lessons to the story: First, the one who puts you in deep dung is not necessarily your enemy. Second, the one who gets you out of it is not necessarily your friend. Third, when you find yourself up to your neck in the stuff, it's sometimes best to keep your mouth shut.

The moral of my story is that things will not always go our way. Money may not always be within reach, people will lack integrity, and border crossings will stop us in our tracks. But if we don't hit the roof with every obstacle, blow, or hiccup that derail our plans, and remain open to what comes next, we may have the pleasant surprise of gifts we could not have foreseen. Perhaps life is simply correcting our course.

NOVEMBER 22TH, 2011

STATE OF MEADOW REPAIR UPDATE

For a few years now, waking up has been accompanied by a physical feeling of intense internal vibration that has been, to say the least, disconcerting *(actually, quite unsettling)* – and this occurs without the jolting sound of a clock. When this happens, the exterior of my body doesn't tremble, but my insides instantaneously aquiver as if they were reacting to shock; the feeling resembles that of an engine rumbling from deep inside. All I can do, is anxiously wait-out the ten seconds it lasts. The same phenomenon has been occurring when I am startled by a sound while resting at night or even during the day. I have a pretty clear sense that this has been an indication that my nerves were probably shot.

The good news today is that I realize it hasn't happened in several days. I can only surmise that my body has accepted and is responding to the "In Repair State" decree. I am picturing my nerves being gently coated by a fresh new layer of myelin *, a protective sheath equipping me for my new beginning. I marvel gratefully at this tangible proof that I am on the right path – a path of healing – and that my Meadow Repair is indeed occurring.

A little TLC ** does perform miracles.

---

* This word just came back to me from my college biology class! Perhaps my memory is also benefiting from the healing process.

** Tender Loving Care.

NOVEMBER 25TH, 2011

COL. EGO'S LAST STAND

I have had a little bit of a cold recently, which has resulted in hardly any sleep for the last eight nights. Two noteworthy observations *(more like one conduct and one observation)* have resulted from this unpleasant state of affairs.

One: In the past *(love calling it the past)* I would have really stressed about it, but nowadays, even in the middle of the night as I labor to find my breath, I whisper words of gratitude. In the midst of my unwellness, I simply tell myself, "Yep, this is not a fun night, that's a fact" and it stops there. Instead of getting worked up, I think about all my recent inner accomplishments, contemplate the transformation occurring within me, and I am grateful. I push it as far as to give myself silent congratulations: "Wow girl, you're really making progress! Do you realize how much you have changed? It's pretty amazing!" What follows is a certainty that such deep transcendence of being can only invite the Universe to be supportive of my new dispositions, and respond with events of like-frequency. I must say: I can't wait to witness and experience this new partnership.

Even physically, I feel my resistances melting. Something is softer inside my body. There is an openness of channels of sorts that I can actually feel. Even with a cold and a stiff neck, there is an ease inside of me. And contrary to the feelings that accompany resistance, insistence and will, this state of openness and inner-smile feels natural and effortless. As I am learning to relax into my life, I feel doors opening: doors of my heart and doors to my life.

Two: My sleep quality is not only affected by my cold. There is also my ego *(mind)* that seems to have taken over my dreams and hypnagogic state (threshold consciousness before falling asleep). He is now running wild at night, multiplying restless dreams that leave me exhausted. I must admit to being a little surprised by this because I am feeling at peace with my current choices *(of societally non-productive and financially irresponsible activity!)*. Also, I am drawing confidence from knowing that I have completed the seminal task of reshaping the template by which I live: I have stopped *(pretty much)* fighting my life – I am accepting my circumstances – I have let go of old hurts, I have realized that I am not a victim of the Universe *(that's the biggie)*, I am releasing my story, and taking care of myself. That's a brand new code for living and I think my ego doesn't appreciate the change.

HIT ME WITH YOUR BEST SHOT

So this morning, I consider that my ego's antics may be his last attempts at exercising control. Since I have unmasked and called him out on his diurnal incessant ramblings, he no longer has free rein during my conscious hours. Consequently, he has resourcefully identified his last remaining playground: Nights, where my alertness is diminished. This is where he takes a desperate stand, puffing up his chest in an exaggerated effort to show me who's the boss. And I understand the desperation: He knows there is some restructuring going on and that there is a new woman in charge.

Yep, I think I am going to adopt this storyline. It will allow me to continue to deal with his outbursts with equanimity. I may even look onto him lovingly, as a mother would her child who is putting up a fight before going to bed even though he is exhausted: "There, there. I know. Give it your best shot. We'll talk about it in the morning."

Ego is a resourceful creature. It will find the hole in your shoe and jauntily seep through. Best to patch the holes, or simply be amused – until you do – by the unbidden guest creeping into your shoe.

NOVEMBER 26TH, 2011

THE WISDOM IN UNSOLICITED ADVICE

A few days ago, I had a phone conversation with someone who was going through a difficult situation. We talked for a while, I listened, and offered a few helpful comments. It was a supportive, positive discussion.

The following day, further ideas I thought could provide additional valuable perspective, occurred to me. Since we hadn't been involved in each other's life for some time, I was reluctant to call her back. So I decided writing an email would be the way to go: not too imposing or intrusive. Knowing she was on the road for several days and that the timing of a thought-provoking message might not be optimal, I figured I would hold off until she returned.

But by now, it simply feels out of context and revisiting the subject with her may be unwelcomed. And that's what triggered what I believe is a pretty smart idea: Since unsought advice is usually undesired – and we should all be the wiser for waiting to be asked for our opinion – I am sending her an email telling her I have further insights about our previous conversation, and that if she is interested, I could email them to her. This initiative is relieving my anxiety of risking interfering in her life: If she wants my additional two cents, all she has to do is ask.

I saved my two cents. She never did reply. But I definitely feel this was a wise way to go about offering unsolicited advice.

Whenever we are about to open a sentence with either: "I know this is not a good time but...", "I know you're not going to like what I have to say but...", "I know this is going to hurt you...", or "I know you don't want to hear this...", perhaps we should count to ten before speaking and make sure there isn't a better time, a better way, or even if what we are about to say should be said at all.

NOVEMBER 27TH, 2011

THE NON-COMPETE AGREEMENT

In my recent search for employment *(the one that's on hold for now)* and past attempts to find collaborators for the marketing of my products, I have met with a few accomplished women: women who have made their mark in the world, or at least in their professional world. I have to admit the encounters have almost invariably left me with a hollow feeling. The "sizing-up" that takes place is definitely not an objective one: it's personal. What really seems to be going on is this: "Is this woman going to steal some of my (spot) light?" If the result of the evaluation denotes the new woman has strong attributes, she is usually considered a threat rather than a possible ally. Sometimes, I think this deplorable attitude may even occur subconsciously, as if the arrival of a new woman in another woman's turf awakens some atavistic conditioning that the newcomer is a rival that could steal her man or her place in the tribe.

I remember a male acquaintance of mine enthusiastically organizing a meeting with a successful female friend. The objective was for her to hire or assist me in finding a job. He seemed proud of having masterminded this match, thinking we would really get along because we were so alike. Knowing what I know, I had my doubts from the get go. But how do you explain this aspect of the female psyche to someone you hardly know: you don't and hope to be proven wrong. But my suspicions of an ill-fated encounter were confirmed in no time at all. The woman, having been briefed by her friend about my many talents, was "expecting" me, and I felt a chill of antagonism the moment I walked in. Women being women, I guess, the lunch meeting went on pleasantly under a pretense of friendliness. Although the man was completely oblivious to the rivalry that had loomed under the surface *(he later even encouraged me to follow-up with her)*, I knew the gig was over.

SISTERHOOD REVIVAL

Over the years, I have found that there are mainly two types of women that stand outside this regrettable circle: Extremely secure women who cannot be threatened by another's assets and who welcome gifted collaborators, and mature women who have pretty much accomplished what they had set out to do and are now ready to leave a legacy of knowledge by taking a younger version of themselves under their wing. Unfortunately, these are two rare breeds and the bulk of the female population would greatly benefit from a revival of the bond of sisterhood.

Just as other behavioral remnants of our primeval evolution are no longer appropriate to this day an age, so too is women competing against one another, antiquated. An era of global connectivity and collaboration is upon us and we should make a conscious effort to catch up to it.

Women should understand that there is enough light to go around: enough for us all to shine. We should not compete against each other but rather applaud the light of the other. Our collective glow can only shine the brighter.

In order to be recognized in the world, we must first recognize one another.

Women-united is a force to be reckoned with.

NOVEMBER 28TH, 2011

18TH DAY OF EGO SOBRIETY

It has now been 18 days since my ultimate psychological and emotional breakthrough that the Universe is good:

18 days since I disengaged from repetitive and useless thoughts;

18 days since I have worried, fretted, blamed, stressed, resented or felt victimized;

18 days into the program without a hitch, without cheating, or falling off the wagon.

As I explained, my only slips are in my dreams, in which I am still misunderstood or feel betrayed, and I know these will soon dissipate as well. I can feel the program working, I can feel it settling in, finding its place, making itself a home.

From the heart of this budding sobriety, I contemplate this field of my life and believe there is no stone left unturned. It has been weeded, plowed, fertilized and seeded; the harsh winter has come and gone.

I celebrate the beauty of the blooms and rejoice in the rewards of upcoming harvests.

I'm on my way.

> ***"She became one who is capable of spiritual flight. Her wings spread like those of an eagle, she lifted her heart heavenwards, stepped from the nest and flew to the stars."* ***
>
> Jade Wah'oo Grigori

* I consulted with Jade in Sedona, Arizona. He is the caretaker of "the Ways", an authentic shamanic lineage, and provides personal healing sessions, spiritual guidance, as well as Shamanic Travel Adventures around the world. His website is www.shamanic.net.

DECEMBER

THE RUNAWAY MIND

DECEMBER 1ST, 2011

THE 21-DAY ITCH

Well, although just a few days ago I was certain that this recently plowed field of my life had been thoroughly sifted, there may in fact have been a few half-turned stones that were left behind, and the winter thaw is bringing them up to the surface: After 21 days of psychological teetotalism *(not "teatoddlerism"!)*, a new itch is now tickling my ego who had, up to now, graciously submitted to detoxification *(except in my dreams)*. This prickling comes from external elements – administrative, social, and familial tasks, obligations and concerns – poking at my serenity. Because unfortunately, although I do my best to keep the outside world at bay while focused on both my Meadow Repair and Ego Sobriety programs, my environment is unlike actual rehab facilities where the exterior world is effectively shut down while recovery is underway. In my case, intruders are managing to filter through the perimeter.

Since my quieter and improved frame of mind is still in its stage of infancy, the smallest demand put on me, or need for justification *(I sometimes have no choice but to offer a vague explanation to acquaintances as to why I am still not working – I have not told anyone but my mother about either my writing or personal improvement programs)*, seems to have the power to push me off-track. Each incident is a temptation for my ego to take charge and thrust me right back into my old thought patterns.

This morning, my protective enclosure was breached by the collective power of a group of phone calls that embodied familial and social obligations and concerns. Fortunately, because the difference between my new and old dispositions is quite striking, I was able to detect the intrusion as it was being perpetrated. Although I do give myself props for discerning that I was being drawn into replaying old dynamics – one of my ego's favorite fixes – it was but a first step: the mere act of identifying an unraveling episode is insufficient in disabling it. Ergo, I stood as an observer witnessing the beginning of my slippage.

At once, in a state of mounting panic, I told myself: "Oh no, I am not done with my 28-day program, I do not want it interrupted. I don't want to give in. How do I stop this right now?" I took a step back, putting enough distance between my self and the negative emotions that were rising, and from that standpoint, contemplated my reaction of refusal. I realized that my "not-wanting-it-to-happen" was a thought tinted with fear and resistance, and thus equivalent to not accepting and fighting "what is" – two things I have learned are absolutely counter-productive.

Determined not to fall back into this familiar pattern, I brought myself to a place of stillness, and rather than fight the feeling, I accepted its presence and observed.

Soon, I noticed the contraction in my body was not very deep: the breach had not yet caused too much damage and was still superficial. Behind it, I could still feel my newly acquired calmness and openness. I intently focused on that, breathing into it. The remarkable thing in this experience was that as soon as I positioned myself as an observer, the fear dissolved.

Once the fear and resistance business was taken care of, I was able to deal with the causes of my recent near-derailment. From my stillness had emerged a clearer mind, which allowed me to see that the emotions – brought to the surface by the morning's phone calls – did not have to be. In fact, they no longer corresponded to who I am now. They were mostly a knee-jerk reaction: an automatic response to old stimuli.

I reminded myself of the new healthy habits I was creating in my life and that slipping into negative feelings was just an old groove I was tempted to revisit. I stayed in that place until I was able to merge what I mentally understood with my recovered physical feeling of peace.

The hours that followed felt a little bit like I was on probation: I would be tested, and good behavior would be rewarded. Keenly aware of the precariousness of my status and conscious of the pivotal and critical nature of the day, I walked through it carefully, as if an old foot injury had flared up and I just had to watch my steps for a bit.

STEP BY STEP GUIDE TO FEND OFF SLIPPAGE

1. When you feel yourself slipping, acknowledge what is happening.
2. Once you do, your first reaction will probably be to panic, feeling slightly helpless: "Nooooo, I don't want this!"
3. Recognize your objection is a form of fear and resistance.
4. Don't fight it. Find your stillness and observe it: fear will dissolve.
5. With a quiet mind, examine the source of your quasi-relapse and its mechanism *(it's probably an old one).*
6. Reconnect with where you want to be and tread gently for a while.

Old triggers often invite old responses. Beware of bringing old baggage to a new situation. Learn to lighten your load and to be discerning of what your carry moment to moment. Proficiency in this skill makes for less strenuous travels.

DECEMBER 2ND, 2011

FOLLOW YOUR BLISS

A couple of days ago I went for a hike in the wonderful mountains in my backyard. Invariably, as I walked, I became acutely aware of everything around me. I noticed tiny morsels of lichen, an insect carrying a load to somewhere, the sunrays hitting a tree a certain way, a light rain of needles falling from the canopy of trees above, the artistic arrangement of a berry and sprig frozen in thin ice under my foot, and the movement of the wind rushing past and around me. I relished in every changing scent and every vantage point, and smiled at the odd behavior of squirrels or at a bird's skillful flight through the branches.

The intimate joy I derive from such a heightened sensory presence is probably why I have almost always hiked alone. Finding a partner who will revere, contemplate and honor the mountain as I do has proven difficult *(actually, it's never occurred to date).*

When I am by myself on a mountain, it is I whom the mountain accepts as a guest; as soon as two or more people are gathered, the larger unit becomes a more dominating presence I uncomfortably perceive as a party disrespectfully intruding and trespassing. When it is only I, a silent communication takes place as I enter the folds of Mother Nature: I ask permission, it is granted, and I give thanks.

I even get quite bothered when I encounter groups and hear people talking loudly about this and that, totally unaware of their surroundings *(need to work on that, everything doesn't have to be so serious all the time).* I find it rude. In nature, I consider myself a guest and behave accordingly. I am mindful of my environment and make sure to compliment my host for the fine home she has graciously invited me to share.

In nature as in life, I try to honor the hallowed grounds I walk on.

We can stroll through life as we do through nature:
Wandering, oblivious to our surroundings and its possibilities,
Or willing and open hearted to be vessels and vehicles
Of its unfathomable promises.

Later, I passionately shared my experience with my Mom on Skype, telling her about the scintillating snowfall over a blue-sky backdrop and about the greenish light turning the endless tree trunks aglow, as if it was the most exciting thing in the world. Despite my fervor, words are never enough to convey the sense of aliveness I derive from my excursions – but I certainly light up trying.

Throughout my life, I have always wished I knew what my passion was. In this sense, being multi-talented has been a double edge sword. It may sound like a full-bellied complaint but it's true: When you have many talents, it is difficult to figure out which one is your passion and which one you should pursue more seriously *(unless you have benefited from someone's help in guiding you to figure it out).*

I imagine that having known where my passion laid would have made my life infinitely simpler: No more uncertainty or hesitation, no more questioning or wondering if obstacles are trying to tell me I am not doing the right thing, or if something else might make me feel more fulfilled. The call would have been clear and irresistible – like Ulysses' sirens – and obliterated any doubt. Even if the pursuit of this passion had come with challenges, I would have rested in the knowledge there was nothing else I could or would do with my life. One single target to aim at and focus on: Easy.

Movies about individuals following their passion (even recklessly), such as *Twister*, have always moved me to tears. I have both envied and admired these characters who, unapologetically and unconditionally, follow their personal grail. The absence of passion in my existence, and my hunger for experiencing such an inexorable drive, has always troubled me deeply.

For a long time, nature and I shared a loving, albeit casual, relationship. Now and then, however, I was given momentary hints that the flirting was intensifying and that the mountains plucked the strings of my core. I particularly remember going to see an IMAX movie about the Everest and having to stop on a park bench upon exiting the theater because I was weeping uncontrollably. My then-boyfriend was stumped, unable to comfort or understand what the heck was going on with me and frankly, I couldn't explain it very clearly either: "*Sniff*... it's so powerful... *sniff*... it's life... *sniff*... I need to be there...*sniff, sniff, sniff.*"

The relationship continued *(with nature – the one with the boyfriend fizzled)*, punctuated by occasional peaks, until the late nineties when I started experiencing the allure of the mountain more intensely. At that time, I had made new friends who owned a B&B in Stowe, Vermont *(lucky me)* and it became my second home. Twice a month, I would take the four-hour drive down to the Green Mountains, and stay for the weekend. Regardless of the difficulties I was facing in my life, I could always muster the energy to go to the mountain, knowing it would replenish me tenfold. Rain or shine, snow or gale, I would be up on the trails, by myself, exploring new terrain, discovering new rocks, knots, and mosses, until I proclaimed myself Queen of Mount Mansfield. This was the first time I felt the embers of passion *(other than in man-love)*. It was the beginning of a torrid love affair *(again: with nature)*.

TEACH WHAT YOU LOVE

What I consider the most fulfilling experience of my life *(to date)* resulted from giving into what was then just beginning to look like passion: In 2001, I was offered to lead my first hiking Wellness Retreat. Although I was enthused by the prospect, I must admit to have been more than a little intimidated.

The retreat (and the ones that followed) was scheduled around day hikes, optional Annie's yoga-stretch classes *(a personal brand of movement since I am not a yoga instructor)*, meditation and/or journaling, and lively dinners complemented by a few bottles of wine *(in my idea of balance between spirit, mind and body; earthly pleasures should not be denied)*.

Needless to say I was nervous when I showed up to introduce myself on the first night. Here I was, proposing myself as their leader without any real technical knowledge to impart or great adventures of conquering Kilimanjaro or trekking the Machu Pichu to share *(which some of the participants actually had)*. In fact, my qualifications were limited to Stowe and my self-awarded title of Queen of this one mountain. Bravely, I laid-out the schedule, introduced the guest-guides who would lead alternate hikes (to accommodate all levels), and spread out the sign-up sheets. Given the experience of these guest mountain-veterans who boasted about all the summits, local and exotic, they had climbed, I was surprise to see my list fill-up. I guess I had something other than conquests to offer; perhaps my love was coming through.

Having never myself partaken in a group hike, I shepherded my first group from the heart. I determined as I went how a mountain guide would lead; I did it my way. To my further surprise, the word of my singular style got out after the first day and participants hurried to put their name of my list for the next outing: something magical was happening on these hikes.

This was another instance in my life when I was reminded of the true meaning of "Teach what you know". Up until then, I had believed it to mean: "Don't try to fake your way through teaching something you don't really know about. Stick to the curriculum of what you can document you have learned or you risk making a fool of yourself and being of disservice to others." But this experience taught me that the true meaning was: "Teach what is 'you'. Teach what is within you. Teach what you love." What makes someone a worthy teacher, or leader, comes from the heart, not from the résumé *(not all of it or all the time anyways).*

The retreat as a whole turned out to be transformative for each of us. Many guests shared with me the depth and lasting effects of the experience, which happened to take place two weeks after September 11th and included individuals from New York, New Jersey, Pennsylvania, and Massachusetts.

For me, perennial seeds had been sowed in the furrows of my being. As I was leading this group, I had felt as though winged feet moved me across the ground. I had been carried by an energy reciprocally given and received, and had experienced a moment in time when I felt on point with my design. Sharing my love of the mountain had functioned as a universal translator for the greater love I hold in my spirit, and which I yearn to give infinitely. Those who had received the message were then free to disseminate it through the voice of their own translator, in their own life, and keep it going.

Paradoxically, leading retreats was at once demanding yet effortless: it felt natural.

A few years ago, as I was again trying to sort out what I wanted to do with my life, someone shared these insightful words with me: "Do what you love, do it for free if you have to, and life will unfold as it should. Do what you love and invitations will come to you." Although I figured it was a very nice strategy for later – when my finances would permit me to do something for free – I proceeded to make a (short) list of when I had felt "at home" and loving what I had been doing. Well, leading wellness retreats not only appeared at the top of the list but I also realized that it had, in fact, already generated an invitation: Years before, at the end of my second experience as leader, I had been asked to organize a tropical week-long retreat, and the group had inferred that, regardless of the cost, they would follow. This consisted of a door opening onto an unforeseen rewarding career: I was being *invited* to do what I loved and would get paid for it *(under the Caribbean sun no less).* What was also revealing was that the offer had occurred spontaneously, without effort on my part.

This could have been a defining moment but I did not recognize the opportunity as such. Well, I kind of did, but as something not doable. My life was in such shambles that I could not fathom how to follow through. Perhaps the timing wasn't right, but at least, the idea had been planted that out of following your bliss, opportunities will come *(okay, maybe I did no see it that way then, but in retrospect today I can recognize it as such – when it happened, I was left upset that I had to pass on something good; further proof that the universe really wasn't on my side).*

Today, I also understand that just as we must live in our truth in order for success to come into our life – and not wait for success before finding our truth – we must sometimes *(always?)* follow our passion *(for free at first or as a sideline perhaps)* before figuring out how we can make a living at pursuing it. "Live it, and they will come."

NOTHING NEW UNDER THE SUN

"Follow your bliss" is by no means a new concept. The phrase was actually coined by Joseph Campbell (whose writing, incidentally, greatly influenced George Lucas' *Star Wars*) through his teachings in the 70's, and was popularized following the posthumous broadcast of *The Power of Myth* in 1988. He himself had derived the idea from a much older source, the Hindu Upanishads. He verbalized the concept by saying that by following one's bliss, a person puts themselves on a track that has been waiting for them; and from that place, they then live the life they were meant to live.

At least I am happy to report that I have learned the lesson *(I think – I hope)*. From where I stand today, I don't believe I will ever let another invitation slip by. I remain alert, aware and open. In a roundabout way, I seem to have found my purpose as a result of following the thread of my passion once more: It is the Coast Mountains and their surrounding nature that lured me here in Vancouver where circumstances would collude and compel me to write. If I hadn't heeded their call in August 2010, I would not be here *(now that I think of it, the same mountain/nature thread lead me to Sedona: another seminal location of my life)*.

PASSION, SIGNIFICANCE, AND PURPOSE

By daring to allow my passion for the mountains to guide me, I have found significance in my life. I am now doing something I love, something that is *me*, something that gives meaning to my life, something I believe will be of service to the greater community: I have entered into purpose. And for the moment, I am doing it for free *(have I mentioned I am not making any money right now?)* – let's see where this takes me.

> ***Let your passion be your guide. Directly or indirectly, it will lead you where you ought to be. If you live your life following your passion, you will live an authentic life.***

TEACH YOUR CHILDREN WELL

I indicated earlier that failure to know my passion throughout my life has been cause for a lot of wandering and dissatisfaction. If I had known my bliss, I would have been living in my truth a long time ago. And I am not alone in this: I've heard the same lament from so many. For most of us, the search is still ongoing – blessed are those who avoided this sludge because they had a doubtless knowing from the get go *(and those are the ones who kindly attempt to teach us that hard work and perseverance will bring success – fine print: if you know your bliss).* Actually, I believe we are all wired with a passion at birth and that if we followed it, we would find and accomplish our unique purpose. Let me rephrase this slightly: We are all born with a purpose and the Universe generously gave us passion as a roadmap to find it. The problem is, with its busy schedule of creating us all, it omitted to inform us of the existence of said map. And this is the crucial lapse that parents and mentors need to remedy today: They must be made aware of this particular aspect of our design and teach the children about it.

In order for our children's lives to unfold as smoothly as possible with the best chances at optimal results (including joy, fulfillment and success), they each must be assisted in discovering their passion and supported in following it. Just imagine what would happen if every child knew for sure that he was good at doing something unique and precious, that he was "the chosen one" to do it on this planet, and that the world needed him exactly as he was *(I have heard of garbage collectors who were passionate for their job – it just goes to show).* We would have generations of individuals who did not need to prove themselves by putting others down, who would respect others for who they are, and who would find worthiness in everyone. If our children were seen and valued for who they are, self-worth and self-confidence would inevitably ensue and spread like wildfire.

Yes, we must teach our children well; we must show them the way is through their worthy passion. I believe it is the greatest gift they can receive. And the gift would not stop there, it would be a gift to the world because I suspect that if every human being realized the purpose for which they were created, not only would they be happy and rewarded for it but every function in the world would be fulfilled with minimum angst and frustration. If everyone did what they love, nobody would be working *(it wouldn't feel like work)*. If everyone followed their bliss, their passion, their love, the world would be a much happier place and purr like a well-oiled machine or run like a healthy body.

LIKE THE CELLS OF A BODY

I do believe we are all born with an innate purpose. Individuals on the planet are not unlike the cells of one body: they have a life of their own but collectively form a whole. Each one has a place to be and a role to fulfill. In our bodies, differentiation occurs naturally whereas in our life, passion is the indicator of where we belong.

A muscle-cell is not encoded like a brain-cell and will not behave as one regardless of how hard a brain-cell may wish it would. Even if a taste-bud-cell gets angry at a fingernail-cell for not helping out, it won't change a thing. Before judging and complaining about someone not doing what we want them to do, let's consider they are doing exactly what they should (and can), given the purpose of their creation.

Overall collaboration and individual integrity is paramount. If a group of cells, calling themselves Lung was to foment an insurrection against the Heart group, or if this Heart Group staged a mutiny against the Brain faction, the Body would have a problem. But if each group becomes the best at what it is meant to do, the body will go about enjoying life and adequately fulfill its own role in the human collective.

A cell is to an organ what an organ is to a body, a person to a family, a family to a community, a community to a country, a species to a genus, a genus to a planet, and a planet to a solar system. Everything that "is" is part of a larger body. And in the name of peace, we would be wise to keep this in mind.

Respect that each person has their own properties, role and function in the world: wishing a liver cell to perform as a heart cell is not only pointless, it is unloving.

Accept your own properties, role and function in the world. Be who you are, be the best version of "you" you can be, with integrity: that** is **perfection and will make the world go round(er).

Consider humanity as one macro-organism composed of billions of cells called humans. If everyone is true to their nature and focuses on doing their job well (being who they are), the larger organism will evolve has it is meant to do.

DECEMBER 3RD, 2011

EMOTIONAL UPDATES

As I write the stories of my past, I think about the complexity of everyone's story. I think about the richness of teachings that can be unearthed, the revelations hidden behind where one has been, and the trails leading to whom one has become. I also realize how crucial it is to keep up with your life and not sweep things under the rug. Our lives are so tightly woven in emotional intricacies that said rug could quickly become bulgy and cause us to trip.

Just as our computer regularly prompts a dialogue-window asking if we wish to update our software, so too we must do with our emotions. Just as with the computer, if we don't get around to taking care of it, our system might slow down, not function properly, or even crash eventually.

A few years ago, several major events congregated and tumbled into my life in a short period of time: I was accompanying my father while he was dying, I had received devastating financial news, all the while my far away beloved one's dysfunctional behavior had reached new heights. At the time, I wisely chose not to allow myself to feel the extent of my broken heart, or dwell on the consequences of my financial loss, because my primary task was being by my father's side. I even had to defer feeling the complete range and depth of what this experience of death meant for my future, in order to focus on being there for him and with him in every moment. The decision was sound and did allow me to be fully present through the months, but sometime after my father died, I started crumbling, and that's when I knew my first step had to be to update my emotional software, reboot my system and go from there. The task of tackling my neglected emotions could no longer be postponed. So very consciously, and with a little dread, I put time aside to review these recent events with my mind, my heart and my guts. Painfully, one by one, the reactions emerged. Reality hit me, consequences were imminent, emotions were raw, and fears surfaced. Nothing was sorted overnight, but the vital process of inner-health maintenance was in motion.

Given the speed at which we live life these days, and the amount of events we seem to superimpose one onto another, it is understandable that we don't always have the luxury to deal with every emotion as it comes up. We have become proficient at managing and storing them, perhaps a little too proficient. In and of itself, the practice is not to be faulted; I believe it is okay to put some issues on the shelf while we deal with more important matters. But what *does* critically matter, is that we not forget to get back to them lest the rug spew them out, leaving us with a mess.

Let's make sure we attend to our updates on a regular basis so that our internal system works at its fullest potential.

Add a list to your list of lists. Call it *My Personal Software Updates* ***or*** *Emotional Updates To Do.* ***When you don't have the time, energy, or psychological ability to deal with the emotional impact of an event, write it down, and get back to it another day. These updates are essential for the good functioning of your self.***

DECEMBER 4TH, 2011

XMAS GREETINGS

Today I took it upon myself to design a Christmas card to send to a few friends and family members. My initial idea was to select a photograph from last month's enchanted trip to Mount Kulshan, print the quantity I needed, and draw my own festive doodles with green, red and silver metallic pens, thus adding a hand-made artistic touch.

As I opened the selected image with Photoshop, I decided to try my hand at computer graphics. After a few strokes, I was hooked and worked on it all afternoon. Being quite pleased with the result, I emailed my card-to-be to my Mom. The moment she saw it, she called me to share how moved she was by the creation. She said the card was in my image: in the image of the new me she had seen emerging lately. She described it as bright, lively, sparkling, joyful, and full of light. As she was talking, I looked at my card through her eyes and began seeing what she was seeing. It moved me. The picture was scintillating, playful, and vibrant; it depicted a world where I saw myself living. The creative process of making the card had not been intellectual or intentional, it had been intuitive and was reflective of my renewed inner being.

This revelation was a comforting, reaffirming moment that the journey I have been on for the past 24 days (and initiated months earlier) is transforming my core and is beginning to spill into my life.

Our inner transformations will manifest themselves in many ways. Noticing the small things that we are now doing differently can be validating and encouraging.

DECEMBER 5TH, 2011

UNEXPECTED

Day 25 of ego sobriety and it appears that I now sport an almost new brain as well as a dusted-off shiny inner-self *(that picture I drew said so)*. There is reason to rejoice. Did I mention that I don't think I have lived worry or drama free for more than a few occasional consecutive days since having three good months in the late 90's? Well, it is so.

Along with my sparkly new self, an unexpected and extraordinary thought has been slowly coming forth in my mind. Timidly at first, but with enough assurance for me to mention today, I've been thinking that I feel like getting a job! Yes, really. As my positivity is requiring less minute-by-minute attention and becoming more natural, I have considered looking for work for the holidays. Slowly, my physical wellbeing is making strides: I have only had three days of nausea last week and my "good hours" *(when I don't feel totally exhausted)* are stretching. So I think I should be able to handle some part-time work in the near future.

A few weeks ago, I met a girl in a gondola on my way up to a local mountain resort to do some gentle hiking. She happened to work at one of the restaurants and told me about the four-hour shifts and interesting gratuities. On that same day, I met an older gentleman who praised the working environment of the resort. Well, combine these "signs" and the fact that getting to work would imply a gondola ride *(there are no public roads up the mountain)*, and you know I made certain to make a mental note of this; something I could pull out when I felt physically (and mentally) ready to get a job.

That moment came days ago and I decided to go out on a tentative limb by contacting the Executive Chef of the resort. I wrote an intriguing and enticing email saying how I would like to meet with him for a few minutes, and that although I had little experience as a waitress *(I worked in a bistro 18 years ago)* and my career had been as an entrepreneur, I was a quick learner and would add zest to his team and become an asset to his restaurant.

I am very hopeful, but the challenge is not to project myself into the future just yet. The past month has peacefully sailed under the flags of Meadow Repair – in order to improve my health – and of my latest concurrent 28-day program – consisting of switching my beliefs and thought patterns – and I must now restrain my ego from fabricating expectations.

I have an idea: Since I have three days to go on my 28-day program, I will remain here and now until it is completed. The anxieties of an unknown Phase Two are futile and detrimental *(Lesson 2: Take 10).* "One day at a time" is how it goes for us addicts of any sort. Only once the 28-day program concludes will I dedicate time to determine the syllabus of the next program.

Yep, that works for me.

Planning ahead is important, but we must also remember that each day suffices in itself. Occasionally, when the future causes anxiety, we may be wise to give ourselves a break and focus solely on the day at hand.

DECEMBER 6TH, 2011

SERENDIPITY

Last night I began reading a new novel and the serendipity is worth mentioning. First of all, it is part of an indiscriminate selection of six summer-read books I recently purchased at the used-book store. On top of that, I only picked this specific one last night because of its cover: a woman and a man from the waist down, wearing blue jeans, barefoot, hugging, ankle deep in the ocean – something perfectly suited for my mood.

The story is about a woman moving to Nantucket with only the little money she borrowed in her pocket*. As she considers this move a new beginning for herself, she sets out into her new life with three rules:

1. "Be self-sufficient" *(that's my plan).*
2. "Don't lie about the past" *(which in my case I take to mean: be truthful, transparent and authentic – and why not write a book while you're at it).*
3. "Exercise good judgment with men" *(not really relevant for me right now but I could interpret it as: be patient a little longer, you will eventually attract the right man).*

---

* *The Blue Bistro*, Elin Hilderbrand.

As the main character arrives in her new town, her immediate priority is to find work, and lo and behold, she coincidentally meets the owner of a famous restaurant. Based on what he sees, he decides to give her a chance as the assistant manager even though she has no restaurant experience! *(That's all I'm asking!)*

SYNCHRONICITY AND COINCIDENCES

We have all experienced synchronicity and coincidences in our lives: As we are driving somewhere, the radio will play the song we were humming, the announcer will use a word we were searching for, our favorite numbers show up as a recurring theme for a period of time, a phrase on the back of a bus unexpectedly answers a question we were pondering, the clock displays 11:11 when we absentmindedly glance at it, etc. Although I avoid trying to find any specific meaning in these happenings, I do, however, welcome them ever so fondly. To me, they are checkpoints along my route, a stamp from the Universe validating that I am on the right track of my life.

> ***Consider coincidences and serendipitous occurrences as confirmations that you exactly where you are meant to be, doing exactly what you are meant to do. Once you get such a nod from Life, continue on your journey with confidence and reassurance: you are where you belong at the moment.***

DECEMBER 8TH, 2011

CONGRATULATIONS! NOW WHAT?

I woke up this morning after a difficult night of sleep. Even though I had told myself to relax, not think about the future, and to just complete my 28 days peacefully, my mind/ego did not cooperate 100%. So the night was not very regenerative. But today is the last day of my program and I intend to give myself profuse congratulations and enjoy it.

During my restless nocturnal hours, I decided that my first order of business would be to email my Christmas card to the Executive Chef of the coveted restaurant, with my best wishes along with a footnote such as: *Still think we should meet.*

As I turn on my computer I am shocked to see an email from him in which he apologizes for the delay and proposes a meeting for tomorrow. I am a little baffled, and I like it. Tomorrow just happens to be the first day following my 28-day program; I am moved by the magical timing. I cautiously dare to consider this the result of the universe's law of attraction: its vibrations are now syncing with my new frequencies and everything is going according plan. It is plausible, right? After all, attracting good things has been the goal behind all my work. So why am I a little uneasy? I want to be excited though I remain incredulous. I guess dealing with hardship and disappointment is much more familiar territory than that of ease and gratification. But I am an adventurer and oh so willing to change my tune. I email him back, agreeing to the meeting *(without the Christmas card though, it would be a bit too much)*. Let's see what the rest of the day brings.

He confirmed without delay, and I spent a peaceful day clearing up all the paper work on my desk, accomplishing all the little administrative tasks I had been putting off, and checking them off my list. It was an efficient, satisfying day.

I was surprised by the quiet mood of this last day of my program. I had imagined a day dedicated to deep introspection, review and gratitude, and concluded by a ceremonial farewell to the "sober facility" *(so to speak)*. But I guess I have done plenty of that lately and going about my day with simplicity and ending it without a marching band, was even better suited. I truly appreciated that.

Some milestones can be celebrated without fanfare. The full flavors of accomplishments and self-satisfaction are sometimes found in the simplest dish.

DECEMBER 9TH, 2011

CAN IT BE THAT SIMPLE?

Another morning that follows another difficult night of sleep *(sure sounds familiar)*. My mind practiced a trampoline summersault routine throughout the night: a lot of jumping around went on *(after all, we did have a public appearance the next day)*. Because my vertigo and inherent nausea have been creeping back up lately, I decided to try a new medication before going to bed last night: bad idea. The moment I swallowed the pill I realized what a dumb thing to do the night before my very first job interview. The drug is supposed to be innocuous but with me, I never know. My reactions are often listed as highly improbable in the fine print of the piece of paper the pharmacist hands you with the prescription. In this case, the result was: I woke up groggy and with a fuzzy head.

Of course, my morning is spent thinking about the meeting. Hoping to clear my mind of its fuzz and maintain a calm demeanor, I stretch a little and breathe some fresh air out on my balcony. Since uncertainty is seeping into my mind, I get back inside, sit down, and write the following: *It's the next step Annie. It is the natural progression. It is part two of the program: Reintegration into the world.* This gives me perspective and tugs at my faith.

Then I tackle the difficult task of finding something proper to wear. The difficulty lies in the fact that I do not own interview clothing. I have been self-employed for so long, working from home, that all I have – as interview options – are blue jeans and two nice summer shirts I can't wear today *(it's winter)*. The rest are very sporty *(cheap)* sweaters and tees. I do own two sport jackets, a sandy colored one *(it's beige – but that sounds so boring)* and a black one, but those don't feel right for today – too formal for the top of a mountain. I end up opting for a crisp new white t-shirt with a beige *(sand)* cardigan and a rich ocher and aubergine scarf. Luckily, I have a new winter coat that looks pretty smart *(a necessity I acquired through discount cross-border shopping)*. As soon as possible, I need to purchase some good clothing because once I'm out in public, I just may receive invitations for socializing, and I should dress properly!

I finally head out for the meeting, drive to the base of the mountain and hop on the gondola *(I'll say it again: how cool is this?)*. I make my way to the restaurant and since I arrive a little early, the hostess asks me to sit at the entrance and wait for the Chef. As I am sitting there, watching the servers and bartender at work, I start doubting the whole thing: "What the hell I am doing here hoping to get a job as a waitress? Can I really picture myself being one of them? With the type of career I've had, my talents, my aspirations... and the Chef is probably going to be arrogant and make me feel inadequate... I want to get out of here." Simply put, I'm scared; but I need to push through those fears. I can do that.

Silently, I repeat to myself: "It's the next step. It is time. It is not the ultimate goal; it's only a step *(think of the puppy)*. You will be out and be seen. It is a first step towards being self-sufficient." But as the minutes pass, I really start slipping down hill. I don't want to, but the feeling is pretty strong. At last, the man shows up. He is energetic, has a straight and honest glance, and he is easy to talk to.

Understand that it is not the job of the Executive Chef to interview new employees. All applications for the resort are to be made online, sorted out by the Human Resource Coordinator and then passed on to the H.R. Director who will call back the chosen ones. The E.C. is responsible for seven food-and-drink outlets on the mountain, including his five-star restaurant; he does not interview neophytes with no restaurant experience. But for better or worse, as I have explained, this dragon that I am has a hard time conforming to established and conventional routes. She tends to look for uncharted, less mainstream bypasses.

The conversation flows and the really funny thing is that, you know that novel I'm reading? Well, it turns out it's making me sound somewhat knowledgeable of the restaurant life. As we are talking, he uses restaurant jargon that I would have never understood had I not been reading that book. I also ask a few intelligent questions because the book describes at length the different roles and running of the staff in a restaurant. Now *that* is serendipitous.

He tells me that after the holidays, he normally just goes back to his usual staff and may not need me then *(it does sound like he'll hire me until then)*. I answer that I'm not worried because people leave all the time. He knocks on the wooden table, meaning that he wishes he doesn't lose his trained staff, and I do the same gesture as I quip, "We're going to confuse the poor wood, I'm not wishing for the same thing you did!" Since I really just want a foot in the door, I make sure to tell him that I will do any work, including administrative assignments. The meeting concludes as he tells me he will look into his needs and call me next week to let me know what he has to offer. Good enough, it actually sounds like I have a job!

So it appears all is well and I can actually start trusting in life. There *is* magic in the air, except it's not magic, it's the result of my inner work. Although again, I have to wonder: Really?

This experience is revealing to me that despite my remarkable strides, I still have a strong undertow of... fatalism, particularly as it relates to anything connected to the elusive prospect of financial autonomy. In this regard, my core belief has undeniably been muddied and is in dire need of TLC. My history has created a figure akin to an apostle Thomas in me: I need to touch to fully believe. As I have mentioned, a succession of financial downfalls has flooded my life from every direction for several years *(the specifics of which, after considerable reflection, I am choosing not to share – so we can forget about the margaritas I once offered)*. If I contemplate the whole picture from a distance, it's actually so absurd that it's kind of funny – just not quite funny ha-ha since I'm at the center of if.

The good news remains that I no longer feel the victim of an unkind Universe picking on me. I have taken ownership that despite the fact that I have lived in spiritual awareness since my youngest days and always strived for betterment, my just-as-long history of not living authentically, has caused karma to bite my behind repeatedly. But no more. I am centered in my truth and henceforth basking in good karma.

Nonetheless, I recognize that my wounds of economical defeats exist and will take time to heal. My trust issues resemble those of a woman who has been betrayed time and again in past relationships, and enters into a new one with a good man: Bit by bit, event by event, proof by proof, she will realize her doubts are no longer appropriate, and her wounds will heal through repeated applications of a balm of positive new experiences. I am myself in a new relationship with life, and little by little, my skepticism will gradually disappear.

Back to today's fears concerning this job. I must continue to tell myself that this job is not about the job per se: it is about the step in the right direction it represents. This is my first day after completing the program, and feeling overwhelmed is to be expected. I suspect I am walking similar steps to that of an addict being released into the world after rehab: The drama has passed, the convalescing has taken place, the breakthroughs have occurred; healing is well underway, faith has been renewed, and the outside world seems mighty big. But the time has come to leave the protective cocoon and fly away. It is the next natural step. *(Go girl.)*

For those who have felt betrayed or beaten-up by life, for whatever reasons, rebuilding trust will take time. After making the necessary changes within yourself and in your environment, do not succumb to the impossible expectation that your world and perceptions will instantaneously turn around. Wounds heal into scars that eventually fade away.

DECEMBER 10TH, 2011

THE SUM OF ALL FEARS

Last night I came upon the repeat conclusion episode of *Why Not with Shania Twain**, a series that follows her on a journey of healing and self-discovery with the ultimate goal of recovering her lost voice; and this was yet another serendipitous occurrence. As her quest proves successful *(her voice returns at the end of the series)* the interviewer's final query is: *"So, the obvious question now is when will we see you perform again?"* Shania replies that her instinctive (conditioned) answer would have been that she was not ready yet, that she was afraid, and that she needed a little more time. But that now, because of this journey through which she had learned to test herself through her fears, performing was "the natural next step" *(yes, the exact same words I had written during the day – hence the serendipity)* and therefore, that's where she was heading.

Whether a next step consists of performing in front of thousands of people, getting a job in a restaurant, or walking out of one's house, the courage required is the same if it pushes someone to conquer their fears. The actual steps may be on a different social scale, but at par on the scale of the soul.

* Presented on OWN television.

COURAGE

Several factors influence how each person incorporates courage into their life, and certainly, different situations will call upon one's courage and test their mettle. One of the factors is that each individual is born with a particular level of innate bravery, plain and simple. The ability is programmed in our DNA: Just as one person has a gift for music and another for numbers, so too is a person wired, or not, for courageous behavior. Some people are natural-born fire-crackers who enjoy pushing the envelope and are fueled by audacity; others possess a more quiet and yielding personality by nature, and are less inclined towards inner or outer heroism.

Whichever the degree of predisposition, this skill can be learned – with more or less effort depending on the individual – at any stage of life, but would be an invaluable aptitude to develop at a young age. I believe that as much as we must champion the quest for passion in our children, so too is it imperative that we teach them, and make them practice, courage. This doesn't mean forcing children to do things that petrify them, but rather to encourage them to get acquainted with their fears, and embrace the thrill of pushing through with an acceptable amount of discomfort. One thing is for sure, practice is essential: courage is an art and an acquired taste they will carry throughout their life and forever be thankful for. There is no downside to courage.

I put courage right up there with the top five keys to living a good, fulfilling life:

— Love as much as you can: Yourself, others, the planet, the Divine.
— Always forgive: Yourself and others. Be kind.
— Don't fight what is: Plan for change but accept today with its who, what, when, where and how.
— Show courage: Dare to jump into what scares you.
— Be gracious: Whatever happens, grace makes life easier.

The Z rewards

Practice your courage so that your become proficient at this instrument. Define, explore and push your boundaries. Be daring. It will add pizzazz to your day, zing to your performance and zest to your life.

DECEMBER 11TH, 2011

SHANIA AND I

Yesterday I mentioned Shania Twain's television series. I had actually watched the whole program back in the spring when it first aired. The moment I had seen the trailers, months earlier, I knew I did not want to miss that show. The previews had instantly piqued my interest and I instinctively let them grab hold of a corner of my heart.

There were several reasons for that. One : I like Shania. I have always been rather fond of her as a person, and if I happen to stumble onto a program featuring her, I will definitely watch. Two : she's Canadian ; it's an added incentive. Three : I also happen to enjoy her music. Four : I have to confess enjoying celebrities' stories. Not the absurd, irresponsible, disconnected-with-the-world-and-the-self type of thing *(okay, occasionally I do, for entertainment, as a disbelieving judgmental voyeur)*, but the human stories. Five : I must further confess to having been a little dubious about her story *(like : Oh no, maybe she's more of an airhead* than I thought)* because really, what did she have to legi-

* Keeping my English vocabulary straight: You say "harebrained" but "airhead", right? Seems a little pea-brained to me. Just saying.

timately complain about that would justify creating a whole public healing-quest over? She is healthy, beautiful, talented, rich, recognized, has a successful career, a good son, and a great man who loves her and whom she loves, and very decent (!) living quarters. I mean, come on: So you were betrayed seven years ago by your husband and girlfriend *(which I agree is a tough break)*, but you have since found a better love, and still have everything else. So get over it! How would she handle a situation like mine: not having good health, or money, or career, or recognition, or man, or home? Now *that* is something to complain about. So I figured she was probably, and disappointedly, not very strong, incapable of gratitude, a little spoiled *(a lot spoiled)*, and needed to prove to the world that deep down, she was just like the rest of us, and also suffering. I figured she needed a come back after such a long absence and that she was following the trend of celebrities opening their lives to the public.

All of this, the genuine interest and the voyeuristic pleasure, made the series irresistible to follow and did not deter me from finding Shania endearing. The opening date was circled on my calendar.

A ROSE BY ANY OTHER NAME

Within the first minutes of the series, I breathed a sigh of gratitude, as I understood why my heart, above anything my mind had brought up, had nudged me to watch. From the onset, I was gifted with a great aha! moment. As I listened to Shania narrate her story, the authenticity of her pain came through, and it dawned crystal clearly on me that regardless of exterior circumstances, when someone is dealing with a situation that pokes at their deepest wound, we are all the same.

A wound is a wound is a wound, and they all hurt when you stick a knife in them. Whenever a person is tackling a core issue, tending to a fundamental emotional scar, or struggling to undo an intricate karmic knot – when a core-belief is affected – pain doesn't differentiate between the haves and the have-nots.

It does not matter that I don't have most of what she has; the point is that my set of circumstances exists to make me face the toughest challenge of my life, and so does hers. Her journey mirrors mine in every essential way that matters.

For both of us, the most personally testing circumstances and events have congregated in our lives, opening a window onto possibilities for elevating ourselves. And these conditions are custom-made to point out our respective heaviest anchors, and to offer the promise of great deliverance.

I have chosen to unshackle the restraints of a deep karmic bond, which will allow my personality to expand and my being to soar; and her choices and journey will do the same. Both our actions required mustering the courage to execute an equally giant leap of faith over an abyss of deeply entrenched fears. The significance of the exploit is identical within the scheme of our respective purpose, growth and life. The release will be as liberating in both cases, the breakthrough as gratifying, and our emergence, as life transforming. *

No matter what you have gone through or what your circumstances are, the journey of transcending fears is the identical process and should be celebrated by all, in every case. For each individual who courageously faces his Goliath, the Universe breathes easier and applauds in glee, and a person of goodwill rejoices.

---

* Note: Shania's relationship wounds of betrayal and distrust happen to have been healed by the unwavering love of a good man who, I am sure, was steadfast in applying a balm of assurance for as long as it took. This certainly seems to support my idea that with time and TLC, my trust issues towards life will also be healed.

DECEMBER 12TH, 2011

I SEE A SIGN

A warning sign.

I thought I had it. But I just received an email from the E.C. of the restaurant at the mountain telling me: "Upon review of my current staffing requirements, I currently am staffed for the winter season. I will keep your résumé on file for future consideration." So, there it goes, another unfortunate notch on my disappointment belt. It's hard to understand: at the end of the meeting, it had sounded like a done deal. Perhaps not abiding by the standardized rules and going over the chain of command ended-up upsetting the apple cart. Or maybe this was just not the next step that I was supposed to take. But I have to say, this job sure made a lot of sense to me.

I am conflicted between the fact that I allowed myself to believe things were changing only to be let down again, and the fact that I want to believe – and actually do believe – things have no choice but to change as a result of my inner transformation. I'm okay, but I feel a little numb, a little confused, a little weary. I have to admit that I am bummed-out: his response has put a tiny limp in my stride and a little scratch on my shiny dispositions. Thing is, I had expectations. I had already conjured up a nice little scenario in my head *(the one from my book)* whereby I met with the chef who was charmed by my presence, instantly recognized my potential, and hired me on the spot *(he wouldn't want to risk losing me to another restaurant).*

I am going to have to reflect on the meaning of this and perhaps take time to work out the content of that next 28-day program. One thing is for sure: I am determined not to let this bring me down. My recent progress is momentous; the changes are too pleasant and palpable for me to regress now. I am enjoying my positivity. But I have to admit the level of challenge of maintaining that positivity has been bumped up a notch because the prospect of being here alone during the holidays and not yet working is rather daunting. And that is the warning sign I see looming on the horizon: *Steep Slope Ahead. Proceed at your own risk.*

After sharing my thoughts with my niece she commented: "A wise woman once said, 'sometimes a cigar is just a cigar'. There is nothing to read into it. It's not even about you. They were just fully staffed."

As Yoda might say, "So smart you are, young Padawan."*

Expectations are just another face of "should haves". Instead of regret and blame for what should have been, they portend the dissatisfaction of what lies ahead for the future will assuredly be different that what is expected. Expectations should be handled with care.

DECEMBER 13TH, 2011

HAPPINESS IS MY CHOICE

I must come clean and admit I did not do so well yesterday: staying the course proved to be beyond me. I found myself putting on a face and I actually could not even pretend I was fine. I went out to

* To state what is obvious to most, this is inspired by George Lucas's *Star Wars*.

run a few errands and I was impatient at drivers, made wrong choices attempting to avoid traffic, went back to the store quite crossed as I realized I was charged $ 6.90 for a tiny amount of coffee *(turns out, it was no mistake)*, and couldn't fake enthusiasm during a certain phone conversation in which the person deserved my encouragement. I had one joyful moment at the supermarket when I chatted with *(to)* a beautiful infant in her stroller. She smiled, giggled, and I welcomed her to the planet – this did make my heart sing for a minute, and I was grateful for it. But all in all, I managed to create myself a pretty crappy day.

Surprisingly, I still purchased healthy foods to cook myself a smart meal; I give myself points for that. I watched television all evening. During one of the many commercial breaks, this loud, over-enthusiastic preacher showed up in a thirty seconds spot. He was really into his message *(dare I say slightly annoyingly so)* but one of his sentences hit me: *"Happiness is a decision!"* Of course. I had forgotten I had already learned that, but this was a timely reminder and I heard it. I ran to get a piece of paper, wrote it in big letters and set it on my pillow to make sure that when I got to bed, this would be my last thought.

The rest of my confession about yesterday is that as I lay in bed wearily – leaving the light on, knowing that even if I wanted to sleep, I couldn't – I surrendered to my sorrow and shed some tears: about twenty of them. They were the first in a quite a while but unfortunately, the news of the day had gotten to me and my heart was overflowing. I had hoped to start soothing my wounded trust and begin the healing process: I had wanted a proof from life. As I said earlier: I believe. But I had wanted to be shown concrete support. I want ease and easy. I believe in ease and easy... can I even say I deserve ease and easy?

I picked up the piece of paper I had laid on my pillow earlier, read it intently, and went to sleep repeating to myself: "Life is good, happiness is my choice. Life is good, happiness is my choice. Life is good, happiness is my choice." And guess what, I had the best night of sleep. I slept for hours: no nightmares, no lying awake, no getting up. I vaguely remember a dream of holding hands with others and leading a ritual of sorts. Then my last dream in the morning was of an old boyfriend from my teenage years *(whom I still hold in high esteem)*, showing up at my door with a big loving smile. We started kissing, holding each other, laughing. There was just so much joy, like the world had fallen into place. Friends and family were there, and at some point, I was insistent in asking if this was a dream: I pinched my brother and asked him to pinch me; I did not wake up. Everyone present convinced me it was not a dream, this was real and all was well. All I had to do was rejoice and enjoy. Then I slowly woke up and thought, "Oh, so it was a dream." But the happiness lingered even as I awoke to this reality, and I was left with the thought that good things were on their way, and that my life could change for the better in an unexpected instant.

WHAT CHANGED?

I am aware of being redundant in asking myself this question but it appears to befall in the category of useful parroting. And I have two reasons to bring it forward: One, what had actually changed yesterday that caused me to stray, and two, what changed overnight to explain feeling my joy again this morning *(other than a dream)*?

Had yesterday morning's email informed me that I had lost a dream job, or that I had been sacked from somewhere? Had anything been taken away from me?

And conversely, in the past twelve hours, did I sign a new contract, or was I the recipient of some great windfall? Did any other event change my long-term outlook or current situation that could explain feeling better? The answers are no, no, no: nothing in, nothing out. My relative financial security *(recent access to a substantial loan)* and insecurity *(it's a loan and it won't last)* have not budged.

Yesterday's feelings of loss and defeat had stemmed exclusively from the scenario I had created in my mind of how my life would unfold from this part-time job in a restaurant, of the imaginary people I would now never meet, and of the few hundreds of dollars I would not be earning. In reality, the blow I felt I had received was only inside my head; the news that nearly broke my spirit had in fact only destroyed an illusion, a fabrication of my ego, a castle made out of sand.

So the warning sign I saw looming yesterday was posted for my consciousness' benefit. It was cautioning me to proceed with care because my ego was now in possession of a few tasty morsels to feed its yet-to-happen-stories-of-fear-and-doom about not working for the holidays. The sign warned that if I should get too close, I might start slipping.

Fortunately, I am beginning to be able to rely on the experience I have acquired in dealing with similar situations, and I will handle this one as well. My life today is not the scenarios of my ego or the emotions they generate. It is up to me *(the real me, not my ego's portrayal)* to choose whether I allow them to dictate the quality of my current state of being, or not. The choice to be in happy dispositions remains mine. Maintaining a positive outlook is still in my hands; giving out good vibes to attract the best outcome is still in my control.

Having a good day is still my choice, and I choose to have a good day.

Sometimes, asking ourselves the question: "What has actually changed?" may point to the fact that nothing other than the script of a fabricated scenario has been crumpled and tossed aside. This realization can effectively bring us back to what is real in the present moment, and help dissipate a false sense of defeat.

DECEMBER 14TH, 2011

PRACTICE, PRACTICE, PRACTICE

Although I successfully maneuvered in response to the warning sign that popped up a couple days ago, I am still proceeding with caution. I am feeling the eyes of my probation officer upon me. I am realizing that, contrary to what I thought just a while ago – when I felt my positivity did not require minute-to-minute attention and I could look for work – staying the course is actually still quite demanding. I am getting more proficient at it, but the skills aren't honed and are not second nature by any stretch. I see that I got a little bit ahead of myself thinking that I was ready for the world. My 21-day itch, whereby the smallest demand sent me off-track, is not only a reality of the past; in fact, my sobriety is still fragile and my new good habits have not yet become well-beaten paths.

I was reminded of this fragility yesterday just as I was getting over the hump. I received a call from an acquaintance recruiting me for a small project. Although it instinctively didn't feel right for the time being, I reluctantly accepted – logic saying there was no justification for me to refuse. But my body was quick to grab a loudspeaker and vehemently announced its opposition to my choice *(I felt sick)*. Quick to follow suit, and happy to jump on the bandwagon, my ego grabbed the megaphone and began chiming-in with old tunes about my dutiful obligation to accept any offer that was money-bearing, whether they compromised my wellbeing or not. And just like that, I was back between a rock and a hard place of my own creation.

This morning, I am agitated and flustered as if immeasurable pressure has been put on me. The mere thought of *having* to produce something within the next few days has prevented me from sleeping and thrown off my balance physically and mentally. This is a serious setback: I am being pushed onto an old path I have been intentionally avoiding to allow regeneration to occur. I really don't want to go there.

As I am writing this, a flashing sign comes on in my head: *You will no longer choose economics over your truth and wellness.*

Right. I've seen this one before.

Then another: *Do not replay old dynamics; they are no longer congruent with who you are.*

Right. Right. Got it.

I did get it. I sent a straightforward and candid email explaining I was currently not equipped to handle even the smallest stress associated with a timeline. If the project could wait, I could attend to it later, sometime in the course of the next few weeks. Apparently, that's okay *(frankly, I would have preferred to be told it wasn't okay and that I was off the hook for good, but oh well).*

Life really does believe practice makes perfect doesn't it? Lessons must be learned by heart, through repetition, until they become effortless. It's like grammar: you have to recite conjugations endlessly and repeat rules over and over before you master the language. Grammar isn't much fun, but I do enjoy writing.* *(And by the way, for those of you who grumbled about English grammar, you would be in for a shock if you ever tackled French.)*

Some paths we travel, even more than once, just to learn they are the wrong ones.

---

* On the subject of grammar, I will take the opportunity to insert a comment about the educational system. I am one of those who are skeptical of new programs that relinquish old-school repetitive practices such as grammatical analysis, multiplication tables, and algebra. One can argue these are pointless robotic exercises – which, in most cases, will never be used in adulthood and that computers render these methods antiquated, but in my opinion, they are key tools of brain development. They trace the pathways of reasoning, organization, association, and deductive thinking; all skills I am heavily relying upon as I write this manuscript and that I am greatly thankful to have acquired.

MY RASPBERRY RIDE

When I got out of the house this afternoon, I noticed that someone has hit my lovely car. I say my lovely car because I love it so, and it holds great sentimental value: It reminds me of my Dad. Here is the story why:

Back in 2005, I had invited my parents for a visit in FriHo, and had planned on driving down with them from their home in Ste-Ville, Quebec. We would stop overnight in Stowe, VT, and turn this into a pleasant road trip. At that time, I was leasing a Honda Civic, a car I didn't like *(I'm an SUV girl)* but that had served me well *(following my bankruptcy)*.

Two days before departure, my well-maintained car stalled on the highway *(with me in it)* and had to be brought in to the garage: it was repaired without fuss. I can't remember what the problem had been but I was glad it had not happened while on our upcoming excursion. The next day, something else went wrong *(also can't recall exactly what)* and I had to bring it back to the dealer once more. Again, it was fixed. At last, it was the morning of our trip; we packed up my car and got on the road. Within a few miles, some other mechanical problem occurred, and as we happened to be driving by the dealership, we stopped-in, mildly irritated by the snag. Mechanics hoisted up the car, identified the problem, but for some reason *(you guessed, I can't tell you what it was)* repairing it was problematic and would require a good amount of time *(can't remember how much)*.

Well, whatever the delay was, it proved unacceptable to my father for whom patience had never been a strong suit *(the apple... the tree... there may be some truth to this)*. He was a driven visionary and entrepreneur who often upset colleagues by bulldozing over what he considered insignificant bumps. His solutions were always swift and grand.

True to his persona, he said: "Annie, that's enough. We have a trip to take and this is ridiculous. Go pick a new car in the lot and let's leave this lemon here. I'll make it happen. And pick a SUV, I want you to be safe on the roads." Stunned, but not really surprised *(we had seen the exasperation rising in my father's eyes)*, my Mom and I stepped out into the lot for a little impromptu shopping. Looking around, she told me that if this were her choice, she would choose the raspberry-red CR-V, and I concurred. Within a couple hours, my father had secured a loan with the only bank who would grant him a loan for a car that would be registered in my name *(the difficulties to juggle with were that no bank would put my name on a loan – not even as a co-signer – because of my bankruptcy, and my father was legally blind – making it difficult to explain buying a car!)*. Eventually, we signed all the necessary papers, they prepared the vehicle my Mom and I had picked out, we transferred the luggage into my new SUV, and off we went in my brand new raspberry ride. I have a picture of myself in front of my beautiful car with Mount Mansfield as the backdrop. We had a nice trip.

To this day, pretty much every time I get in my car, I am grateful, and I think of my Dad. I love my car, I take care of it and it takes care of me. I have always been safe in it. This is why yesterday, I felt pretty bad after noticing someone had "disrespected" my precious belonging *(it is also the only thing I [almost] own in the world – a seven year loan, five months to go!)*.

When I noticed the damage earlier, I sent an email to my landlords upstairs wandering if perhaps they had had a delivery truck come by recently, or any other careless guest who could have "inadvertently" hit my car while it was parked. This is a shared driveway between the residents of this house and the neighbors' house, and the way it is set-up, everyone leaving must back up next to my car before continuing down the hill and onto the road. I sent the email without holding much hope it would deliver a culprit because obviously, whoever had done this had chosen to cowardly hit and run. To my surprise, Mrs. Landlord told me she was the one but had thought she had barely touched the car. Problem solved: she readily volunteered to pay for the repair. I am so happy to have gone forward with my fishing email, and so relieved that no one had been malicious enough to cause me trouble and disappear. I am also quite pleased for not feeling too sorry for myself *(God, why me?)* or overly upset earlier. For the few hours I did not know what had happened, I actually managed not to spin too much of a sorry story.

All is well.

Intuition will at times drive us to take actions that defy logic or reason. These inner compulsions are often on the mark. When you get a sense of "I** must **do this", don't question it: do it.

DECEMBER 15TH, 2011

MIRROR, MIRROR...

Getting my hair done is always such a stressful experience. It's been years since I have been able to relax on a hairdresser's chair *(and that has only occurred a few times)*. I don't know if that's how it is for many women, but in my case, every appointment is a source of anxiety: anxiety and anticipation because by the time of the appointment, I usually can't stand my hair anymore, and am desperate for a pick-me-up.

Before each session, I promise myself to explain as clearly as possible what I'm looking for *(bringing in post-it marked magazines to illustrate my views)* and psych myself up for an enjoyable pampering experience.

Today is no different. I cheerfully sit on the chair, optimistic, and start explaining my vision. But right away, I get my first twitch: the hairdresser is distractingly nodding, but not really listening. I gently insist but it's a fine balance: I can't get under her skin because she must like me in order to be inspired to do a good job. Hoping to lighten the mood, I crack a few self-deprecating jokes about the finer points of my micromanagement-prone and insecurity-based personality. A rapport is established. I should be okay.

The critical highlighting and lowlighting process begins, and because I once had a very good hairstylist *(another Quebecer living in Arizona)*, I can tell there is no order in the way the colors are being applied: the dark shade is being put on top rather than under, there is no rhythm to the sequence, the color mixture is not quite painted all the way to the roots. I feel the amount of hair per foil is too large, and the delicate sideburn area is being clumped into a single foil. Distress is around the corner.

We go to the sink where my hair is washed and rinsed within seconds. I internally cringe as I remember my "good hairstylist" explaining to me the importance of washing and rinsing off the products thoroughly for several minutes. We return to the styling chair as I dread what removing the towel will reveal. In her distracted state, she must have misheard the "natural streaks look" I had stressed because what I get is a "natural skunk look". The products are brought back out and a touch-up session gets underway.

Time for the haircut. By now, my apprehensions are full blown. I pull out an after-my-good-hairstylist picture *(stylists must hate that)* to dispel any possible misunderstanding. With the first clip, I bite my lip. I specified a full-length look in the back and hair is being layered short at the top. I interrupt her and say, "Hem, excuse me, I would really like the full length in the back!" She acknowledges that it is what she is doing, and continues. There is no turning back. To my grave dismay, I can tell there is no technique to the haircut either: the back length is cut last (!), there is no crosschecking of layers, no comparing whether both sides are the same. The sad part is that she is such a sweetheart and I really like her. My hair is blow-dried and styled *(she does make it look good)* and I leave thanking her. At home, I get out my comb and scissors, and equalize both sides of my head as best as I can, and ruminate about how long it will take for my hair to grow back.

I don't know why a haircut can affect me so much – I had an easier time dealing with the car damage than this. And it's not even a disaster. It's not like I'm going to be stopped at the supermarket and asked what happened to my hair. So what's the deal? I know it really bothers me to pay for a professional and not be satisfied. It's a question of principle and integrity. More than that, I think my ill feelings are due to the fact that I have put my trust in someone and I feel betrayed. Yes, this rings right: Because I feel I have been burned so many times in my life, my hair drama reflects my trust issues.

Nah. That's hogwash: It's just plain vanity.

Here is my honest conclusion about my day: I am meant to be rich and get the best hairdresser in town. Period. Yes, I should probably reflect on the reasons for my vanity and the inflated role of my ego, but screw that. I just need to have money.*

Mirror, Mirror... give me something to say!

I wish I had wise words to convey.

But I don't.

---

* April 2012: I am not rich yet, but I have just returned from an (expensive) appointment with Ali and Patsy at a downtown Vancouver salon. Wow. Now that's what I'm talking about: worth every penny *(and a twinge of guilt)*. Next time, I'll be able to relax and enjoy myself. Between this salon and the Cutie Pie Wax Bar, "The best little waxing house in Texas" *(...I mean Vancouver – FYI: this refers to an 80's movie title)*, I am creating a nice little network of personal care in my new town.

DECEMBER 16TH, 2011

STALLING, IDLING, OR RALLYING

So this is the eighth day since I completed my 28-day program. I am not displeased with myself: Under the watchful guidance of my awareness, I have diligently recognized and monitored the various temptations of my old ways, and successfully resisted their allure. I am still standing. But obviously, my discourse has changed. I am no longer experiencing the great moments of illumination and elation that have faithfully punctuated my recent journey and spurred me forward; my preoccupations are definitely more rudimentary.

Perhaps it is the result of a convergence of elements: With the end of the 28 days, I was divested of the motivating structure of a program; then not getting the job I believed was right for me undermined my get-up-and-go, and there is the possibility that I have simply reached a plateau and need to integrate the lessons for a while. This is not unlike the plateau one reaches when dieting, at which time, after significant and constant weight loss, the body appears to stop responding to the same efforts as though needing time to accept its new state – identifying it as its new normal – before moving towards the next milestone.

The latter, I have taken under consideration. Although I am under the impression that I am losing steam, I am also cognizant of the necessity of an adaptation period and this is probably why – half consciously and half instinctually – I have been less demanding of myself and not getting right back on another systematic program. You just can't go full steam ahead 100 % of the time.

So despite the fact that I am beginning to blame myself for

slacking-off, I must be mindful not to. I must be loving of where I am now, and understanding that there is a rhythm to all things of life.

Plateaus should be expected during our inner journeys and we should not allow those calmer periods to make us question our progress or determination. Assimilation time is in fact essential: it is when our being integrates lessons, experiences, and new information. Once these notions are incorporated, a new baseline is set. The nifty trick is to discern whether we are being a slacker when we should be pushing forward, or whether we are wisely sitting back in order to take it all in.

DECEMBER 18TH, 2011

A GIRL'S BEST FRIEND

In harmony with lovingly allowing myself to slack off and to take some distance from my daily grind of consciousness, I took a break yesterday and went shopping down in Washington State. Prices truly are more advantageous compared to British Columbia and I wished to take advantage of pre-Christmas sales *(traffic reminded me that I was not the only with this thought on the last Saturday before Christmas! What was I thinking?)*. My shopping list was a short one: I wanted to purchase a tiny diamond stud to replace one I had recently lost. It may sound frivolous *(and it may indeed be)* but it's my one purely narcissistic indulgence *(although my hair may fit in that category too)*

– actually one of seven since I wear seven studs: four on one side, three on the other. As a young teenager, my ears were pierced thrice. As a young adult, I bumped it up to five and owned an impressive arsenal of earrings that I pinned like butterflies onto a very large cork-board. For years I held out for numbers six and seven, which I symbolically associated to my sixth and seventh chakras, waiting for the day I would consider my self and my life to be whole. Shortly after meeting Richard, I gifted myself with what I deemed a complete set of earrings and ever since then, I have exclusively worn seven studs, day in day out, except for very rare occasions such as my recent meeting at the restaurant.

As it turns out, not only did I purchase a pair of diamond studs yesterday but also a pair of pale citrine stones. Since Kohl's offered a 70 % discount, in addition to a 25 % scratch-and-save I was lucky enough to get, I went all out and decided to replace the zirconiums I had be wearing as well.

The ride home proved not so smooth and found me stuck in an endless border line-up as well as highway stop-and-go traffic. These unexpected delays afforded me time to think – too much time. And that's when my self-rewarding day of shopping turned into a return trip ridden with pangs of conscience. The reprieve had been short. Confined in my car, I had time to feel guilty about spending money *(a reasonable afterthought, but useless at that point)*, silly about wasting a day, and worried about not having a job for the holidays. Not what I thought I was bargaining for with a day off.

Once I got home, and in spite of a lot of loud singing in the car, those feelings lingered and began to seriously threaten my sobriety. I felt weary, despondent and vulnerable. In that moment, my wiser-self made a very astute observation:

"Annie, you are tired, frustrated from traffic, and hungry. This is not a good time for objective, rational thinking. Working yourself up and getting all anxious tonight will not change anything, will make you miserable, and will result in a rotten night's sleep; so let it go for now. You can think about it tomorrow morning, rested, and if you want, you can make a new plan then."

"Okay."

This morning it occurred to me that instead of feeling the energy of not working as anxiety, and beating myself up for being jobless, I could celebrate the quasi-miraculous fact that I am gathering newfound energy; by doing this, I would basically be transforming destructive angst into constructive life-force. Thinking it was the smart thing to do, I headed out to the mountain, caught a ride on the gondola, and pushed myself on a demanding and wondrous winter trail. I returned exhausted and satisfied: pleased to have positively honored my vitality.

Energy is meant to circulate. If unused, it becomes stagnant, festers, and can infect our psyche and body. If it is misplaced or misused, it can turn into a destructive force. When our energy is not working for us one way, it is up to us to channel it through a different outlet.

DECEMBER 19TH, 2011

WHAT ABOUT TODAY?

I am presently drinking my morning coffee wondering what today will consist of. The first order of business should be to finish emailing my Christmas e-cards; I've been putting it off. Then I could go up to the mountain to try to "accidentally" cross paths with the Chef to remind him of my continued interest in working in his restaurants *(I tried yesterday when I went up, but he wasn't working)*. Transforming my not-working-anxiety into life-force doesn't mean, by any means, that I have given up the idea of working for the holidays. I am still seriously teetering between acceptance and panic.

While on the subject of coffee, and since I claim to be so keen on working, you may be wondering about the coffee shop job. Let me tell you about it: After being turned down for the mountain restaurant job, I did drive down to the shop to ask about work for the holidays despite the fact that I was unsure about being able to complete full days of work – the mountain's four-hour shifts had been reassuring. But on my way there, my ego mused: "How the heck are you going to take orders and punch-in the register when you need a different pair of glasses to look at the client and to read that register?" The reason for this is that I need progressive lenses* but I have been reluctant to get them because of my vertigo – it doesn't seem to be the right time to add an element

* As I am writing this, I see a dark shape strolling by my window (less than ten feet away). I know it's an animal, but I can't tell which one because I am wearing my reading glasses. All excited (this has to be wildlife), I scramble to find my other glasses under the piles of notes scattered on my desk. When I finally put them on, I catch the butt of a bear walking away. Now what if I did not recognize a client before I saw *his* behind walking out the door? It wouldn't be good business.

of visual adaptation – and also, the cost has been prohibitive. Well, this shilly-shallying led me to turn around before reaching my destination.

You tell me: is this another trick of my ego or a sign that I am not meant to be a barista after all?

Back to my... my what again? I forgot. What is it that I am *supposed* to be doing right now? What is the business at hand? Focusing on an alternate job? Getting back on a pure positivity track? Outlining my new 28-day program? I must say: I am uninspired this morning.

Soooo, not actually doing much yet today *(although I always consider writing this book a very good something)*. I do have my plan of finishing my Christmas cards... let's see.

EVEN NATURE GETS CONFUSED

I ended up going for a walk on the Seawall and what I saw when I arrived baffled me. I was greeted by nature in a state of disarray. What I witnessed, along with other bemused onlookers wondering what the fuss was about, appeared odd and confusing. The sizable waves were incoherent, as if arguing with one another: big and small ones coexisted side by side indiscriminately – at times perpendicular to one another – and the surface was rippled as if by an independent impulse.

It was all very perplexing and I would not have been totally shocked to see some huge extraterrestrial vessel emerge from the waters. All the while this was happening on the surface, the sun was shining as a watchful patriarch looking over what he knew would only be a passing dispute amongst his brood. It was a fascinating scene.

> ***If waves can have an off day, so can we. During those days, let's simply remind ourselves that what we perceive as tumult is but a momentary ripple in the greater scheme of things.***

DECEMBER 20TH, 2011

SPIRITULIN

Well, yesterday did not turn out so great. Although it did begin with relatively good intentions, they did not pan out. After completing my e-cards *(one small check mark in the "good" column)*, I puttered around the house and suddenly just felt exhausted and deflated. I convinced myself that in such glum dispositions, my idea of going to the mountain resort to try to "accidentally" cross paths with the Chef would be unwise. That's when I decided to go for a walk *(second check mark)*. As usual, time spent in the company of nature was soothing, but the feeling did not last; in the hours that followed – and out of the blue *(blue-ish)* – I began to feel singularly miffed, irritated and generally annoyed. I had officially toppled over.

That's were I stand this morning, mulling over *(and over and over)* what has been happening to me lately. This growth plateau I urged myself to embrace is not very flat and it's getting old. I am definitely reacting to the feeling that I am not doing enough *(Oh no! not that feeling again!)*. This state of limbo – between what was and what will be – is taking its toll on me. My failure to maintain steady levels of certainty and focus is wearing me out as it keeps me bouncing from peaks of faith to troughs of doubts; kind of like the crash that follows a sugar rush. I need to regulate my "spiritulin" level.

A BANQUET FOR MY EGO

My situation is actually not much different than say, two months ago, but my once-found virtuous circle has long been broken *(further cause for feeling bad)*. For some time now, I have neglected my morning meditation and yoga/stretch *(sorry for not being a better example)* that were so beneficial to me *(silly humans : what we know and what we do are too often two different things)*. I have also mostly foregone my outdoor walks and hikes since not getting that waitressing job. Furthermore, and although I am eating healthy food, I have been consuming too much of it and put on a few pounds. And there's more : I have not been dedicating as much time to writing, or at least, I have not delved into more penetrating subjects. And finally *(for now)* I have not started working on my friend's project and it is seriously gnawing at me.

Bottom line is that Not-Doing-Enough has been standing arm in arm with Should-Have and I've backslid right into them. I guess I didn't heed the warning of the sign after all and ventured too close to the edge of the slope : I will not have work for the holidays and my ego is enjoying a feast I am both catering and serving *(could* this *be my waitressing job ?)*. I have begun to skid down the icy pitch of the foreboded hill.

This is not where I want to be and there is still time to catch myself so that I don't end up battered at the bottom of this black diamond run. I need a plan : a plan to insure that when I get on the other side of the holidays, I am happy with myself. I don't know what it will consist of yet, but just in case I should decide to get back on track with a plan that would include meditation, I meditate for an hour and it helps.

Accepting things as they are should be effortless, mindless, wordless : it should simply BE. Let us BE, simply.

"The miracle is not to fly in the air, or to walk on the water, but to walk on the Earth."

Chinese Proverb

DECEMBER 21ST, 2011

TEETER-TOTTER

It's official: I am experiencing amnesia's second trick. Not too long ago, I perceived as inconceivable that I could ever go back to being stressed and anxious or thrown off my center, and now, I am having a difficult time remembering how to find my center and how not to worry. Really, really neat trick. All my seesawing has yielded a not so peaceful and easy feeling because I am now standing on shifty ground* *(gone is the sense of steadiness I once had from standing on the solid ground of my truth when I was happily experiencing the much more pleasant first trick of this pony).*

By repeatedly standing-in, feelings of uncertainty and unease have surreptitiously challenged the permanence of my good-spirits; nowadays, when I knock at the door expecting my joy to show up, I don't always get an answer.

I woke up this morning from a restless night of too many unpleasant dreams, again, and joy did not answer the roll call. I.do.not.want. this.anymore. Never again. I have known the joy of joy and I want it back in a permanent capacity. As I have said before, I have acquired enough tools by now to work my way through and out of this tight spot.

> *Gentlemen, I can rebuild. I have the technology. I have the capability to make myself a joyful woman. I can be better than before. Better... stronger... happier.*

---

* I would not want to infringe on anyone's copyrights, but this sentence is making me hum a melody reminiscent of the sounds of a certain popular flock of birds of prey that vastly filled the air *(waves)* in the 1970's.

Right now, a friendly wave from the Universe would go a long way; or even better, a reassuring two-thumbs-up accompanied by a gesture of concrete support. Something along the lines of a job prospect *(or an actual job)*, an invitation to something fun, unexpected money, a miraculous health recovery, or a love interest. You know, something palpable in this human and physical world. Something nice to make me smile for a while.

SIDEBAR PLEASE : THE PERFECT-MAN-FOR-ME

As "feministless" as it may sound, I do include a man in my wish list of life enhancements. I would definitely consider this addition as a great gift. In my mind, going through life "by-two" would change everything. Some may argue that relationships add to the complexity of life *(those are usually serial relationship lifers)*, but my opinion is that unless you have gone through years of difficult times by yourself, without a true confident and partner, without anyone to scratch an itch in the middle of your back, your knowledge of the question is greatly limited and your sentiment may be best kept to yourself. By no means am I robbing the invaluable treasures that are found while spending a few years alone. I actually think that if more people spent a (considerable) period of time unattached – and used that time to define and grasp the full nature of who they are – they would show up in relationships not seeking self-determination from the other, and unions would be healthier for it.

Nonetheless, those who hail eternal singlehood as the ultimate status don't have (or picture) the type of relationship I have in mind. I do not believe we are meant to experience life as freestanding entities but rather as side-by-side *vases communicants*, between which energy flows freely, in a perpetual movement towards equilibrium. And until I dance this dance, I will dream of it. The important distinction is that I am not talking about your run of the mill any-man-will-do-to-assuage-my-loneliness kind of relationship; I am talking about a genuine partner in heart, body and soul: and this is of a different realm than companionship. David Deida is an author and speaker who hits all the right notes of my idea of a (real) man-woman relationship.*

His three stages, or types of relationship, clearly explain how my desire to share my life with a man has nothing to do with dependence, and exists beyond companionship. From a woman's point of view, he describes the stages as:

1. I need a man. I depend on you to be whole.
2. I don't need a man. I am whole by myself.
3. Being whole is not enough. I can take care of myself. Myself *is* good enough but I want more. I want my spirit to be open wider than I can alone, and through union experiences with a man, I want to reach beyond *me*.

With these (paraphrased) words, he has captured my life-long yearning. In every other way than monetary, I am absolutely self-sufficient; but I want more.

Back to the central issue of the sidebar: I would welcome a man *(my perfect-man-for-me)* in my life. I want it, I pray for it, I magnetize it: I'm ready for it. As I said, some people argue that being single is the way to go, and others *(perhaps the same ones)* suggest that if it hasn't happened for me yet, it's because I have not been ready *(I wonder: were all of them 100% whole and ready when they met their mate or did they mature within the relationship? – moving on).*

My girlfriend's concern is that I should achieve financial independence prior to getting involved in a relationship. As I was readying myself to move to Vancouver, she strongly advised that once I settled

* www.deida.info

in my new city, I should avoid any man-distraction until I was "all sorted out". Although I understand where she was coming from, I do not concur. In my view, I don't need to be independent from my man: I want to be in communion with him. And in my vision of a partnership, both partners bring to the table what life has given them or what they are proficient at. In a world where money is almost almighty, this idea may be considered naive and idealistic, but just as I believe and strive for my greatest potential, I also believe that humans can elevate themselves above the energy of control money can generate. And certainly, I trust that the perfect-man-for-me will be such a man *(or he wouldn't be him)* and that I will be such a woman if the tables are by then turned *(although I do want a man who is skilled at handling the materiality of this world!)*.

It is rather obvious that I have difficult karma with money *(however, I may be settling my debt with the Universe as we speak)* but I don't feel I must have resolved all my issues before meeting my man: he can be part of the solution and we can mutually support each other in the different aspects of life we have yet to master. I don't want a tit for tat relationship. I don't need itemized equality: I want the bottom line of a life-and-spirit assets balance sheet to be of equal value. Whether money comes into my life from my partner, from my own successful business endeavors *(this book qualifies)*, or from a lottery *(I guess I have a fixation on this one – it's my elusive magic pill)*, it is all the same to me. The Universe will meet me where I am, and decide on the modalities of the transaction itself. In any way, I'm ready.

But as if to comply with my girlfriend's admonitions, a rather strange thing has happened since I moved here: with the exception of my new Squamish friends who appreciated my presence, not a single interested glance has been directed my way. Not a hint of anything that resembles flirting or even akin to acknowledgement. Not one second look: absolutely nothing. Not one man has been intrigued by me (or even addressed me) or made any kind of effort to be in my vicinity. Men have generally shown absolute indifference when it comes to me. I am the one who has initiated conversations while on a hike, in grocery stores, or out on the Seawall, and without fail, they have unmistakably cut the conversation short and continued along their way. I know I am no spring chicken but I am no ugly duckling either, and I am certainly not standoffish. I walk around open, in no hurry, friendly: and yet nothing. It is rather disconcerting, I have to admit. I do hope there is a bigger plan behind this and that my perfect-man-for-me and I are somehow making our way towards each other, and that the eventual timing will be perfect. But still, a little attention and ego boost would be appreciated.

End of sidebar.

I'm still not smiling.

I scroll back in my document and read my last thought from yesterday; the one about needing a plan to make the best of the next few weeks in order to be pleased with myself once the holidays are bygones. Who was I trying to fool? The question is a crock: I know exactly what the plan has to consist of *(we usually do, don't we? – it's more a matter of implementation than definition).* The various options of my plan are: A) Get my body, mind and soul into shape *(exercise, stretch, meditate).* B) Get serious about my nutrition, cut back portions, and lose a few pounds. C) Commit to writing more. D) Do a good house cleaning before the end of the year. E) Any combination or all of the above.

"Get it together Annie. You know you can commit to this: you recently completed a great 28-day program. Just do it. Make yourself a shorter 14-day program if that's less intimidating, and commit. This way, you will enter the New Year positively."

"You're right, I'll think about it."

"Don't think about it too much, you know what will happen if you do: just do it."

"Right, let me mull it over and get myself there."

"Uh-huh, as you wish."

Any ambitious journey will be comprised of a variety of footsteps. There will be some long strides, occasional jogs and daring leaps but also frequent small steps as uneven terrain is negotiated – some backtracking may even occur in order to find the right path. But overall, each step is necessary to reach a destination.

DECEMBER 22ND, 2011

THE BIG STUPID

Okay, so I'm still humming and hawing about clearly defining and committing to a new program, even a 14-day one. For whatever reasons, wise or not, I am reluctant and/or lazy about doing so right now. Still, in the event that I did eventually decide to sign-up for a yet-to-be-determined program *(can't really be less committal than this – do I need to consider I have commitment issues too?)*, I did pretend that I was on such a program yesterday and meditated, stretched, went for a walk on the Seawall, ate well, and wrote quite a bit. By having done so, if I do enter into a program today, I would count yesterday as Day 1, which would mean I would only have 13 left to go *(I've decided not to consider the two-day old meditation as a sufficient effort to count it as a day of program).*

I know, I know. This is a bit *(a lot)* of a "psycho-semantic" game I am playing with myself. Deep down inside me *(not even that deeply actually)* lies the conviction that I have to do this in order to end the year on a high note and begin the new one with a sense of self-satisfaction. Even though I am not committing to a formal program, I know very well that I will not allow myself to nullify all the work I have put in to this day. Letting myself down now would be tantamount to scratching out a lot of my efforts to date, and would set me back greatly. I will not do this to myself. I will continue to raise my level of self-confidence by getting on a track that will provide me with a continued sense of accomplishment. Since it is clear now that I will not be working for the holidays, I will make the best of it.

As I went to bed last night, I pondered the idea of going for an early hike in my backyard mountains: "Maybe first thing in the morning, before anything else... something different that could feel exciting." Upon awaking at early dawn this morning, and instead of going back to sleep for a couple hours, I decided to get up – still gently toying with the possibility of getting dressed and heading out. I had coffee, read auspicious predictions about the upcoming year of the Dragon and... wait for it... yes! I got dressed and went for a hike.

I began walking towards the trail, simply pleased with myself for having stepped outside; the length or difficulty of the outing did not matter. Then I got on the mountain and the energy started to seep inside me and to steadily build up; building me up and gathering joy. At last, joy was back.

At the first junction, I had a choice: left and right for the *Baden-Powell* trail, or straight up on *The Big Stupid.* What do you think? I chose *The Big Stupid* of course! And it was a little bit of a punishing *Big Stupid.* Actually, the big stupids would be the bikers who can use the trail. I would personally be petrified riding a bike on the way down. I could honestly not even imagine it being doable. But for this hiker, the trail was beautiful and perfectly challenging. The stillness of the early morning hour created an aura of magic. The path was an ingenious stairwell of twisted gnarled roots that crisscrossed and intertwined to offer noble footing. There were suspended pathways built from chopped logs that swirled up and down, dipped recklessly, and angled sideways. It looked like a roller coaster in the middle of the woods. In another spot, there was a ten-foot long weathered board balanced on a fallen tree like a walk-on seesaw, four feet in the air. I had to walk up *(or cycle, for the big stupids)* on it up to the middle point and as I stepped onto the other side, it tilted and brought me onto a log floating in a swampy area. Cool! Very cool!

Around a bend I saw a heron standing very still in a large puddle. I stopped to observe him and began talking to him: "Good morning beautiful, how was your night? I am very surprised to see you here; you seem out of place. How will you fly away with your big wings between all these centennial trees? How will you reach the sky again?" I walked very gently towards him, carefully placing each step, avoiding twigs, minimizing noise, making sure to maintain a non-threatening energy not to spook him off *(although I was curious to see his prowess flying between the trunks).* I got closer and closer, it was an amazing moment: Me and the crane in the middle of a quiet ancestral forest amidst rays of sun streaking down around us... *still closer...* Then I thought how much of a good joke it would be for someone to bring stuffed animals and put them along the trail, like a bear maybe... *closer...* At this moment it occurred to me that maybe the name of the trail was not for the daredevils recklessly flying down the hill but rather for the fools who thought there was actually a heron in the middle of the woods letting them get so close. You guessed it: the heron was a fake! Who's the Big Stupid now!

The whole hike was lovely, demanding, and energizing. I went up *The Big Stupid* and came down *Ladies Only*. I hiked pretty hard for two hours: Very good for a second day of *ex parte* activity. And when I got home... I vacuumed. Right on.

Happy New Year! Last night was the Winter Solstice – actual beginning of the New Year.

Mother Nature is a most generous one. She always gives and never denies. In her home, we are her children and she provides boundlessly. She will nourish, replenish, amaze and entertain; fill our hearts with joy, our eyes with beauty, our bodies with energy, and our soul with solace.

DECEMBER 23RD, 2011

THE GREAT ALCHEMIST

This morning, my inbox contains a New Year's greeting from a personal-growth center. It says this upcoming year is a year 5, in numerology, and that the number represents the quintessence of matter and its transcendence. If one pictures the corners of a square as four dots, it suggests, and adds a fifth dot above the shape, a pyramid is created and thus, the fifth dot symbolizes the new transcendent dimension.

Conveying this concept of transformation, the image for the e-card is that of an ice crystal. The idea being that although a crystal is but solidified water, it is also entirely different from its original liquid state: the crystal is a new self-created structure, which emerged from within the stillness of water.

THE GIRL WHO WANTED TO BE A CRYSTAL

At this moment in time, the image resonates with me profoundly. We too are matter, and the same potential for transformation lies within us: A new transcended "us" can also emerge "overnight" from within our stillness, given the right environment *(a little more than cold weather as far as we are concerned)*. Take a moment and picture a close-up of a water crystal: its delicate, intricate and beautiful nature. If *that* is the potential of water – a simple molecule – imagine what the potential of our being can be.

This is the kind of life-transforming process I aspire to experience. And although I am aware that I cannot will for transmutation to occur *now*, I can devote myself to creating the necessary conditions for a transformation to take place. I am only responsible for mixing and providing a yummy love-rich petri dish for my soul. From such a propitious environment, God is free to perform his alchemy and elevate the living.

THE GREAT MATHEMATICIAN

It appears that when God created the world, he had a few mathematical aces up his sleeve. Not only did he (arguably) have the intention of his great vision but he may have been the greatest mathematician that ever was. As the numerical underpinnings of the universe, and all its constituents, is becoming more and more common knowledge (through literature, movies and television), the equations of creation are coming to light for everyone to contemplate in wonderment.

Today, the general scientific community is aware that the Golden Ratio (PHI) and the related Fibonacci series are pervasive in the totality of creation.* From the leaf arrangements in plants, to the growth pattern of flowers and seed florets, to spots on a leopard, or the spiral

* Physicists and other scientists, please forgive my over-simplification and probable blunders.

of the nautilus; from our body's proportions to that of a dolphin, or the sections of an ant all the way to the dimensions of planets and trajectory of their orbit, all these manifestations of creation are fundamentally ruled by a similar life-impulse that can be linked to a ratio of 1.618, PHI, the Golden Number. Architects of Ancient Egypt and of Greek Antiquity were fully aware of this life-creating and eye-pleasing ratio (common examples being the Pyramid of Giza, the Parthenon and the Acropolis). These peoples utilized the Golden Number in their architecture and "urban planning", as a gauge in their art *(as did later masters)*, and also as an optimizer of power in their rituals. They also used it to provide life-enhancing properties to their healing tools.

Furthermore, present-day exploratory (and somewhat marginal) scientific research attempting to measure the wavelength of love has revealed that the frequency emitted by the body's electromagnetic field when in a state of unconditional love (as well as the voice's harmonics when expressing love) is also associated with PHI, or Golden Mean ratio. Now *that* is information than can carry us over the threshold of our current belief system and into the realm of a new life-altering paradigm: Love is literally a life-generating force and can therefore physically affect all that *is*.

These notions have turned on a kind of pinball machine in my head where lights are flashing and points are being feverishly tabulated as various universal, religious, and scientific precepts are being hit by a mercurial orb. *We are stardust,* Ping! *God is Love,* Ping! Ping! *Love is PHI,* Ping! Ping! Ping! *We are the Universe,* Ping! *PHI is creation,* Ping! *God created the universe,* Ping! *We are made in the image of God,* Ping! Ping! *Love is the highest of emotions,* Ping! *We are creators of our life,* Ping! *Love heals,* Ping!

A playful game of mix-and-match can yield a syllogistic insight into humankind's age-old propensity for conceiving a God that is the Great Creator:

The mysterious universe is God;
God is Love;
Love is PHI;
PHI is Creation;
Therefore: God is Creation.

Score!

Depending on each one's beliefs, regardless of them really, and however we choose to incorporate these ideas about the power of love into our respective lives, it can translate into amazing wisdom that can transform how we live every day.

I digressed again. My point this morning is simply that I like the imagery of the water transformed into crystal. It connects me to my infinite and unforeseen possibilities. I also like the idea that this type of transformation will occur spontaneously, notwithstanding my will *(preferably without its hindrance)*, given I provide a favorable substrate.

Love's frequency is in harmony with the mathematical principles governing creation. Therefore, we are surrounded by manifestations of love in everything that is. When we feel love, we are attuned with creation and become creators ourselves. "God is Love", and through love, we too become Supreme Beings.

This bridging of the gap between God and science will certainly create ideological turmoil and spark fiery controversy. The sleeping lion will be poked and the timeless feud against such a natural merge will be reignited – as, for a moment still, some will mistakenly think that one denigrates the other.

DECEMBER 24TH, 2011

THE LAND OF MY MIND

Yesterday was not the best or the worst of days. I did not shine my brightest light but although partially dimmed, it stayed on. Physically though, I was spent. The previous day's hike was taxing on my body and I could feel my depleted energy awaiting being replenished; I even attempted and afternoon hook-up with a caffeine-drip but to no avail. Generally, my outlook remained fairly positive.

MIND MINES

The night, unfortunately, was a different matter all together. I woke up at 3 A.M. with the stark realization that I hadn't gone to the bank to transfer my credit card balances to a 2.9 % offer, and with the deadline looming amidst the holidays, I may have really messed up. Or I may be just fine. But these anxiety-filled thoughts acted as a turbocharged ignition to my ego's engines and they rumbled through the night.

I travelled to and fro and again between earnest resolutions, rehashed scenarios, and worn-out worries: I drummed into my head that the theme for 2012 had to be financial autonomy, fretted about finding a job ASAP *(to be consistent with said theme)*, teetered between finding any job or looking for the right job *(really old stuff)*, and even second-guessed the validity of my excuses for not returning to the coffee shop way back when *(I'm not kidding, I went there)*. To be thorough, I also revived the stress caused by the friend's project, which I have finally initiated but is getting more demanding everyday.

Once I had explored every inch of what I was doing wrong, I ventured further into the confines of my mind and expertly reprimanded myself for being unable to sustain my joy, for not making the most of each day, for failing to commit to a new program, and generally, for not being a super-human.

LET GO MY EGO

At that point, I made a much-needed pitstop. The break allowed me to take a breath and remember that I was human, and that perfection was a fool's goal. My wiser-self told me that I should not be so harsh on myself, that I should show compassion towards this well-intended person that I am, and that I should be accepting of where I stand in this moment. *(Sure sounds a lot like "accepting what is" to me. Now where did I hear* that *before?)*

That was better. I went back to sleep.

This morning, as I took stock of my nocturnal trek, I realized that the entire journey was peppered by exploding bombshells of "should haves". Whether they consisted of "should have done better" or "should be doing" or "should be kinder to myself", they amounted to "should" nonetheless and were indicative that I had been on the wrong path *(again)*.

STARTING OVER

I then decided to try a fresh start without "should haves"; silently reiterating that they were the fabrication of my mind and they were absolutely useless *(one day, I'll get it)*. One question could help me reset the night's clock: What is good today about how and what I'm doing? My answer was as follows:

— I am health-wise better and physically stronger: my nausea only occasionally manifesting itself.
— I have been more active physically in recent days and even meditated a few times.
— I have been more mindful of eating well during those days as well.

— I did not slide down the black diamond slope *(a little skidding, but nothing dramatic really).*
— I am anxious to work, and that's a good thing.
— I have written every day.
— It is Christmas Eve and I am not too nostalgic.

The reality that surfaced was that I did have cause for celebration *(or at least satisfaction)*, and so why not simply be pleased and proud of myself for those reasons. I knew that as the New Year chimed in, making money would most likely be #1 on my list*, but this was still December.

I decided to appreciate the things I had to be grateful for today.

THE GIFT HORSE

From this brighter perspective, I am now thinking of something else: How foolish I have been to think I could dictate that *early-November-to-mid-December* was the finite amount of time necessary for my mind and body to undergo complete regeneration, and that the process should now be finished. Who am I to know? Once I went into the Meadow Repair program, I must have missed the part where it said that I had to relinquish control and that the timeline was not up to me. Now, I wonder: Could it be that the Universe knows better and that I am not quite done regenerating? Is this why I'm not working?

If I look back in time, I can recall that much of those suitcase-laden years were spent praying and begging the heavens for my space, my time, my rhythm, my undisturbed reflections, and my un-violated energy field. The truth is that last fall, from the moment I was unable to work, my prayers were being answered in a relatively sweet way.

Sure, I have had to contribute to the fulfillment of my plea by demonstrating awareness, venturesome willingness, and courage

---

* I say most likely because one thing I have learned is that we can never be certain of what the future will be – September was also supposed to be about making money.

(which luckily I had). Also, my financial and health situations have not been what I would have readily chosen for a hiatus but nonetheless, the manner in which events and circumstances have come together has in fact afforded me the opportunity of time for myself. I got what I wished for. And although some of this time was spent flirting with fear, guilt, and discouragement, it has all been part of my coming of age process.

So, as hard as I was being on myself last night, if I mentally compare where I was two months ago to where I am and how I stand today, I can only recognize that I have made great use of the opportunity: the time gifted to me was not wasted, and it just so happens that I am given a little more still. So how about it?

How about I find the befitting poetry in ending this year with time for myself and for attending to my wellness.

How about I chill out, knowing that next year will unfold under a different theme, for as much as 2012 will be about financial autonomy, I now realize that 2011 was *(and still is)* about my physical, mental, and spiritual wellness.

How about I conclude this year relishing these days dedicated to myself, as if they were the last days of an unexpectedly extended tropical vacation.

Yes, I will fully enjoy the next two weeks.

And if some of those days I don't have the energy to conquer a volcano or explore the jungle; if some of those days I do not accomplish "should do" tasks, so be it. That will be okay too. *Mañana.*

"So relax girl, these are days divinely gifted to you. 2012 will be something else and will take care of itself. Now, you have these days that you have prayed for, for years. Receive them with gratitude and know the time will come for change."

I feel my belly softening. Peace on Earth and within me.

If we choose to have faith, whether in God, a Greater Consciousness, or the Universe's Wisdom, we must consent to relinquish some control.

DECEMBER 25TH, 2011

DIVINELY GIFTED DAYS

Merry Christmas to all!

The good news is I am doing just fine. Yesterday's realizations really were game changers. I made the flowing poster-card: *Relax, these are divinely gifted days*, and it's working for me. I did make it in the nick of time to the bank and everything is set. Once that bit was done, I drove myself down to the waterfront and had a delightful walk on the Seawall. It had been really dark and rainy for the last three days but at 3:30, the clouds parted and gave way to a generous blue opening.* So I caught some rays, enjoyed the sunset, and concluded my contemplative walk at nightfall. It was absolutely peaceful and beautiful. I live here. How privileged am I.

Christmas day and it's already noon, I have been Skyping with my Mom, making phone calls, emailing last holiday e-cards, and responding to emails. Time to move on with my day, gently and gratefully.

---

* When I moved to Vancouver, I was warned about the dreadful six months of darkness and consistent rain and so, I expected to suffer from gloom. But two things have contributed to diminish the impact substantially: One, this year's local weather has apparently been clement. Two, as a new member of the West Coast's insider circle, I was informed that Vancouverites were in cahoots in propagating a bleaker than reality myth in order to prevent a mass westerly exodus.

In the spirit of abundance and gratitude, I splurge on myself today with pleasurable simplicity: I am just a little bit more generous with the ingredients of my daily routine. I do not skimp on my deliciously nutty *Andalou Organic Body Butter** or with my seldom used and too expensive *Kerastase Care Volumactive Conditioner with Complexe Ampli-Ciment* (!). I put on my favorite knickers and slide on a brand new pair of hiking socks I had been saving for a special day *(I love new hiking socks)*. At breakfast, I liberally spread butter *(not real butter: Earth Balance)* on my homemade blueberry-bran-walnut muffin. Each of these simple gestures of bounty is experienced with presence and fills my heart with joy.

What do you know: The grey skies are clearing again, looks like we're in for more sunshine! **

Abundance can be experienced through the simplest of gestures. Joy can be found anywhere and only depends on our ability to see it, receive it, and generate it. An open heart is all that is required for joy to rush in.

---

* A few weeks ago I used a medication in the form of a patch (applied behind the ear) for the first time and within a couple hours I felt drowsy from the effects of the drug. I was astounded by the speed and efficacy with which a quarter inch of my skin could distribute a substance to my entire body. For many years now, I have chosen organic skin lotions because of a general sense that they were better for me but I had not I realized how vital a choice that was. Just imagine: Everything we put on our skin goes right through our blood stream, brain, and various organs. Something to think about.

** I must apologize to my new community for not participating in the conspiracy – give me time.

DECEMBER 26TH, 2011

EVERYTHING IS GOOD, EVERYTHING'S OKAY

So yesterday was my first Christmas in Vancouver without family or a loved one. I was prepared for some nostalgia, a few tears, and anticipated an output of deliberate effort to make myself enjoy my day but, not so. I simply had a delightful day. I went up to the mountain and had an exciting winter hike. Even though it was warm at home, it was all stormy snowy weather up there. The winds were blowing, making all the trees sing, the snow was falling *(sideways)*, visibility was limited, and it was fabulous. I had planned on taking a short stroll but instead, spurred by the beauty of this lively nature, I embarked upon a real grind, the official Snowshoe Grind of the mountain, without snowshoes. Since my intention was to go for an easy walk, I was only wearing blue jeans and the wind quickly turned my thighs into painful popsicles. For a moment, I considered the smart thing would be to turn around, but instantaneously I thought: "There is no way the wind, or my popsicled limbs, is making me turn back. I am loving this." I had a fantastic time. Once I returned via the gondola *(still loving that)*, I treated myself to a *Grande Latte* at Starbucks and drove home to Skype with my family gathered at my mother's to celebrate Christmas in Ste-Ville.

Thanks to our computers, I was given a virtual seat at the end of the dining table, was poured a glass a wine *(which sat in front of the screen)*, and participated in the festivities for nearly an hour, chatting and laughing with the group. Earlier in the week, my mother had mailed me her famous Queen Elizabeth cake so when desert time arrived *(appetizer in my case)* we shared in the same delight, which added to the feeling of closeness. When we signed off, I felt I had had my family Christmas and it was actually perfectly satisfying for me.

Having been invited for Christmas dinner by my landlords upstairs, I proceeded to get ready to join them. After having my taste buds teased while watching my family enjoy my mother's cooking earlier, I was happy to partake in an actual home-cooked meal with all the trimmings. The chef was the Italian mother of the brood *(assisted by her English hubby)*, so you know I was treated to a feast of the senses. The conversation was lively and it was half past ten by the time I walked home, down the stairs, satiated.

The only glitch of the day was that I could not get to sleep. I watched television until one o'clock then read in bed until six-thirty in the morning. Following months of quiet isolation, I was probably over-stimulated by the merry chatter. Unfortunately, my insomnia was accompanied by queasiness. When I woke up earlier, I felt as if I was hung-over and the feeling is persisting. The thing is, the only way to explain a hangover would be that I got drunk on life because I have not drank any alcohol in a long time.* Regardless, I had a great day and I am not letting this put a damper on my joyful dispositions. All this does is make today a "down-day": couch, television, gentle food and baking cookies, and taking it as it is. I trust this too will pass and that one day, along with the rest of my health issues, it will be permanently remedied.

For now, I'm all right and tomorrow will be fine.

---

* This is one of my peripheral health problems: I have always enjoyed wine with my meals, and an evening cocktail or two, but 18 months ago, alcohol began making me feel sick. It gradually escalated to the point where half a glass of wine would condemn me to several bed-ridden days of battling nausea and total exhaustion. I did consult professionals and had a bunch of tests done but everything seemed normal.

Joy can be stretched backward and forward: we can feel it ahead of time, as we anticipate a joyful event, and we can also bask in its aftermath. Let's be sure to make the most of it.

DECEMBER 27TH, 2011

ALL IS FAIR IN LOVE....

First of all, I had a very good night. I slept for several hours and I am mentally back *(physically not quite, but better)*. My first words this morning, as I opened my eyes, were "Happy December 27th!" I know, there was nobody to hear the greeting but eh, I guess that's what happens when you live by yourself for too long.

Last night, I resumed my reading of another bedtime novel *(while I am writing this book, I am making it a point to exclusively read mindless stuff)*. This one is a story in which the cheating husband of the main character leaves her on the day she gives birth.* Some aspects of the story made me reflect on past relationships and revealed a hitherto unnoticed level of insight *(not so mindless after all)*.

The storyline goes like this: Following months of separation, the wife and husband come together to discuss their situation. In a stupefying move, the husband ends up turning the tables around and manages to almost convince her that the demise of the relationship was her fault, due to her difficult character and selfishness. He goes as far as telling her that because he still loves her, he would forgive her

---

* *Anybody Out There*, Marian Keyes.

(remember: he's the one who cheated and left) and take her back if, that is, she agreed to change certain aspects of her personality. After a few days pass they meet again and she says something to the effect that if he loved her, he would not ask her to change into something less than who she is or try to control her. Most of all, she is irate about the fact the he made her doubt herself and that she had willingly considered changing who she was for him. At the end of her sensible and justified tirade, he confides that his motivations had been honorable: what he had done and said had been for her own good.

I can definitely relate.

I can relate to the effects of emotional blackmail and manipulation; to the feeling of smallness and malignant sense of self-doubt they instill. The process can be quite insidious and begin under the clever disguise of love and support. In my younger days, I had a boyfriend who demonstrated great interest in helping me find my way in the world. To be fair, he put in a lot of time and effort guiding me professionally as well as in my personal growth. The problem was that as he built up my confidence, he kept control of it. He used to tell me that I was smarter than him, that there was no limit to what I could accomplish, and that I had the world by the tail. But he was like the designer of a computer security system who, unbeknownst to the client, leaves a back door access to the master program from which he can insinuate himself and wreak havoc if he chooses to. And he did: When he got angry, he would tell me that he had *made* me, that I was nothing without him, and that I would never accomplish anything on my own.

Finally, one day, I found the gumption to leave the relationship, but even though my resolve was strong, any backbone I had was steamrolled in the process and suffered injuries that took years to heal.

During the long course of the agony of separation, he would often scream uncontrollably using his secret access to my core, and then suddenly get quiet, and tearfully tell me, in the gentlest voice of confidence – as if he was about to reveal something he wished he never had to – that the main issue, because he loved me so much, was that he was afraid *for me*. He was afraid I was making a terrible choice because not only would I not make it in the world if I left him, but above all, since I was such a difficult person, no one would ever love me again like he did. And that made him so sad... *for me*. Just as the man in the story who claimed his contemptuous behavior was for the good of his wife and made her doubt herself, he too was playing with my inner circuitry and nearly convinced me of what he was saying.

As I mentioned, my injuries were serious and because of that, were vulnerable to future flare-ups, and that's what ended up happening. Years later, as my life experiences had helped me grow into a stronger and freer woman, I entered into a new relationship. Eventually, the man who had fallen in love with my spunk would threaten to kick me out if I did not change into something meeker and more agreeable. He too told me that he was afraid that if I left, given my self-absorbed nature, I would probably never find anyone else to love me. Now, although I instinctively knew that I really was not unlovable, the fact that I was hearing those words for the second time troubled me : could there be some truth to them ? Both men had held the same discourse, had made me feel like the bad guy, and had accusingly fingered my self-centered and immature behaviors while claiming they, on the other hand, had only loved and supported me. Both demanded I altered my personality – as a favor to myself.

Until I read the passage echoing this experience in the book last night, I was still missing a piece of the puzzle. Although I had made peace with the past, grown from my stories, and acknowledged that it took two to tango and therefore these men had not executed this dance alone *(they may have had the square pegs but I had the square receptors; I was there of my own accord)*, somewhere in the recesses of my mind, I still thought my "difficult personality" had played a part in these stories.

But last night, I saw the light as it dawned on me that if an author had created these characters, then she had witnessed this in her own life and my story was not unique but shared by a whole community of women. The insidious manipulations I had been subjected to were the result of a widespread programming of the brains of a certain breed of men, and none of it was grounded in the truth of who I was. But why do men do that? Why is it that the first line of defense for (ill-advised) men who take strong-spirited women as partners, seems to be breaking the woman's spirit and making her doubt herself?

I don't exactly have the answer but certainly the onus is on women to know and believe in themselves, as well as on the mothers, fathers, and brothers who care for the girls who will become those lovers. If women grew to know their worth, their empowerment would disqualify them as partners for an unhealthy tango of manipulation and control: the men who like this dance would roam the dancehall alone.

TRUE LOVE

Women. Girls. (Boys and Men.) Do not accept to be manipulated, debased or demeaned. You *do not* deserve this. Believe in yourself; believe you are perfect just the way you are *(of course, we can all work at some of our minor glitches)*, and know that the right man (or woman) will love *all* of you, flaws included, and will always strengthen you. Above all, love should never make you feel lessened; it should always make you feel heightened.

If you are in a difficult situation you know is wrong and can't find the strength to take a stand, find support. Find someone who will boost your self-confidence or physically stand by you as you speak your truth. Personally, at some point, I wish I had had more of a spine, or the use of a friend to act as my bodyguard as I said or did what needed to be said or done. What I would have liked to say was: "You are wrong: I am not the bad person you paint me to be. I am leaving because *this* is wrong and I will be okay." Furthermore, I would have loved to retrieve precious personal mementos and childhood photographs I did not have the guts to collect at the time, for fear of wrathful retaliation.

I do realize that since you have been made to doubt yourself and to believe you are at fault, reaching out is very unlikely: I know because I didn't. But perhaps if I had had someone to encourage me to do so, I would have. So today, I am here to encourage you to reach out, to take a stand, and to pay attention to the pit in your stomach telling you something is wrong. You can do better. A moment of courage will open up a new world for you. Beware of the Trojan horse inside your head. I am with you.

A true partner should hold you up and wish for you to shine brightly. Always. They should neither want nor have the ability to dim your light. Ever.

Love does not diminish anyone; it elevates everyone.

DECEMBER 28TH, 2011

BELOVED

Two days ago, Richard, my beloved King of his Street Kingdom*, called me. I was lying down *(dealing with nausea)* when my phone rang and I instantly thought: This is Richard. And of course, it was.

* To be accurate, I wish to specify that Richard has not consistently lived on the streets. He has also shared the shelter of various roofs for some periods of time.

We always had this insane connection. Understand that his phone call is a rarity: in the past nearly two years, he has left three messages and talked to me once *(one of the messages was the night before I moved here, and he wasn't even aware I had plans to move – it goes to show).*

I picked up the receiver and the Arizona area code confirmed my knowing. I smiled and greeted, "Hello!" and he replied, "Mmmm, how I love hearing your voice." In an instant, I feel regal. The immediacy of my transformation is staggering – although no longer surprising. As soon as I hear his voice, my insides respond with wholeness as if gates were opened and energy floods through me, filling any void. The moment we connect, I know I am seen completely, that I stand in my totality, and that I am free to express myself without an iota of censorship. He is, to this day, the only person with whom I have experienced this ultimate state of being.

For this reason, I will probably always anticipate connecting with Richard, in spite of the frowns and admonishments the mere mention of him triggers in people who are aware of our history. What can I say: some fibers of our souls were intertwined at inception, and to tangibly experience this primordial weave from time to time, is a rare privilege.

THE STORY OF US

Richard and I met in Sedona during the summer of my hiatus in 2006. As I mentioned earlier, it is a twist of fate that lead me to this land of the Red Rocks *(and it was fate as well that had brought him there, two months earlier).* Three weeks after my arrival, I headed to a local brewery for some R&R *(very cool little place with an enclosed covered outdoors area complete with a firepit in its center and greenery around the edges).* As I was standing at the bar, a man came over said, "Hello, I am Richard. How are you tonight?" Since my mind had been playing tricks on me that day and I was not in great spirits, I answered, "I'm okay. It's been one of these days." He *(and his imposing stature)* stepped closer, looked me in the eyes for a few seconds *(his were rather mesmerizing)* and then put his arms around me. As he held me tight he whispered in my ear *(with his deep husky voice)*, "Give it all to me" *(meaning the weight of my difficult day)*. And I did, willingly. Although I was slightly bewildered, something in me had instantly let go while in his arms. Our first exchange was limited to that moment. He moved on to talk to someone else. His rugged good looks reminded me of my first crush as a young girl: the Malboro Man!

Unknowingly, I had come to the Brewery on Drumming Circle night – something that was absolutely foreign to me. Richard, on the other hand, was an adept at drumming. One by one, more than a dozen drummers set-up in a half circle (including Richard) and the music started. I stood in the doorway separating the inside and outside areas, gently swaying back and forth and side to side as the music penetrated my body. I was being drawn into the rhythm but still resisted surrendering to it, as I was self-conscious of being in a public place and it is not my style to ignore such a fact: I maintain respectability and decorum. After some time, Richard stopped playing and came towards me. Without a word, fixing me with his eyes, he extended a callused and powerful hand, inviting me to dance. *(He would later tell me that he had been watching me undulate to the music, bewitched by an apparently glowing aura, had found me to be the most beautiful woman he had ever seen and had been irresistibly captivated by me.)* A battle raged inside me: I wanted to go but was shy; I wanted to let go of my control but was afraid of making a spectacle; I wanted to allow my spirit to fly but was afraid of opening the cage for fear of what may happen. Mainly, I wanted to go with this man. The stakes were high and the decision was a huge deal to me: In a few seconds, if I said yes, I would be moving to the center of a circle, with Richard, for everyone to watch *(nobody else was dancing)*, and I knew that if I did, I was going to let go. The spell the rhythm was casting on me was quickly overpowering my will. After a last attempt from my ego to hold me back *("you're gonna look like a fool")*, I gave in, stepped in, and went all out. The experience was mind blowing. It was the first time in my life that my mind was totally relegated to second, third, or even understudy fiddle. My body contorted into shapes stemming from some monadic visceral knowing; it was transformed into a powerful vehicle of primal rhythms grounded in the depths of Mother Earth. Richard and I were entranced by the beating of the drums and joined in primordial rapture.

I felt the beauty of the continuous intuitive movements my limbs were freely expressing. Limbic memories were being awakened. My pulsating postures were responding to ancestral rhythms encoded somewhere in my DNA. My awareness reverted to some atavistic state of oneness in which I was no longer dancing but being danced.

After some unknowable amount of time had passed, the drums waned and Richard grabbed me once again, lifted me off the ground, and swirled me around in celebration of what had just occurred. I was elated. People in the room trickled out and I staggered to the washroom. As I was waiting in the dimly lit antechamber, Richard came in with a resolute stride, grabbed me *(yet again)* and kissed me passionately. He then looked at me and said, "If I had not done this, I would have regretted it all my life!" and he walked away. Needless to say, I was swept off my feet and left breathless. I entered the washroom and stared at my reflection in the mirror as I uttered, "Woooow!"

The next day, I emailed a girlfriend, and although I did not mention the inexplicable dance, hug or kiss, I said I had met this *"strange, older, magnetic guy"* who had triggered a serious case of fascination in me.

Two weeks later, back at the Brewery, I was sitting at one of the wrought iron garden-side tables when Richard showed up. He walked up to me and asked if he could sit. Meaningfully I said, "Of course, I've been waiting for you *(my whole life)*." He sat down next to me, picked up one of my sandaled feet, removed the sandal, and began massaging my foot as we started talking for the first time. And that was it.

We spoke until the place closed down, he came over to my place where I laid a mattress on the balcony *(of my fabulous perched house overlooking the tremendous Red Rocks)* and we spent the starry night talking *(and kissing – but actually mostly talking this time).*

The following week, we went to Drumming Circle together where once again he dragged me out of my reservations and this time pushed me to drum. This too was way beyond my comfort zone: I usually don't do things I'm not proficient at in public. But remembering the rewards of the previous week's breakthrough, I complied. And it happened again. After only a few minutes of timidity, I entered a rapturous trance and discovered I was very gifted for drum playing. Next to Richard, I delved into the experience body and soul, interjecting syncopations, enhancing the fundamental rhythm, adding unexpected stresses and accents to the backbeat, and even (sometimes) blending into the whole until the singularity of my sound was inaudible. I played until all of my fingers were swollen and raw, and I shivered from a sense of deep freedom and fulfillment. At the end of the session, just as when we had danced, people lined up to thank us for the offering of this inspired performance. We would do this again often.

In the course of the two weeks that followed, we spent time together. He was working on a construction project then, and I occupied my days hiking. During the evenings, I recounted my summit-conquests-running-from-bushfire-lost-trails-hummingbird-mistaking-my bandanna-for-a-flower-snake-encounters adventures to him over home-cooked meals and under the golden skies of breathtaking sunsets.

Then came our magical day trip to the Grand Canyon. We awoke at dawn, next to one another – after having spent our first night "together" – and prepared for our exciting outing. Neither of us had ever seen the Canyon, and as we drove closer, we held hands as tears welled up in our eyes. We had a premonition that this was going to be a momentous experience. The plan had been to hike down and up for a few hours while taking in the scenery, but so overwhelmed were all our senses by the grandeur of the scenery, and so transported were our spirits from roaming these sacred grounds, that all we did was stand on the edge of the Canyon for seven hours. We stood and sat, talked and contemplated, cried and laughed. We must have radiated a remarkable glow because couples stopped and watched, and children tugged and their parents' sleeves and pointed at us in curiosity. In a mystical moment, as we were standing and staring into each other's eyes, my breath was taken away as I saw his eyes turn to pure gold, like the eyes of an eagle. Tears ran down my face as I told him what was happening, and in the middle of my words he said, "I know, yours too." Gratitude spilled from our hearts and we wept with joy.*

I clearly remember my feeling as we later walked side by side along the banks: for the first time in my life, it felt as though I was walking next to my equal. The feeling was not related to accomplishments, education, social status, or intellectual ability; it was about having found a twin spirit belonging to my long lost tribe. Throughout the afternoon, we kept looking at each other gleefully and incredulously, asking for confirmation: "Really?" And one or the other would answer, "Yep. Really." After a lifetime *(or lifetimes?)* of waiting, we were at last reunited.

Upon our late night return, Richard stayed with me and moved-in the next day for what was left of my time in Sedona.

Leaving was hard, but amidst my sadness I rejoiced at the thought that I was no longer journeying on the planet alone and that I had finally found where I belonged in the world: next to Richard. The

* I did not think I would ever mention this experience publicly, but after reflection, I decided it honored what Richard and I once shared.

future would not be simple – living in the USA and starting with limited funds – but it was linear. The goal was clearly circled; now began the work to make it happen. That's how, once I returned to Quebec, I contacted a lawyer to figure out how to be able to reside in Arizona, and began working assiduously on my USA residency visa, which would take me 18 months to complete.

I returned to Sedona three months later, as I would many times over the next three and a half years. At the airport, Richard was waiting for me at the gate. As we saw one another, my heart expanded. My eyes fixed on his; I slowly walked towards him. I stopped when I was about six inches from his chest, we looked at each other deeply, I dropped my purse and carry-on, and we began to kiss. We kissed until a guard interrupted us and apologetically asked us to move over because we were blocking the flow of passengers.

Signs of Richard's lack of follow-through and unreliability came to light early on. In truth, I was repeatedly and frustratedly dumbfounded that, despite his determination, best intentions and promises, he would end up not contributing "whatever it takes" to our future together. The discrepancy puzzled me: First, if you make a commitment or a promise, you keep it *(that was the world I lived in)*. Second, if you know what you want and what needs to be done to make it come true, then you do it. Simple. I had never been confronted with someone with an addiction and it took me a while to somewhat understand the inherent complexities and painful ramifications.

Despite the obstacles, there was no doubt in both our hearts that we belonged together, which meant I was willing to give it whatever it took and to make up for whatever he couldn't do. I mean, we had found each other: the rest was details as far as I was concerned. If he needed more time to heal right now, as hurtful as events were, I would pick up the slack. Our future was at stake and my hopes that he would come up to the plate were constantly renewed by his relentless efforts and new beginnings. Once I became aware of the problem, we tackled his drinking issues and sorted the past and present collateral damages. A lot of time, energy, and money were spent to allow us a fresh start... several times over.

Richard is (was) an immensely gifted spiritual man. His perceptivity, insights and visions are profound. He is astute and possesses a swift intelligence, which unfortunately, in his compromised state, he uses towards craftiness, manipulation and deceit. Children and animals are instinctively drawn to him, which attests to his veritable nature. When he is sober, he loves and cares for all creatures, he is attentive, a constant gentleman *(he would never let me open a door)*, will always offer his arm to the elderly and make them feel seen and valued. When drunk, he has shown me a dark side of man I had never witnessed in my life.

Our years together were a vigorous roller coaster ride. Manifestations of our incredible connection showed up at every corner and elevated us to dizzying peaks where we were infused by glimpses into the great expanse of spiritual and emotional possibilities. But ineluctably, vertiginous drops followed.

After obtaining my USA visa in the spring of 2008, I moved to Sedona, but that's when things did not go as planned: Richard's dysfunction was causing serious mayhem, many of my hopes for income had been dashed, I contracted one of those super-bug bacterial infections in both my legs, and I learned my father's cancer was claiming victory. Within two months of my arrival, and as soon as my legs allowed, I flew back home to live with my parents until my father's final, glorious breath a few months later.

This experience was life altering, I *(we, the family)* was privy to a truly divine experience that moved my core, and also took a deep toll on me. After months of 24-hour-a-day presence and care for my father – and subsequent weeks of administrative after-death business and emotional aftermath – I was beyond exhausted, a ghost of myself. At that point, I was in desperate need of the teeming stillness of the desert and longed for the rich red dirt to replenish me. And also, to be honest, despite the severe Richard-drama that had transpired in my absence, I needed him to help me through this. Upon my arrival, I pried him out of the alcohol soaked burrow he was hiding in, and brought him home with me. He rose to the occasion comforting and restoring me like no one else could have by reaching out to the essence of my soul. After a few months, my finances imposed yet another return North and Richard had spiraled downward once again.

As I wrote at the beginning of this book, my health degenerated dramatically in 2009. My body ultimately collapsed under the strain of years of holding together the myriad shattered pieces of my heart. Actually, it was the realization that true love did not conquer all that proved too much to bear. A broken heart or a challenging life I could deal with, but this time, it was my soul that had been smashed, pieces scattered then doused like a campfire at the end of the night. An ember of hope was nowhere to be found. In my extreme weakened state, I *knew* this was most likely the end of my journey. In a survivor's last instinctive attempt at holding on to life, and despite the incomprehension of people around me, I gathered my last smithereens of vitality and decided that, even if I needed a wheelchair to travel the corridors of airports, I would make my way to Sedona again. The faint agonizing voice of my soul had whispered that the only thing that could bring me back from the brink of what I understood was to be death, was love. And the only way for me to access unconditional love was with Richard. Ironically, the cause of the destruction could be my salvation. After nine months of complete radio silence from him, I knew that if I was able to locate him, he would be far-gone, and himself in the eye of self-annihilation. If I found him, I knew he would willingly accept me as his lifeline; and in allowing me to love him to health, he would in turn become my own lifeline. If I found him, love would pour out of my heart and I would be alive once more. I was perfectly aware that only a miracle would keep him sober permanently, but this time, it actually wasn't the point: I had to feel love lest I die.

So I made my way to Arizona *(without any wheelchair)*, drove to a neighboring community of Sedona where I presumed he still roamed the streets, and began looking for him in the shadows of the underworld. After a several unsuccessful attempts, I sat in my car in a city park, took a few deep breaths, and in a prayer state, began talking to him, "Richard, my beloved, I am here. I need you and we should connect *now*." As I opened my eyes, I saw the top of a baseball cap moving behind tall grasses across an open field. My heart skipped a beat. I stepped out of the car and the person *(the hat)* had disappeared. I told myself it had been my imagination, that there was absolutely nothing to tell me it was him, and that I had never even seen him with a baseball cap. Regardless, I walked across the field, and to my surprise found several paths heading into the abutting woods. After a second's hesitation *(I was not feeling very secure and was very weak)* I followed one of them into the thicket. After a few hundred feet, and across a bend, there was a little decrepit stone bridge laid over a stream. A man with a baseball cap was sitting there, hunched over, crying. It took me a moment to realize that it was Richard *(he no longer looked like the beautiful man I knew)*. I walked near him saying nothing. He looked up and quietly muttered, "Hi. I knew I could feel you. I was crying for you." I sat next to him and we started talking. Soon after, we packed up his tent and belongings; he vowed he would never return, and we went home together.

Nursing him took everything out of me *and* healed me. Love flooded my whole being; the wilted blossoms of my heart were revived, and I grew alive again.

THE ESSENCE

The greatest gift Richard gave me was to allow me to discover the full woman that I am: her gambit of emotions, her intuition, spirituality, quirks, mischief, and humor. By bringing out, seeing, and loving every single aspect of me, he permitted I explore, express, and act out all of me. He loved me when I was angry or abrupt, when I was afraid, had doubts and lacked self-confidence, when I was childlike and silly, when I was wise and inspiring, when I was a goddess, a nurturer, a business woman, a seductress, or a prude. He allowed me to flow from one to the other and embraced it all; and that was the most liberating and life-changing gift I was ever given. Together *(during the sober times)* he was a real man and I was a real woman with everything this implies. With him, I experienced the heightened state of union I had believed was possible all my life.

When we talked, nothing was taboo, there were no eggshells to walk on *(on the lighter side, I remember commenting about a present he had given me, telling him his thoughtfulness warmed my heart but that it was the tackiest thing I had ever seen)*; there was no shame or embarrassment for any thought either of us could have. Nothing the other could say or think was unworthy of consideration. Anything that was born from either of us was worth listening to and exploring. We could never offend with something that was part of us. I could tell him that although I loved him completely, I could sometimes imagine the relief that would come from his demise. He would consider this and thoughtfully reply: "I understand why you might feel that, and I can imagine how painful it must be for you to acknowledge you have these thoughts. What I am putting you through is a great burden." More than once did he ask me to leave him because he hated that he was introducing such ugliness in my life and felt he was sullying the purity of my soul. I would understand but always maintained that the strength of our union would see us emerging at the end of this tunnel.

He could tell me reprehensible things he had done and together, we would identify the source of his behavior and discuss the impact his action could have on his (our) personal growth and healing.

When I learned he had cheated on me, I told him what he had done was ugly but not the end of the world. I expressed my deep hurt, said that I would feel anger *(and I did let him have it)* and disgust *(I did cry when he later touched me)*, and that it would take time to work through it. But I also said that if our love was meant to make us whole and heal us of the respective wounds we carried in this world then this was part of the journey and it would ultimately elevate us *(in this instance, I was betrayed – which was my thing – and by cheating on me, he had invited anger and disdain upon himself as if to insure the best person in his life would reject him – which was his thing).*

Beyond this particular instance, we both understood that his self-destructive and disrespectful behavior was part of the tango our personalities were dancing. Sure, he was the perpetrator and I was the sufferer, but we had both chosen to be there, in body and soul. The roles were equal except he was playing the villain, and I, the victim. But the storyline could not unfold without the participation of one or the other. We were being true partners because we prodded the pitfalls and wounds in one another, and by recognizing and addressing the issues – given a willingness to do so, of course – we would heal and grow. As soul mates, we pointed an unforgiving spotlight onto every blemish of our selves.

During some of our great no-reservation conversations he would compassionately tell me: "How long will you accept to be so mistreated? You know that's one of the things I'm here to teach you: to no longer take abuse. And the longer it takes you to get it, the worse my behavior will become; it's subconscious, but it's my soul's purpose. So get it already, say you've had enough and won't take it anymore so that I can move on to something else myself."

And I would say: "I know, I'm hardheaded and stubborn, it is taking me a long time. And the degree of pain you are causing me is really escalating."

We discussed our hopes that once I "got it" and asserted that I would no longer accept to be mistreated– which meant leaving him – he would be free to sort himself out, and we would ultimately find our way back to each other and continue on side by side, enjoying our love peacefully, and blossoming together on this Earth. This was the optimistic option. The bleaker one we also unenthusiastically considered was that the longer it took (the worse his behavior), the more likely the outcome was to be a permanent separation. And if this were the case, he would be condemned to explore the depth of his darkness alone, and would probably not make it out alive.

And the permanent separation is the option that came true; and exploring the depth of his darkness alone is where he has been for quite a while now. Whenever we have talked since, I have made comments such as: "So. You're still choosing to go deeper into this hole and not use all your exceptional gifts?"

And his answers have sounded like: "Yeah, even though I am miserable and suffering like hell, and really hate it, I don't think I'm done. It sucks."

When I eventually made the decision to leave him and told him I had had enough and had to move on, the first thing he told me was, "You're welcome." He was acknowledging that he had accomplished his purpose in my life. I had learned self-respect: I had learned to honor myself.

This may sound crazy, but it is the truth: our communion existed beyond our personalities – although I must say that I had the best times of my life when our earthly personalities were in sync too.

I believe we got very close to enjoying the purest form of communication available to mankind. If he had conquered his demons – he would have then had my back and been a reliable partner – we would have. I remember watching Sandra Bullock's Oscar speech about having found exactly that in her life and saying to the TV screen, "Good for you girl. Happy to know a woman has it. I'll find it too." and then being so pissed when it was announced she had been duped. I even wrote her an empathy letter!

THE GREAT PARADOX

Within a situation where undependability *(to put it gently)* abounded, I actually learned trust. By having a partner love all of me, I finally experienced a relationship in which "who I am" was never undermined and "what I said" never used against me. The great paradox is that the most authentic relationship of my life was with a compulsive liar.

THE PHONE CALL

So two days ago, Richard called me.

After I picked up the phone and heard his savory "Mmm..." he continued to say, "How are you my darling?" Since small talk was never something we did, and a question was never posed in a trifling way, he knows that if he asks how I am, he will get a forthright answer. It has always been like that. If he asks, I will unceremoniously unwrap the naked truth of my thoughts, emotions and state of mind for him to look at plainly. So I told him where I stood in my mind, heart, and soul; I told him of my challenges and hurdles, of my daily diligence requirements to keep on track, and of my book *(he is aware that I live in Vancouver because the one other time we spoke – briefly – was for my birthday in October)*. I told him I was the proudest I had ever been of myself, that I was transforming my life, and that I finally no longer functioned from my wounds. He told me I was the greatest woman he had ever known, that my book was exactly the right thing for me to do, and that he was proud of me.

Then I asked him how he was. He said he was okay but that he would not share specifics about his current life. I understood (his shame) and did not pry further. My next question was: "Do you have any plans to try something different for the years you have left to live? Do you plan to give a shot at being all you can be?"

He replied: "I do have ideas in the back of my head, but I don't have the courage to act on them."

Richard is a manly man: he is exceptionally powerful, proud, protective, and prime to defend that which he loves and believes in. But we have discussed how, strangely, he lacks guts when it comes to daring a leap of faith for himself. Actually, that's not even true: I have witnessed admirable bravery on his part when it came to confronting his demons. But there are a few problems: He needs someone present in his day-to-day life who believes in him *(which he had with me but I was also away for long periods)*, he is clueless as to what to do after a valiant and victorious battle *(he knows how to fight, all guns blazing, but not how to build on the success)*, and his resolve is sporadic – his grit comes in spurts – which means he cannot sustain his efforts.

The conversation continued and he added that he was not as strong a person as me. I replied that the fact that he was my twin soul said something about who he was. But that if he needed to, he could draw from my courage whenever he wanted. He could carry my love as a torch to bring light to his path.

I suggested he pack up a bag and leave without telling anyone, and try a fresh, sober start somewhere else. At worst, the local guys would always take him back, and he could always return to being king of his street kingdom. So why not give it a go?

"Really, just go for it!" I said. "Why not? What do you have to lose? What is the worst thing that could happen to you? End up homeless and drunk?" We both chuckled.

"I know you probably think you have relationships where you are, but we both know none of them make you a better man or make you want to be the best you can be." He silently agreed and said:

"I heard you. Enough said."

"Okay"

Soon after, the time he was given on a friend's phone was over, and we said goodbye.

The good news is that for the first time, ever, his phone call did not make me tremble from head to toe. It did not even make my breathing laborious. I was happy to have talked with him, and I had enjoyed the connection and its beneficial lingering after effects.

AFTERTHOUGHT

I hung on to the dream of Richard and I for a long time; I have been tempted to say for too long. But in truth, it was the perfect amount of time for me to learn what I needed to learn. Of course, I still sometimes wonder what it could have been like if our love had succeeded in piecing together his shattered soul. But maybe that would have interfered with his own destiny; maybe there is a reason for his journey; maybe I would have interrupted a design greater than our personal desires.

Who knows: Perhaps we are blissfully happy in an alternate reality, experiencing our love as a unit, and manifesting our potential as a team. We did have so many dreams of how we could serve humanity together, and I hope that somewhere, in a parallel universe, these dreams have become reality.

ALMOST PERFECT

Whenever I think or talk about Richard, I always say he was the love of my life "to date". I do not think that he was the best I will get. He was almost perfect. No, he was perfect for me then, because of who I am now as a result. And a future man will benefit from his gifts.

The next perfect-man-for-me will correspond to who I am today and I believe it will be splendid *(and less painful)*. I was going to say that the bar was set very high because the next man would have to be everything Richard was *(less the broken soul)* and more. But as I write this, it occurs to me that it may not be necessary to find the same thing with someone else: someone else can teach me something else. My new man can take me along new adventures in the land of love, and we can venture into yet unexplored territory. I have never been one to return to the same location for an adventure anyway. That's good news. "Hey my man out there, do not fret, I will not compare you to anyone else. You will not be measured by another man's yard-stick" *(forgive the pun, or not)*.

THE END

Our last reunion was in the winter of 2009 when I travelled to Sedona to bring myself back to life. After getting healthy, Richard got a job, and a door was ajar giving us a glimpse into a possible future together. I spent the best Christmas of my life volunteering at a soup kitchen with him. We truly had a jolly time. I was alive, joy had returned, and we were reunited. We spent New Year's Eve holding hands, sitting on garden chairs in the middle of a quiet street, under the glow of a Blue Moon. It seemed a miracle had occurred. I wanted for nothing more than what I had. All those years of suffering had had their reason and were behind us, and we were about to start a life together. On that night, I pledged my full commitment to our relationship.

Sadly, Richard's inner malignant forces claimed him again. I left at the end of February for the last time.

I still think of him often, send him my light and pray that his suffering ends, and that he finds peace. His life is not a happy place: because he is aware of his potential, the punishment is cruel. But it is now his road to travel.

Thank you Richard for introducing me to the woman I am in her entirety.
Thank you for teaching me to love myself enough not to accept abuse.
Thank you for widening my heart until it pushed the boundaries of the universe.
Thank you Richard for I can say I know Love.
Your gifts are eternal because they are now intrinsic parts of my soul.

A failed relationship may not always be a failed relationship. Perhaps it has simply run its course and served its purpose.

DECEMBER 29TH, 2011

GUESS WHAT? (...)

CLARITY, CLARITY, CLARITY

I have finally completed the portion of my friend's project I had said I would handle. Phew. What a relief. Because the project could go on, I had to, once again, make my position clear to my friend, myself, and the Universe: I had to decline any further involvement. What I had said initially remains true: I am not in a strong enough state these days to manage obligations, and my wellness must come first. Although I had previously grasped the concept that the Universe was making me practice choosing my new path by making me take the same stand over and over, I had missed the fact that it also required clarity. As it happens, I had been kind of wishy-washy in my position hoping that my excuses, delays, and hesitations, would make the project go away. But when it comes to dealing with the Universe, half-assed doesn't cut it: speak clearly, avoid subtext, and stay away from fine print.

This morning, I woke up unrested. Through the night, very unpleasant dreams repeatedly startled me awake and I just could not shake them off when I attempted to go back to sleep; so I had to get up several times. You know the type of dreams, right? The ones that seem more real than this reality even once you're awake? They're pretty disturbing.

So I ultimately got out of bed late, having caught up with some sleep in the morning hours. I hate getting up late because I'm a morning person *(I sound like the Grouchy Smurf)*. My favorite rhythm is to wake up at dawn, mostly in the summer when it means I'm up at four-thirty. This gives me such a feeling of aliveness: I feel in sync with creation, stretching my body as the first birds open-up their beaks and announce the miracle of a new day as enthusiastically as if it was their first dawn. Now that's a lesson in being fresh in every moment.

My morning *latte* performed its magic and my early grumpiness kindly gave way to contentedness. Sipping my coffee, I took a deep breath, leaned back in my chair, and reminded myself of the timeliness of these gentle days – my ongoing nausea certainly reinforcing the idea that the Universe did know better then to let me get a job.

(...) I'M WRITING A BOOK!

"A job? You don't need a job!
All you have to do is talk, talk, talk; just tell your story."

Honey-and-garlic man, Farmer's Market

A few days ago, after welcoming the gift of these days, I decided to skim through parts of this story I have been writing. You see, since October, I had not reread my words; I had simply kept typing my thoughts daily as they showed up and stacked the printed pages. But when I took this pause to leaf through my own writing, the strangest thing happened: I realized I *was* writing a book!

I know it may sound silly to you since I have been putting words onto paper – in an organized fashion with the expressed intention of publication – for months now, but perhaps because my idea of a book is ten years old, it had not sunken in yet that this was the real deal.

As I read some of the hundred-plus pages sitting on my desk, the possibility of becoming a published author became an outcome within reach. So cool! The idea got me so excited and proud of myself that I hurriedly called my Mom to tell her the good news, "Mom, guess what! I'm writing a book!" She was enthusiastic but not quite as surprised as I was... since she has been a daily supporter of my writing efforts since October 1st.

PARADIGM SHIFT

This morning *(after I got over my Grouchy Smurf state of mind)*, more earth-shaking thoughts rumbled through my mind. Now that I have come to truly realize that I am actually writing my long-awaited book and that I am therefore fully embracing the validity and worthiness of my endeavor, it occurs to me this morning that the urgency of finding a job, as soon as the holidays are over, is vanishing. Just like that. Since I began writing this book, my efforts have been mostly directed at expunging my guilt about not working, at welcoming the opportunity to regenerate, and at finding inner peace in recognizing that I have been making the best of this time that was bestowed *(imposed)* upon me. But now, it's a new ballgame: My book is a book, and it must and will be written. And the time is now. Ergo, finding employment can no longer be my priority. I am well aware that once I get a "real job", there will be little opportunity for me to write *(I'll probably need to rest when I'm off)*.

So here is the paradigm shift: Not only will I write with renewed ardor while I am not well enough to work or can't find work, but I will also postpone looking for a job until the bulk of my book is completed.

Let me clarify one thing: Even though I am seeing the light, it has not yet converted me into a blind believer. Although I am more convinced than ever that writing my book is the right thing to do, let's just say I stand at 97 % conviction *(3 % will probably come when it is actually published).* I stated in the first paragraph of this book that I have grown cynical of happy endings, and even though I have come a long way since, this small part of me still relates to a sentence from the movie *Mr. & Mrs. Smith*: *"Happy endings are just stories that haven't finished yet"*; the greater part of me is determined to disprove this and become a full, born-again convert.

So my immediate plan is to keep on writing this *(real)* book. I understand it will not be completed within the next two or three weeks, but my intention is to tackle the more exacting subjects I wish to include during this allotted period of time. There are key events of my personal history that have made me who I am today that I plan on sharing, as well as some philosophical and metaphysical concepts that I would like to broach upon.* Many of them are outlined throughout my journaling but will need to be expanded upon, others have yet to be written. I consider these to be fundamental to my book and my sense is that this is the foundation I need to lay before getting a job. Digging for footings and pouring concrete is certainly not the most exciting part of architecture, but it is nonetheless absolutely essential to the construct of my book.

The other aspect of this project – which I equate to the much more stimulating job of raising walls, putting down a roof, and installing window and doors and steps** – is the ongoing chronicling of my cur-

---

* What you have been reading is of course the final version of the book and therefore includes those personal stories and concepts that I was planning on tackling.

** Since you will have been there with me from the beginning, I will gladly invite you in my bright and comfortable finished home when it is completed. It will be a sight to see.

rent journey of finding my voice and of manifesting the fullest expression of myself. This part, I anticipate being able to pursue concurrently to having a job. I am definitely more enticed by this journaling facet of the book. This was, after all, the very premise that inspired me from the get go: documenting my story from the murky middle without the luxury of hindsight or comforts of a happy ending, writing with the sole vantage point of the present looking into the unknown, and telling the tale as it plays out without the clarity retrospection indubitably provides.

I had also predicted the ups and downs of a mad roller coaster ride, and boy was I ever served. I am quite enthusiastic about continuing on this ride and curious as to what it will reveal and yield, where it will lead, and how it will end.

ON THE WAY TO GET THERE

In order to continue writing though, I must believe that my story is worth telling *(Oh jeez, this again? Haven't I established in the very beginning that it was worth telling because, like a reality show – except more real – it would be relatable?).* I must believe that it will inspire others to persevere in their own quest of finding their voice and of being the best they can be, while living the life they were given to experience. As I wonder about this, I realize that this story-from-the-middle is meant to be an example not only that the quest itself is noble but also that the journey truly and literally is the story *(literarily as well in my case).* That even without a happy ending in sight, life is rich on the way to get there.

Our ultimate destination merely gives a direction to our travel. Yes, like a road trip. Imagine having planned a road-trip from Alaska to Peru. Along the way, the thousands of miles and hundreds of stops provide an abundance of memorable occasions for you to fill the memories of your camera, mind and heart with masses of snapshots. Once you will have come to the end of the trip, how many of those do you imagine would actually be from Peru? I'll even one-up this rhetorical question with another: What would your photo album (and memories) be like if you hadn't made it to Peru at all and had had to end your trip, say, in Ecuador? I will venture to say: pretty damned exciting nonetheless. Without regrets, you may forget you had even meant to go to Peru.

If my journey was to end today, I would feel accomplished as a human being *(well, maybe more so right after this book is finished).* Wherever I am distance wise, this trip was already worth it. I have had countless adventures, got stuck in floods and stood on mountain peeks, ran out of gas in the desert and found an emergency gallon in the trunk of my car, witnessed mighty storms and breathtaking sunsets. I have encountered unpleasant characters who have spiced up certain legs of the journey *(and made for good stories)* and was embraced with open arms by others. I have oohed and aahed, laughed and cried; I was scared and fearless, determined and flexible. I have taken-in every landscape presented to me and my albums are bursting with memories of the fullness of every moment: I have lived. And because of that, my soul can soar.

But the adventure is not over yet. My travel is ongoing. I forget though, what was my destination again? What's my *Peru*? The pretext and theme of the trip may have been finding my voice, but the destination has always been a place under the sun with either my perfect-man-for-me, and/or a plump bank account, and/or life-fulfilling projects. Which would mean that any of those is my Peru. So until I plant my flag in some of that soil, do I actually have a story to tell? Is Peru the only worthy happy ending? Could a book entitled *From Alaska To Peru: My Personal Journey* be published before reaching Peru? I can see the reviews:

Readers beware: This is the story of a woman's journey from Alaska to Peru, but the title is deceptive. In this book, Peru is like the Sasquatch: you'll here about it often but never actually see it. The author never gets there.

With a little tweaking of the mindset and a slightly modified title such as *Forget Peru: My Journey From Alaska To Ecuador Was A Blast*, could my story warrant publication, be marketable, and reel-in the interest of readers? Maybe Peru is Part II, the next book, and my readers could be left with a last page cliffhanger: *"Will she ever make it to the elusive Peru? Find out in her next book."*

Or again, reality may be that without even noticing, I have already crossed the border into Peru because finding my voice was not only the theme but the destination as well, and I am already there, simply because I am writing this book. *(Sure. But I still really like what my initial Peru looked like – and I do plan on seeing it one day.)*

As of today, the questions remain unanswered. At this point, I don't know what the title of this book is going to be (*although you do, since you are reading it)* and I don't know what will constitute an appropriate ending. But my working title, since the first day I began writing, has been *To Be Continued...*, and so for now, I will just continue writing and see where it goes. At this moment, I consider the story of my journey is worth telling.

A life well lived is a life during which every aspect of the journey is embraced – the good lucks, the bad lucks, the days that are spent lost and those that go without a hitch, the flat lands and the bumpy rides.

On your way to Peru, whatever is your "Peru", remember to take-in every view and experience the fullness of every moment. You may never pass that way again.

DECEMBER 30TH, 2011

EVEN SANTA CLAUSE GETS THE BLUES

I have no motivation today. Sleep is still playing hide and seek with me and that doesn't help with my dizziness and nausea; and feeling queasy is getting really old. So here I go again, telling myself everything is okay and embracing this quiet day for what it is: except I don't.

Did I mention the ebb and flow, the crests and troughs, the highs and lows and ups and downs of being on this quest *(with this mind of mine)*? Did I mention the freakin' roller coaster ride? Well the turns are giving me whiplash and the drops still take me by surprise and make my stomach churn. The joys of the ride are definitely eluding me right now and I am beginning to wonder if maybe I'm bipolar *(you may have formed an opinion on this by now)*. I may be on a noble quest but my indomitable spirit feels whipped. Looking into the unknown may sound real' romantic but I'd give a lot for the beam of a lighthouse. And right now, I would gladly give-up the turbid waters of this quagmire for a cushiony seat on the *Happy Ending* sailing into the sunset.

This is insane: As certain of my direction as I was yesterday, and as inspired as I felt by my journey, today, I wonder if my story has any business being told, let alone published, or if it's even a story at all. It is beginning to feel like the ongoing ramblings of any ordinary chap. To be fair, not quite ordinary I guess *(if everybody's mind worked like mine – or if people publicly admitted theirs do too – there would be a whole other kind of problem in the world)*. Maybe I'm a little more kooky than the average Joe. Maybe I am slightly marginal and something of an oddball; maybe I am part of the eccentric fringe of the human mind. Or am I just complicated, or high-maintenance? *(Could these words be a diplomatic way of saying certifiable?)* On the other hand, if you are recognizing yourself in my ramblings, than the margin may be wider than commonly presumed and there's a major party going on.

Regardless, at this point, I'm thinking it's a bunch of malarkey: the story in general, and my certainty just as much as my doubts.

So I have an enduring spirit. I'll give myself that (...)

(...) Jeez, I'm stuck. A writer's block of sorts.

No clue where to go from here. Zip. Nada.

I've got nothing. (...)

[...crickets chirping...]

Can anything resuscitate this blank-drawing downcast mind? Sorry, but I must forget about inspiring you right now, I've got to get myself back and put on my oxygen mask first.

[Breathing. Brain cells getting oxygen.]

Here's and idea: I'll read some of my notes and journals, and hopefully something I once knew will clear the molasses that has slowed me down to a halt and engage my gears forward.

I know I've already underlined the importance of writing down conclusions we come to and illuminations we get. But I don't think I have given the practice the attention it deserves. What I have been meaning to do, was give the idea its own heading. I shall right this wrong right here and now:

WRITE YOUR ILLUMINATIONS

Last time I elaborated on the subject, I highlighted that by writing down our illuminations, we can be succored from the pitfalls of an unwitting habit of pattern repetition. By recording our lessons, understandings and conclusions, we are effectively mapping the topography of our journey – a very useful tool to avoid stepping in the same gunk, tripping over the same rocks or slipping in the same rut. This roadmap for the forgetful-pattern-loving-individual is only one of the reasons why keeping a revelation log is so valuable.

Another precious benefit of such a log is inspiration. On a day like today for example, when I've got the blues and can't, for the life of me, find an uplifting thought off the top of my head, or spot a guiding light inside it, said log can come in very handy. This morning, although Zeus has summoned his Muses and I am afflicted by their absence, hope is alive because on previous days, when I was graced by one of their presence, I had jotted down my thoughts and I am now in possession of my own inspired material. I don't need to be a victim of Zeus's temper or his unpredictable desire for a family reunion.

So I pull out my journal and begin leafing through* *(Preacher, heed your own preaching)* and with surprising ease, I stumble onto the perfect passage:

> *My gift is the perspective I have of my journey, the capacity to always see growth opportunities in whatever comes my way, my dispositions for love, forgiveness and gratitude, the ability I was given to understand others and the willingness to share my experiences as an example that all is human. My gift is my desire to use my life to understand and inspire others; it is a talent for putting my experience into words and articulating it unabashed, in written and spoken forms.*

This expanded second iteration of defining my gift was written last year when again I wondered what I had to offer the world. At the

* Of course, books can be a good source of inspiration as well, but words you will have written during your own moments of divine clarity are sure to resonate much louder in your consciousness.

time, I did not suspect the importance of defining my gift, or how often I would forget what it was, and how helpful it would be, time and again, to read it back to myself. Even until right now, I had not realized the power and necessity of doing it. Everyone should indulge into this kind of introspection and ask themselves this vital question: What is my gift? It is actually not an obvious or easy question to answer but that answer is possibly the brightest beacon a person will find in their life. It ties in to finding one's passion – fulfillment – and living an authentic successful life. I am reminded of last year's process of writing my résumé and the list of insightful questions I had written: *What kind of person am I? What kind of person am I not? What do I like? What do I do? Where am I at my strongest?* Perhaps these are the main headlines of our individual instruction manual. Perhaps everyone would benefit from writing a Personal Mission Statement *(and remember to revise it periodically).*

Back to the matter at hand: The fact that I am inspired yet again by something I had the foresight to scribble before. Not only that, it also essentially echoes yesterday's conclusion *(which I had forgotten)* that my journey *is* worth sharing because the story of my life is my gift, my legacy. The fact that the same theme keeps coming back to guide me could not be more à-propos, and validates my point that writing our illuminations can serve as precious personal memorandums for when our memory falters *(apparently a lot in my case).*

As if by some pre-ordained correspondence, I just received my mother's wishes for 2012.* Roughly translated, she tells me:

---

* My parents were always very attentive to the special occasions that dot the year. On those days, we, their children, have without fail been on the receiving end of thoughtful words, gestures and gifts. On Valentine's Day, we could count on waking up to a beautiful candlelit breakfast table set in red and white *(a performance repeated at dinner)*, decorated with hearts of every size my mother would have cut out herself days prior and accented with loving messages displayed in her familiar handwriting. On our birthdays – once we had flown the nest – we were always serenaded with birthday song duets over the phone, either live or on the answering

> *My wish for you is that your innermost dream of reaching out to others be realized. May your desire to awaken consciousnesses, to open new horizons, to guide others in discovering the inner strength that resides in each of them, and to communicate the deep joy of being in contact with nature, be fulfilled.*

I am deeply moved. This *is* why I am writing this book: to fulfill this inner desire of reaching out to a community of kindred souls. I have long felt that I was meant to share my experience and outlook on life, that it does have a unique flavor, and that perhaps it could inspire. And even though so many times I come to be blasé and uncertain of its worth, I have witnesses first hand what effect sharing it can have on people. I must hold on to this knowing that is so easily forgotten.

When we are graced with a flash of understanding, a glimpse of the bigger picture, an insight into our psyche, a key to inner peace, a faith resurrecting thought, or any aha! moment, we must write them down because we *will* ***forget. Having the possibility to go back to these moments of clarity can provide a life-enhancing boost just when we need it the most.***

---

machine. For the New Year, my father would write each of us a letter of appreciation, and in an envelope, would include a few crisp bills that reflected the ease or difficulty of the year. On Mother's Day, as an adult, he would send me flowers even though I have no children *(a reality I properly grieved in my late thirties and then transformed into a freedom of joyful possibilities)*. He maintained that my heart beamed motherly love for the world and that as such, I deserved to be included in the celebration.

[A benevolent Muse is back from Zeus's family gathering and I am on a roll.]

THE GRACE OF OUR GIFTS

Mention of my purposeful gift brings to my mind *(in a sideways, ricochet, second-cousin kind of way)* a conversation that took place a few years ago while laying supine on the table of my yogi/healer chiropractor. As he was expertly untangling some knots, I shared that I feared I was wasting my God given gifts: My art was not breaking through *(no longer publicly displayed)*, my yoga inventions were sitting on a shelf unknown to the world, my ability to bring joy to others was grossly underutilized *(I spent most of my time in my, albeit beautiful, attic)*, and my talent for opening hearts was laying unexploited *(same spatial reasons)*.

I was feeling a great sadness and a fair measure of shame that I was somehow insulting God *(or the Universe)* who had gifted me with so much. My sense was that as the recipient of such divine largess I was responsible for not wasting a drop of it and making the greatest impact possible on the world. He listened to me empathetically and voiced an observation that gave me serious pause.

First, he told me to simply savor the whole of who I was: my artistic abilities, my creativity, entrepreneurship, awareness, consciousness, and compassion. Then, he suggested that I should realize that even if my art, products, and interpersonal qualities were not widely spread on the planet, I could still proudly love who I was and what I was doing. I could do so because within my world, regardless of its reach, I was in fact producing art, inventing products, bringing joy at the supermarket, and touching the hearts of the few people in my surroundings.

He continued to explain that the scope of one's action differs from one individual to the next and that it is often a matter of destiny, karma, or simple luck of the world, and not a reflection of their work or brilliance. For some people, impactful success even came without them seeking it *(his wife was an example: she had been doing her thing, minding her own business, and was approached to do something in a large arena – now that I know what I know, I suspect she must have been following her passion as well).* Some people are simply destined for prominence: it is their experience to experience. And if I was not meant to affect humanity in a big way, it did not take anything away from my genius *(his word).*

He emphasized that I *was* using my gifts, that I was not wasting them, and that as a soul, I was being all that I was everyday; and the scale on which I was doing it was of no importance. He concluded in saying that the only offense to God *(or Life or the Universe)* would be to not recognize, appreciate, and use the gifts. And since I did, I was indeed honoring them.

Ali MacGraw brilliantly mirrored this wisdom when on *Oprah*, years ago, she addressed the fact that many people considered her current private life in the mountains of Santa Fe as a step down from her days as the "it" girl forty years ago. She deplored that starring in a popular movie was somehow perceived as more important than lovingly taking care of cats and flowers. *"What a jip!"* she said.

We honor Life when we recognize our particular gifts and use them in our lives. The breadth of the platform onto which we perform is irrelevant. Whether we care for a flower with love and earnestness or inspirer millions with our words, it is the heart and integrity with which we accomplish the task that pays homage to God.

[Unstoppable now. Thoughts are showing up in droves. The Muses' sisterhood is putting in an appearance for an after dinner "digestif".]

HUMAN DESIGN

His words effectively dissolved the unsettling sense of guilt I had been feeling. I now understood I had not been denying my gifts or wasting them in any way. Throughout my life I had in fact honored my many blessings and nothing in my actions had been insulting to the life-force that had presented me with such an abundant endowment.

Despite the relief that came from this realization – and it was a major one – an unshakable malaise lingered. Now that the fog of guilt had been lifted, I was left with a clear sense of frustration: Nothing new, it had always been there *(and still is)*, but without the haze blurring particulars, identification was a one-step process. This frustration stemmed from a deep knowing that I was meant to make a significant impression on the world and that I kept missing the boat. Given my awareness of the devious tactics of Ego *(who is a great friend so long as he does not delude himself in thinking he is the master)*, I meditated and inquired to my God within as to whether this was a desire of my ego or a knowing of my soul: The answer came through a peaceful, deeply rooted sensation: without thrill or excitement – which would have indicated that ego was involved – I understood it came from my soul.

DESTINED.... OR DESIGNED

My need to understand the discrepancy between what I *knew* and what my current life reflected, was at last quenched by a flow of insights and data that were provided by a remarkable self-discovery tool called Human Design. A few years ago, a friend introduced me to this *science* and I was fascinated the moment I was shown an example of the personal interpretation-chart it generates. Soon thereafter, I contacted a professional for consultation.

Human Design is a relatively new system for charting one's personality, inner mechanisms, and soul's purpose. It shines a light on one's unique nature by pointing out – with impressive accuracy – their limitations and vulnerabilities as well as talents and strengths. It describes the various strategies for decision-making that will work for each individual and deciphers between "real" aspirations and those conditioned by the outer world.

I am not one to rely on interpretational systems to define who I am, but getting acquainted with Human Design proved to be a most empowering experience. The reason is that it validated the totality of who I was: It confirmed the soundness of my choices *(many of which unpopular)*, gave reason for my propensities, explained my inabilities, justified my failings, legitimized my yearnings, and authenticated my beliefs and desires. It substantiated so much of what I had suspected about myself that after my reading, I felt vindicated, relieved, and unshackled. The information that was unveiled and the new valuable insights that were revealed made me feel better equipped to navigate my life with less self-doubt and blame weighing me down. The knowledge that it imparted allowed me to love myself more. *

In Human Design, the "self" – body, mind and soul – in which we are born, is likened to a vehicle we were given to drive: some were given race cars, others all-terrains, tractors, or an ultra-light. All have worthy though different purposes. Knowing what we are piloting allows us to choose which roads are better suited for our features. *(If I am a capricious, quirky, and high-maintenance machine, it's not my fault: my vehicle was designed that way!)*

---

* Of course, just like with every other valuable insight, I have often forgotten what I had learned and have had to go back to my notes multiple times. But the tally is way up there.

A QUICK TOUR

Human Design is based on four ancient wisdom traditions: astrology, the chakra system, the *I Ching*, and the *Kabbalah*. According to your date, time and place of birth, it provides a chart with 9 centers (chakras) connected between each other by 36 channels (inspired by the *Kabbalah*) and 64 gates (inspired by the 64 hexagrams of the *I Ching*). Centers, channels and gates are shown as activated or not on your personal chart.

Individuals are also categorized in four Types: Manifestors, Generators, Projectors, and Reflectors, and each of those exhibits particular characteristics. Your Type determines which way of approaching life is the most efficient for you and offers the least resistance: this is called your Strategy. Centers, gates, and channels offer a deeper interpretation of your character. The chart also differentiates between your Personality and your (unconscious) Design.

A reading provides information such as: Should you make decision from intuition or reason, are your emotions reliable indicators or not, what are the outlets for relieving pressure in your life, is your ambition natural or conditioned, do you need to finish what you start or not, will you blossom in a community setting, are you designed to take risks to find meaning, do you need others to fuel you or are you self-sufficient, and are you meant to be a leader, doer, initiator or follower *(it takes all – none is "better")*. These are but a few examples out of thousands more that can get quite specific. But even this gross overview gives an idea of how this *science* can promote understanding and acceptation of ourselves and others.

Here are a few insights I got from my own consultation: I am a Projector, which means that "waiting for the invitation" is my Strategy. Out in the world, this translates into: "If you try to sell anything (ideas, products or your talents), you will fail." Coincidentally, attempting to sell something, in one manner or another, is what I have done all my life *(overall unsuccessfully)*. According to my Design, what I am supposed to do *(and the only way for me to achieve success)* is to put myself out there, wait to be *seen* for who I am, and eventually receive invitations *(kind of like what I did when I led the retreats)*. Luckily for me, writing this book seems to follow this model; I couldn't possibly be putting myself out there to be seen much more than this. Yippee! This might just work out.

As a Projector, I am also apparently an eternal student of humanity *(this fits the bill)* and here to know, see, and recognize others for who they are, and act as a guide of sorts *(interesting)*. But this comes with the warning that if I do so without invitation, I will find resistance and feel deep bitterness *(I can attest)*.

My personal reading mentioned that my life was meant to be a living example and that communicating my experience was "in the cards" *(really promising for this book)*.

In Human Design, four of the nine centers are considered "motors", which exist to generate and procure you with energy. Uncommonly, none of these four centers are activated in my chart. This means that I need to interact with people in order for those centers to light up and give me energy. I can imagine that having lived my life in large part as a hermit has not been helpful for my stamina. This could explain why I feel I have been running on empty – I have – and also why my early days of gregarious living in Vancouver felt so good. Since my design also reveals a profound need for solitude, reconciling these two aspects will require a balancing act I look forward to performing.

PARTNERSHIP READING

Another most interesting use of Human Design is partnership reading, which is done by merging the charts of two people. The resulting image makes it possible to observe which channels and centers are activated by the relationship, and provides insight into its dynamic. This can be done for any pair of people, whether siblings, business associates or life partners.

When Richard's chart and mine were combined, the thing lit up like a Christmas tree. At the time, the counselor had said: "No wonder you feel the way you do when you are with him, this is pretty exceptional! You could not, not have met this man in your life."

LATE LATE BLOOMER

I began this *a parte* by mentioning that Human Design had satisfactorily clarified my bewilderment regarding the fact that I felt my gifts were not being used in the arena I believed they belonged. The fact is, the reading of my chart not only confirmed the likelihood of manifestation on a larger scale for me but also revealed that I would have to deal with being a late bloomer. I was told that this would indeed greatly intensify my frustration because it conflicted with the main characteristics of my design, which were leadership, living example, and an abundance of gifts. And just for the fun of it, not only would I be a late bloomer, like many Projectors, but in view of my lack of motors, I would be a late late bloomer!

So, although Human Design explained the cause of my frustration, it did not relieve it. The current state of affairs is that I remain frustrated, still striving to accept using my talents on a modest scale while practicing not feeling like I am being wasteful, and earnestly praying that "late late bloomer" means *exactly* 47 years old.

Perhaps "who we are" is predetermined by the stars, destiny or divine design. But who we become is always of our own choosing. Every moment presents us with a multiplicity of possibilities that collapse into one reality with each of our choices. Such is the quantum reality. We exist as many *selves* ***but live as*** *one*, ***and that "one" is entirely up to us.***

DECEMBER 31ST, 2011

SO LONG, FAREWELL, AUF WIEDERSEHEN, GOODBYE

THE FORGOTTEN LIST

Taking stock of our life is a Year-end tradition for many of us. It gives us perspective and allows us to observe the landmarks of our journey. Through my journaling, I have found that extending the practice of writing an annual progress report to a quarterly (or bi-annual) affair is not only a guiding and rewarding habit but a most beneficial one when I find myself down in the dumps and in dire need of a pick-me-up *(never enough tricks for those too frequent days).* In those moments, basking in a little self-appreciation is good for the soul, builds self-esteem, and fuels me to push on.

In my opinion, we too often forget to take the time to acknowledge what we have accomplished. Instead, we are quick to beat ourselves up about how far we still have to go and how much remains to be done. We have an almost innate tendency to dwell on how unsatisfied we are with our current situation and how unfulfilled we feel at the moment; we too often forget to take a moment to pat ourselves on the back.

I am particularly a fan of making a list of less tangible achievements whether spiritual, psychological, or emotional*: A list of fears that were conquered or lessened, of stands that were taken outwardly

---

* I know I have mentioned a whole lot of lists and notes to keep (emotional updates, illuminations, affirmations, lessons learned, self-appreciation, yearly review) but once you get the hang of it and experience the benefits of doing it, the rewards will outweigh the effort – not everyday, but overall. And most likely, some months or years will grant you a sabbatical from this homework. Personally, I look forward to those!

or inwardly, of resolve that is growing, of emotions we got a grip on, or of steps that were taken in the general direction we aspire to go. Recognizing these types of improvements does require more attention than noting our exploits of the material world but for those of us on the path of awareness, it can prove to be essential, because the long road is usually walked small step by forgotten step, and we do tend to forget where we have been.

We must give ourselves credit because we work hard at our life and we work damn hard at our growth. Right now, the fact that you are reading this book means that you are actively proceeding along this road and that you have not given up despite "everything". You deserve kudos.

When someone tells us (or we tell ourselves), "Why don't you do something good for yourself today?", the first thing that usually comes to mind is some kind of R&R, pampering, or shopping therapy *(which are all nice)*. But perhaps a more enduring alternative would be to indulge in a good session off self-appreciation therapy: A gentle day of self-love, of compassion, and of kind thoughts for ourselves; a day dedicated to self-congratulations.

Gratitude towards life is an indispensable attitude to cultivate out of respect, of course, but more importantly, for our own happiness. But just as we take time to be grateful to God, the Creator, Life, or the Universe, so too and perhaps foremost, must we take the time to thank ourselves for our strides, our courage, and our strength.

— Be kind to yourself, always.
— Be thankful for your timeless desire to elevate yourself.
— Recognize your strength, perseverance, and tenacity.
— Congratulate yourself for your improvements.
— Acknowledge your efforts and successes, and that you are moving forward.
— Be grateful that your journey is about being a better human being.

— Be proud of who you are because you have not given up.
— See the love and beauty within you, everyday.
— Show compassion and be gentle on yourself when you take a day off your quest.

THE TIMES THEY ARE A-CHANGIN'

Last day of 2011. I am so grateful for this pivotal year. I feel I have at long last extricated myself from a well-dug, too familiar, sunless rut, and that in so doing, I have given myself a chance at blossoming. Well, that's not quite accurate. I must revise that statement: I *am* blossoming. It's just that I look forward to the sweet perfume of my blooms to fill the air for miles yonder. Honestly, I am just thankful the year is over. It has certainly been a formidably give-it-everything-you've-got kind of year.

As a partisan of the tradition of Year-end-stock-taking, I always *(pretty much – there have probably been years I haven't)* take time to reflect on the past year. I actually reflect with paper and pen, and write down the salient points that have punctuated my story for the past twelve months. As a fan of listing less tangible events – in addition to covering more obvious ones such as geography, finances, family events, health, and relationship status – I also like to document the various markers found along the road of my personal growth. It is always gratifying to note that regardless of my current state of mind some distance has inevitably been covered *(even if some years, I may not have readily sensed any advances)*.

This year, for the purpose of feeling really good about myself and to put my progress into broader context *(and to paint a more dramatic picture too)*, I will recap 2010 as well since it appears to be the watershed where events and decisions determined in which direction the rest of my life would flow.

I'm back. As if you could know I have been gone! But earlier, I decided to interrupt my train of thought and head for my morning *(noon)* shower. I felt the meaningful exercise of a two-year review warranted some degree of decorum : A touch of elegance *(getting out of my pajama and bed hair)* to honor the value of the process. So here I am, fresh, dignified, and dressed.

2010 was a year where everything that lacked clarity in my life was clarified. Whether it did so gently, of my own volition *(some of it)*, or through life's abrupt way of pulling the rug from under me *(mostly like that)*: clarity and resolve it brought. Let me set up the year by taking a further step back and reminding you that I nearly made it through the fall of 2009, which meant that being alive was already a strong beginning for 2010.

2010 : THE PRECURSOR

—On New Years day, I had 100 % committed myself to making a life with Richard, and by February, I had made a definitive and final 180°. *(I put my belongings in storage and got out of Dodge for a while.)*

—The gallery exhibiting my art in Sedona closed its doors, and being active as an artist was a condition for my residency visa. Finding a new gallery would prove difficult from the East Coast. *(It was beginning to feel as though Dodge was spitting me out.)*

—On a pleasant spring day, I received a letter informing me my visa was not renewed because the person responsible for my mail in Sedona, during my absence, had lost some papers, which resulted in a missed deadline. *(At this point, the message about getting out of Dodge permanently should have really been sinking in.)*

—In April, I was denied entrance to the USA. *(Oh! So Dodge was not a metaphor for Sedona? It was a metaphor for the whole USA? Ooookay!)*

— Following years of expectations, I received the final verdict about some personal loot caught in a hostage situation: It was all gone. I finally knew where I stood.
— In August, I had the failed fated business meeting in Vancouver, which not only brought me here the following year *(of my own free will!)* but also made clear that it was time to let go of my yoga products and move on.
— In September, I began drafting my résumé, determined to get a job in Vancouver.

2010 was a big year too.

2011: THE YEAR AT HAND

I began the year rather discouraged with the fact that I could not find work in Vancouver while living on the East Coast. I felt at an impasse. April graced me with the resolve to throw caution to the wind. Well, we know the story. Let me just list some milestones.

— Made the decision to move to Vancouver regardless of financial and health circumstances.
— Closed the Sedona chapter. Shipped all my stored belongings to FriHo.
— Closed the FriHo chapter. Shipped all my belongings to Montreal.
— Got out of Dodge. Closed the USA chapter all together and became a Canadian in Canada.
— Boldly left my familiar security.
— Spent precious tight-knitting bonding weeks with my Mom.
— OMG, moved to Vancouver.
— Got my own place: suitcases were put away for the first time in ages.
— Cleansed myself of medications: first time in 25-30 years.

—Healed my emotional body of some deep scars.
—Worked through deep-seated fears.
—Overcame doubts.
—Transmuted a paralyzing panic.
—Honed my faith.
—Started writing my book.
—Oh yes, and got a complete set of earrings.

All in all, this has been a very good year. As it comes to a close, the door is about to open onto the next. I am excited for the year to come. I am more than hopeful: I feel that I am standing on the most promising land I have ever known, that I am grounded in fertile soil as well as connected to my higher purpose.

Once in a while during the year to come, let's take the occasional time-out to list the milestones of our inner life and benevolently evaluate our nonmaterial performance. Let us compare ourselves with where we were emotionally and spiritually three months ago, six months ago, two years ago, and hand ourselves a few medals. Celebrating oneself is not egotism.

Note: In my current book document, I am ending this year on page 47. I am 47 years old. Also, the total of my continuous book pages is 111, and as I have mentioned, 11 is my favorite, lucky, ever-recurring number. I will choose to perceive these as nods of approval from Life.

JANUARY

SOULSHINE

JANUARY 1ST, 2012

HAPPY, GLORIOUS NEW YEAR!!!

Last night was a private, quiet celebration. Celebration is actually a big word. I went to bed at ten o'clock after finding nothing to my taste on television, read, tried to go to sleep, and then got up at ten to twelve. I was actually in fine spirits: the simplicity of this New Year's Eve was okay with me. Since it was just a few minutes before midnight, I thought, "I might as well feel the transition into 2012." So I put on my coat and stepped outside: it was a clear night. A few minutes later, fireworks started going off. I could hear their sounds bouncing off the mountains as if they were coming from every direction. From my elevated vantage point, up on the hills of the North Shore, I could see the shimmering city of Vancouver and here and there, from East to West, the tiny sparkles of fireworks. At midnight proper, the amount of explosions intensified, the boats in the harbor tooted their horns, and I could hear the clamor of distant crowds. At this moment, contemplating my new city, I envisioned it from space as a tinny dot at the Western tip of my country. Drawing an imaginary line from the East where I had come from to that speck, I felt a surge of joy, hope and faith. I felt the satisfying warmth of a job well done: I had listened to the whisper, devised ways to get myself here for my destiny to unfold. I imagined and perceived powerful heavenly arms holding me tightly and making me fell everything would be okay.

I wished myself a very Happy New Year several times, out loud, and tossed my hat in the air *à la* Mary Tyler Moore *(except I could not catch it)*. I gazed at the city and whispered: "You are my friend Vancouver. I heard you, I came, I am here; you are my city. I live here with you. We are now joined. Let me flourish with you."

I came back inside and figured the celebration deserved some bubbly, so I went to the fridge and took a swallow out of the bottle of soda water.

I do wish this to be my last New Year without my perfect-for-me-for-the-rest-of-my-life-loved-one *(just to make things clear, I'm talking about a man here, not a cat or any other old-maid creature).* Having someone to kiss at midnight has been a rare occurrence in my life and I miss it so. This is definitely at the top of my wish list for 2012.

This year's list does include some serious personal redundancies as I have wished the same wishes for many many years, but just as I feel that my affirmations now have fertile soil to be rooted in and blossom, so too do I believe that this year has a greater potential of receptivity and that my wishes have a shot at fulfillment.

Here is the list:

- —Strong Health.
- —My darling love by my side *(the yet unknown one).*
- —Financial peace and security.
- —My book being published *(that's a new one).*
- —Said publication being a blockbuster and yielding fulfilling life's work *(new too).*
- —More welcomed visitors in my home *(since I moved here in July, I have had a single guest, my cousin).*
- —And on a very material plane, a new, quiet, beautiful home that is not someone else's basement *(no more people walking over my head – maybe a nice guest house).*

As for New Year's resolutions? Well frankly, I cannot ask much more of myself than what I have been doing. I'm on the right track and I am giving it all I've got. My definite goal though, is to be financially independent and self-reliant in 2012.

A distant cousin just gave me a call. Her and I have always felt a closeness even though we have sometimes gone several years without talking. We chatted for a while, updating our lives to each other. I told her about my ups and downs and twists and turns, and hesitantly decided to confide about writing my book.

Still, as of today, none of my friends or family members *(except my Mom)* are aware of my literary endeavor; the ride has been bumpy enough without bringing other people's opinions and judgments on board. As I mentioned back in December, having to deal with the occasional intrusions of administrative, social, and familial tasks, obligations, and concerns, has been disruptive enough. No need to provide anyone with my choice to write as ammunition. Despite numerous temptations to share this important journey, I have held my tongue, instinctively knowing that adding the voice of others *(or even their inner thoughts)* to the already loud cacophony produced by my ego would result in my surrender to the logic of reason. And my soul has refused to let this happen. It has bravely held this treasure-holding fort against the assaults of my ego and has wisely kept other adversaries at bay.

The moment I voiced the existence of my secret garden to my cousin, I knew it was a mistake. I had thereby laid down a bridge and permitted an invasion. Her instant reply was, "Well you know writing a book has nothing to do with making a living, right?" I got hot with regret and anger, and began boiling inside. I felt my defenses rear-up, my soul ready to fight for its life.

I replied: "No, I don't agree and I wish you would not say that. I will be one of the rare ones whose book changes the direction of their lives. I will be one of those who make a living from it. This is my calling. I believe I was meant to write this book, that it will inspire people, that it is meant to be, and that it will be a success." Trying to camouflage the hotness of my outrage I jokingly *(forcefully)* added, "I forbid you to harbor thoughts of non-success for my book, or of me being naive."

By the end of our two-hour conversation, I think she had somewhat changed her opinion. I couldn't blame her of course; she was simply talking from personal experience. But what I did learn was to keep biting my tongue next time I considered telling someone I was writing a book.

It certainly appears I have a serious regression problem when I interact with family. The last time was back in October, remember, when I got all sorry for myself with my visiting cousin? Today had some of the same flavor. During our conversation, I actually did rehash a little bit of my poor story of risking everything, living on credit, being alone, and of having iffy health. What is so interesting is that even though I spoke these thoughts, it's not even how I feel anymore! I'm doing great! Good thing I moved across the continent to give myself time to deal and be done with this bad habit of reenacting an old role that no longer suits me.

Chatting with my sister this very afternoon, I was so tempted to share that I was writing a book. If it hadn't been for my morning experience being so very fresh in my mind, I would have. And even though I was standing in the wake of that conversation, I came dangerously close to doing it; thinking it would be different with her. Did I mention it's a good idea to write down your conclusions in order to avoid making the same mistake twice? "Today, I have learned that I should not share that I am writing a book until the fortress of my resolve has less cracks. I shall keep my mouth shut until that day."

Perhaps my problem has more to do with memory. Can one get senile at 47?

Whenever you seek approval from someone other than yourself, not only are you taking a risk, but chances are it will not satisfy your needs. Whatever support is provided will never be quite enough unless you first have the solid endorsement of your inner-self. Once you are self-assured, then you can share your conviction with those who will encourage you and fuel your resolve.

JANUARY 2ND, 2012

HAPPY 2ND DAY OF 2012

I got some relatively good sleep last night and I do hope it is a new trend for 2012. I consider this even more of a feat since I managed to find the arms of Morpheus in the wake of an interesting *(disturbing)* event. As I was reading in bed, just about to fall asleep, I noticed the headlights of the neighbor's car coming down the driveway – nothing unusual there – except that the light was followed by a sound: the sound of crushed sheet metal. Yes. Mr. Up-the-Hill, my other neighbor, backed-up into my car! Really.

I jumped out of bed to look out the window thinking, "You've got to be kidding!" only to see him drive off. I put on a coat, grabbed a flashlight, and went outside to assess the damage: much worse than what Mrs. Landlord had done two weeks ago, and also, right on top of it. I was glad her dint hadn't been repaired yet; maybe the lapse had been intuitive.

I wonder what kind of omen this is for 2012. I'm sure there is a way to interpret a New Year's Day one-over-the-other impact within two weeks. I am a little anxious about how this will play out because this neighbor displays definite curmudgeonly dispositions.

He just came by. It's 11:11 *(something is aligned)*. The conversation was fine: He does wish to do right by me, but he and his wife also feel like sticking it to my landlord for assigning me an inconvenient parking space and making him pay for the damage. They do not get along. We agree to talk in a few days.

To be continued.

Consistency. This is the word that emerged in my consciousness last night as a goal *(not quite a resolution)* to strive for throughout this New Year. As I reflect upon my life – or on a smaller scale, my recent time in Vancouver – it is pretty obvious that apart from a steady awareness, all other aspects of my life exhibit a definite proclivity for fluctuation. I do have an inkling though that committing to a daily routine would yield benefits. As you know, I have aspired many times before to establish a regular regimen of meditation and exercise but with little success. Although I am a perseverant and dedicated hard worker and person in general, I paradoxically lack discipline. Or more specifically: structured discipline.

I think it has a lot to do with how my brain is wired. Just as I was never able to accept "because that's the way it is" as a valid explanation *(I also took such an answer as a direct affront to my intelligence and as an insulting mark of presumed superiority)*, it is almost inconceivable for me to plan my actions days in advance. And this creates a problem when one is attempting to establish a set regimen. In my little mind, both the hollow answer and the idea of planning ahead seem to deny the value of my presence in the moment: "Because that's the way it is" rudely dismisses that I am right there, with my brain and awareness, and "planning ahead" repudiates that each moment comes with its own set of prerogatives. Something as insignificant as picking out my clothes the night before is an exercise in futility: chances are that the color and fabric that felt right at the time of selection will no longer correspond to my energy the next day *(you could say I'm not the simplest person there is)*. So imagine how I feel about pre-determining that I will be meditating thirty minutes after waking up, or hiking Monday, Wednesday and Saturday, "regardless of circumstances!"

The problem with my goal is that "consistency" was extracted from the same ore as routine, and as I explained earlier, routine is Kryptonite to me. Still, I suspect that I could benefit from consistency. If I were to begin everyday *(this already sounds dreadful)* with meditation and stretching, and developed a routine *(this is making me quiver)*, certainly I would reap great rewards.

But here what's happening already: I am telling myself that some exceptions are acceptable. For example, if I wake up with an inspired thought for my book, I will make the book my priority, obviously. Or, if I have the urge to go for a hike before my coffee, it would certainly replace my meditation and stretching, right? I'm so sneaky: anything to avoid a sentence of routine. But I also know that so much resistance on my part indicates that I definitely have something to learn from it. And so, I will renew my efforts.

OHM-SPACE™

This morning, in the spirit of my night's desire to begin dismantling the wall of resistance standing between me and discipline, I decided to start the day with a meditative moment. Throughout the years, I have found a few tricks that help ease me into the quiet state that favors surrender of the mind. *(They don't always work, but invariably help.)*

My first trick is to physically maintain what I call an Ohm-space – a space in your home where you stop, sit or lay, and connect with yourself. Those of us who have any kind of awareness practice have certainly heard, learned, or discovered the importance and benefits of establishing a consecrated space where we practice *our thing* – whether the thing is yoga, meditation, prayer, chanting, or simply breathing. Returning to a dedicated area helps to focus on oneself, or non-self, by triggering a kind of reflex-response from the body, mind and spirit. Furthermore, with time and repetition, the space seems to cumulatively retain the energy of our previous appearances, which allows us to slide more easily into the state of being we aspire to reach: relaxation, letting-go, going inward and shutting out the world, are facilitated because something inside us *knows* that once we enter this space, it's "me-time".

Another aid that seems to trigger such an automatic response is music. On occasions when I have neglected my practice for a while, or when getting into it presents a greater challenge than usual *(today would qualify)*, I find that playing music already associated to this activity can be quite helpful. I have a handful of CDs that I have listened to for years while meditating or doing yoga, and playing them on such days is a godsend. Stepping into my dedicated space while playing sounds reminiscent of previous moments of stillness appears to prompt my mind to release its grip and grant me access to my inner temple.

My morning meditation benefited from these tips and I am pleased with myself.

5000 PIECES

Since realizing I was writing an actual book just a few days ago, a motivating sense that the pieces are coming together is mounting. The inside of my head resembles the surface of a working table where thousands of pieces of a puzzle-in-progress lay. The grunt work of sorting through and organizing colors and patterns in separate piles is completed, all the outer edges have been linked, duos are locked together, patches of the image have been assembled, and I can definitely imagine the big picture.

At this point, it is getting harder to put aside, and I am aware of further sacrificing a certain healthy balance in my life – hence the need to give routine a shot. Although the gargantuan undertaking is now highly stimulating, a lot of work remains to be done: empty spaces need to be filled, open-ends await their counterparts, and a few more stray pieces still elicit a question mark. I predict there will be days when I will think it's all too much, but overall, it is exciting.

I am writing a book.

The day is coming to an end and I have been working at it all day long. My energy is now waning and I must stretch my muscles, get some food in my stomach, and some distracting thoughts in my mind. Reluctantly, I get away from my table knowing the puzzle will still be there tomorrow.

As far as distracting thoughts for my mind go, I have a humbling confession to make: I can't wait until the reality shows start their new season. I am a willing junkie, and their mindlessness is the perfect antidote for my overwrought mind.

Create an ohm-space in your home: an area – or even just a display if the space is scarce – that will retain the energy of your stillness, facilitate reaching your center, and remind you to take a breath when you pass by it. Train your brain to respond to the memories of a particular space and to the sounds of a specific music. Cellular and energy impressions are powerful tools at our disposition.

JANUARY 3RD, 2012

IT'S ALL FOR THE BEST – NAH

My prayers were answered! Reality TV season started last night with *The Bachelor*! *(I'm in training: first, wish for a TV show, then move on to bigger and better things)* I admit to this guilty pleasure. It is one of these shows I enjoy in a kind of sick voyeuristic way that makes me squirm *(but only up until the finale, at which point I find it rather moving – I am a sucker for witnessing happy endings, even temporary ones. Despite being jaded, I still believe).* Kind of like when they show painfully bad auditions for *American Idol*: I want to change channel, but I can't. As I have said, these shows do the trick for me: they are an escape beyond the confines of my mind. Not that I'm complaining about my mind: it is a lovely dwelling *(although maybe a little crowded)*, but getting out from time to time is a necessity.

So last night, early on during the show, one of the girls said, *"I believe that everything happens for a reason"*, which to me, was a different kind of cause for squirming. This saying, along with "It's all for the best", always gets a rise out of me. Blanket statements make me uncomfortable and I find that these two expressions are in a state of raggedness from being over-worn and misused. Personally, I keep swinging back and forth between the somewhat naive everything-happens-for-a-reason "True" camp and the apparently more grown-up "No way" camp.

The fact that I have realized that everything that has happened in my life has led me here – doing what I believe is my life's purpose – would put me on the "True" side. But then the fact that I also believe that haphazard events do occur in the cosmos without "reason" – and that occasionally, we may find ourselves in a random collision course – would put me on the "No way" you-should-wise-up side. As for

"It's all for the best", I consider that finding yourself in the midst of a tsunami cannot belong in this category, nor is getting sick.

So I guess I'll remain an "undecided" and keep swinging back and forth between the two camps. But one thing I do know for sure is that we can always find gifts and growth opportunities in all our life's circumstances. And the more we embrace and evolve from tragedy and challenges, the more, in retrospect, will the events appear as though they were custom-designed for our betterment. Perhaps one way to look at it is to accept that from up close, some strokes are messy, but by the grace of our willingness, the big picture will be inspiring.

When something bad happens, it is legitimate to say: "This sucks." Everything that happens is not always *intended* ***for the best. The secret is: we can always*** *make* ***the best of it.***

JANUARY 4TH, 2012

AMAZING GRRR...RACE

How serendipitous! I have a perfect example of using a bad situation to make something good out of it. Today, I had to deal with the double hit on my car. By the way, this is one of those instances when I can state with no uncertainty that having my car run into twice is not *for the best.* It's a pain and a drag, and I wish it hadn't happened.

But, here is how it transformed into a peace mission with *"moi"* as the mediator.

APPLIED SCIENCE

As I mentioned, Mr. and Mrs. Up-the-Hill do not get along with Mr. and Mrs. Landlord, and that's putting it mildly. There is bad blood between them. Mr. and Mrs. Up-the-Hill believe that no car should park in my spot because this is a shared driveway and space is limited. Coming up the hill, members of both households have to go back and forth a couple times to maneuver the hairpin bend in order to access their respective garages, all the while avoiding my car. Mr. and Mrs. Landlord say they are within their rights and Mr. and Mrs. Up-the-Hill do not appreciate their attitude and harbor several other grievances. There are stories of flat tires due to alleged negligence, of rubbish being an eyesore, and of previous car damage that was the fault of one or the other without offers of compensation. Anyway, it's not pretty. A lot of ammunition lying around. To this day, I have just listened to the stories and appreciated the legitimacy of each point of view.

When Mr. Up-the-Hill hit my car, I was not forward in mentioning that he was the second act. The damage from the first incident paled in comparison to the second: his completely overshadowed the dint underneath. I did feel somewhat dishonest about my censorship, but knowing there was bad blood, I had not wanted to poke the fire and watch the sparks fly. I also had a feeling that this could play out nicely: somehow, I felt the omission was perhaps intuitive.

When Mr. Up-the-Hill had come down to talk to me about the incident, we got along just dandy. Ever since we met, his fundamental demeanor of negativity has been disarmed by my constant kindness and jolliness – which I put forth even when he smashed into my car. But although he left no doubt that he would pay for the damage, he also expressed that he was seriously miffed at Mr. Landlord and that he would confront him about the responsibility of this situation. Since I really did not want to be in the middle of the crossfire, I told him I understood his point of view but suggested that perhaps he should let me do the talking and see what I could come up with. He was dubious, but agreed.

So today, I went upstairs and explained the situation to Mr. and Mrs. Landlord. I told them of my deliberate omission, and presented that since they would have been out of pocket to fix my car from Mrs. Landlord's accident anyway, perhaps they could agree to pay for half of the current repair and use this as an olive branch towards building neighborly peace. They saw the particular wisdom of the semi-trickery and agreed.

I walked up to convey the good news to Mr. and Mrs. Up-the-Hill and it made them speechless. After saying that this was a step in the right direction, Mr. Up-the-Hill proceeded to grumble about his other issues, at which time I promptly shushed him and suggested he enjoyed this New Year's gift. After chatting a while longer, he actually mentioned that he might go see Mr. Landlord with some friendly words. I was given a full tour of the house and on my way out he affectionately took me by the waist and said: "Well at least, we got a new friend out of this."

The war is not over but the weapons are down – at least lower than they have ever been.

If Mr. and Mrs. Up-the-Hill ever read this, I hope they can smile at my little orchestration.

How about *this* turn of event. That's what I call making the best of a situation: lemonade for everybody!

I still don't think there was an "intent" behind being hit twice, but I certainly was alert for ensuing opportunities.

Making the best of the bad is a lot like found-art. It takes flair, alertness and vision to create beauty out of scraps.

JANUARY 5TH, 2012

SAME SAME

I have had the intention of sharing with you the story of my encounter with a Tibetan Lama. Up to this point, I had not found the appropriate moment to do so. Then last night, as I was leafing through a book I hadn't opened in years, his bookmarker fell out onto the floor, and there he was, looking at me with his beautiful youthful smile. I took it as a sign that today is the appropriate day to tell my story.

I met with Tulku Lama Satsang* in November of 2008, while in Sedona. His presence in Arizona was part of his first travel to the United Sates – if I remember correctly. Through my years of spiritual quest, I had never, until then, been called to study or meet with an Eastern teacher. But for some reason, as I arrived in the land of the Red Rocks frazzled and in dire need of some centering and inspiring encounters, when my eyes fell upon the ad for his conference, I was instantly drawn-in: something had strummed the strings of my inner being.

This trip to Sedona was the one that followed my father's death and corresponded with a time when I had to perform a serious emotional update. My mind and soul were not only overburdened by a great sense of loss, but I was also untangling the remnants of months of intense family interaction and propinquity, and dealing with the deep stirring caused by the vast amount of inner-work I (all of us) had done in order to allow my father to go free. Furthermore, I was managing my guilt for leaving my mother, and reacquainting myself with the proximity of Richard.

---

* The name is fictitious – I am not sure if it would be appropriate for me to do otherwise.

DEATH'S GLORY

My father's death was the most glorious experience of my life. And so, the sense of loss I felt was accompanied by an immense sense of responsibility. This feeling stemmed from having been one of the few who has had the privilege to experience and witness death as the most beautiful event of life. *(I will even venture to say greater than birth because of the awareness an experienced human being can consciously bring to the moment.)* In a world terrified by the looming specter of the Grim Reaper, I felt it lay upon me to become a vocal emissary of the truth by lifting the veil of fear that shrouds the myth of death.

The days and weeks prior to the event were filled with rich moments of silent presence, comforting touch, singing of childhood camp songs, laughter*, occasional witty irreverence for death, abundant tears, and absolutely open and intimate conversations.

My father had one special wish he would discuss freely: He wanted to be aware of the moment when, as he put it, the switch would be turned "off" and then "on" again. He wanted to consciously experience the moment the light would fade out on the physical world and then illuminate the land of spirit. He did get his wish, and we were there to witness the bestowal.

In preparation for his death, my father wrote his own obituary in which he acknowledged each of us with carefully chosen words. Befittingly, because he was nearly blind, the title of his last words was:

My Eyes Finally See The Light.

The text began with:

Here we are! As you are reading theses words, I have rejoined with the Universe that created me and afforded me this first

---

* One funny example comes to mind: When it was time for my father to take his numerous pills, my (adult) niece would playfully call him over by saying, "Grandpa, time for your snack!" And he would come to her, sheepish and grinning.

beautiful trip on Earth. I wish to tell you that I feel privileged to have been surrounded with so much love and friendship.

And concluded with:

This is why I leave serene and curious to undertake this second trip... I know the best awaits me in this Mysterious World...

At the magical moment of death, during his last breaths, my father looked like he was blown away by what he was seeing. He looked as if he could never have expected what was being revealed to him. His expression of pure wonderment was that of a child who just walked in a candy store as big as a stadium. He was in awe, elated, amazed, rapturous. Family was surrounding his bed and spontaneously, as we were witnessing the gates of heaven opening, we began cheering him on, excitedly, encouraging him to go for it. It was absolutely surreal.

I heard that Steve Job's last words were "Oh wow! Oh wow! Oh wow!" I think they saw the same thing.

It is in that eternal instant that I was given a glimpse into the light. Not only because of what I saw, but because instantaneously, any minute piece of resentment I may have harbored towards him were melted away and dissolved. I was left only with pure love. And from the pureness and fullness or the sensation, I knew this emotion I was now feeling towards him was to be permanent. I had never experienced anything like it. In that moment, I understood that all negative emotions we develop in life, for any reason and towards anyone, are merely earthbound: they do not survive this purifying passage.

This feeling that engulfed all of us was so powerful that it carried us through the following days as we glided across the various funeral ceremonies. Incredibly, as we were illuminated from within by immense joy and divine gratitude, the greetings we received were oddly mostly "thank yous" and "congratulations" rather than "my condolences".

My life would never be the same because I no longer feared death.

Besides the immeasurable gifts bestowed by my father's passing, it also left me in a state of deconstruction of sorts. The only way I can explain it, is that his departure had affected my elementary structure. Although he was not actively involved in my life decisions, my father boasted a very large and powerful aura, and consequently, his unconscious influence was ubiquitous throughout my life. Despite the fact that I had long been aware of the weight of his shadowing *(and to be honest, had imagined his eventual leaving would bring relief, in this respect)*, I was very surprised by the depth of the effect of his departure on my very foundation. I was left feeling like my primordial building blocks had been scattered on the floor, and I was now faced with the task of gathering them and repositioning them my way. I was acutely aware that all this would result in my own empowerment and could even foresee my future state of gratitude, but what I had to deal with at the moment was frightening and bewildering.

Hence, my quest for some appeasing, enlightening and guiding encounters.

MY LAMA

Back to my Lama, or my Tulku Lama. The title of Tulku is an important differentiation in the Buddhist vocabulary. Tulkus are traditionally considered to be reincarnations of Buddhist masters who, out of compassion for the suffering of sentient beings, willfully choose to take rebirth. It is said they can deliberately decide on how, when and where they will do so, as opposed to other lamas who have no choice in these matters. Following their formal recognition, Tulkus may be enthroned and are then entrusted with responsibilities. After years of training and meditations designed to develop their powers of insight and compassion, and studies designed to infuse them with knowledge, Tulkus are deemed ready to take on the role of teacher.

The evening of the conference finally arrived. The center hosting the event was nestled in a valley amidst the deeply rich Red Rocks. The antechamber to the conference room was set up with tables strewn with various items relating to this Lama in particular, and Buddhism in general. There were pictures and books, and other items all dutifully tented by kind devotees. It was not a bric-a-brac by any means: the items were beautiful and thoughtful, and not over-abundant. I entered the main room, sat down near the front, and waited. A single cushioned chair was set on the elevated stage, and although I was inhabited by curiosity, it was nothing that resembled enthusiasm – I was way too exhausted for that. But I could appreciated the fact that I had made the effort to reach out for support when I needed it, and that I was taking steps towards newness at the onset of this new chapter of my life.

The Lama entered the stage to a deferential audience, and began sharing. He had a thick accent that took some getting used too, and I definitely responded positively to his energy and enthusiasm *(unlike me, he had plenty)*. I don't remember much more of the evening other than at the end, I registered for a weekend workshop beginning the following day. I can only conclude that the experience was impactful enough for me to want more.

I recall the weekend being lively, interesting, funny and energetic. There were verbal teachings as well as various physical practices. One of the principles he taught explained that because of the illusion of our minds, we all lived in a constant state of lying: we lie to ourselves and to each other. According to this idea, on this plane of existence our relationships are therefore inherently based on lies *(his explanation was more factual than doom-laden)*. He went on to say that lying was sometimes acceptable if it was done in order to prevent unnecessary hurt. He gave the example of being hosted for dinner by a family who was greatly honored by his presence and who, despite their very modest means, had gone to great trouble to prepare a meal worthy of their distinguished visitor. As she was serving him, the hostess proudly asked if he liked the particular dish she was presenting to him. Aware that she had prepared it especially for him – as it was a dish all Tibetan were known to relish – he told her he loved it when the truth was that he usually avoided it at all cost. This is what he called "compassionate lying".

Later in the day, he went on to offer another teaching. For whatever reason, through this one, his English was particularly sketchy, and as a result most of us stared blankly at him. Noticing the lack of reaction from his audience, he asked, "Is my English okay?" Almost in unison, the class answered, "Yes, it is good Lama", although it evidently was not. Feeling perplexed by this united reply, I decided to speak up and quipped, "No Lama, the English is terrible, we all lied!" He cracked up laughing and so did the rest of the class. We had just participated in a demonstration of "compassionate lying" *(albeit a slightly misguided one).*

Over the course of the weekend I felt a true connection with Lama Satsang and so, at the end of the workshop, I went to speak with him privately. I told him how I had appreciated his presence and teachings, and explained how I had never been one to readily accept "teachers" or "masters" because they always exuded self-importance, and believed they held the *one* truth; something I could not accept. But, I said, "With you, it feels good." As I spoke, I intuitively used my hands to support my words, as we often do when language presents a barrier: I put one hand on my naval chakra and the other on my heart. At this moment, we looked into each other's eyes intently and held hands. I asked him if, in the individual consultations he was offering in the coming week, he could perform a healing with me. Although the consults were not supposed to take that form, he answered that yes, he would, and I did feel privileged. He then put one arm around my shoulder and I spontaneously cradled the back of his head in my hand; we held each other this way for a while. I eventually, and respectfully, gave a subtle bow; he bowed back to me. I bade him farewell and left the building.

On November 11th, I had my private meeting with Lama Satsang *(11/11, my favorite number again! I must have been at the right place at the right time)*. After the initial pulse taking, and without touching the rest of my body, he told me that he sensed something different in my abdomen: not necessarily a problem, he stated, but different. That's when I shared with him about my surgery, my tinnitus, and my father's death experience. After listening to me, he brought his hands over my body and as he began his healing, I felt his energies merging with mine.

The contact was powerful and tears rolled down my cheeks. At some point, holding hands once more, we gazed into each other's eyes for the longest time, recognizing one another. "I see you", was the mutual message we silently communicated.

He instructed me in a meditation practice to help with my tinnitus. It involved using a mental image of your master, (or someone you felt strongly about), like Jesus, he suggested. I reminded him that I did not hold anyone in such a position because I was never able to consider anyone my "master". He thoughtfully altered the meditation, supplied a different imagery, and together we practiced for a while.

Towards the end of the meeting, we were still sitting one in front of the other, our heads perhaps a foot apart, holding hands. I looked at him and said, "Same, same." At this moment, we both leaned in, bringing our heads together. We stayed like this for a several minutes: hand in hand, forehead to forehead. An intense feeling of peace submerged me. After some time, he looked up, shared his respect for me, and said that he was giving me his heart and taking mine in his; and also, that I could be his student and he, my master – specifying that it was not because he was better or greater than me, but just so I could *use* him. His understanding and offer moved me deeply. Even as I write this today, tears of gratitude fill my eyes.

When the meeting was over I said, "Thank you, I hope to see you again." He replied, "You will. Now go sit under the sun and meditate for a while." I complied. I would not have been able to drive away even if I had wanted to. I had to assimilate all this energy.

After sitting in the sun for about half an hour, I stepped back inside, wishing for a few more words with him. With perfect timing, he was in between consults and I was invited in once more. Standing in front of him I said, "Okay, I will take you as my *master* so I can *use* you." He nodded and replied that when we would see each other again, he would give me my spiritual name and do a little ceremony. I welcomed the offer. I was now sitting with him and looking at me he added, "Why don't I give you your name right now and we will do the ceremony next time I see you." Obviously, I wholeheartedly accepted. He took a few long breaths, gazing at me intensely. "Satsang Khandro, that is your name." Since I didn't understand what it meant, he tried to clarify, "Dakini… ?" Seeing no sign that my puzzled look was fading, he called in his assistant and asked her to write the name down for me and to explain its meaning. I said my grateful goodbyes to the Lama and stepped outside with the assistant. She looked at me incredulously as if to say, "Really? He gave you *that* name?" With a hint of reservation she spoke: "This is a good name. It's actually a very nice name. It is like a goddess dancing in the sky, a 'sky dancer'. In Tibetan, the word means 'she who moves in space'."

When I got home, I researched the word and found that Khandro (or Dakini) is the female embodiment of enlightened energy. Dakinis are associated with the path of transformation into enlightened awareness. They are committed to helping all sentient beings recognize their own Buddhahood.

To this day, I remain humbled and hold sacred this spiritual name he bestowed upon me. I gave much thought as to whether or not I should mention it in this book. Today, I choose to – even though uncertainty about the judiciousness of the choice still lingers. A part of me is cautioning that given the beauty of this name, my ego could be enjoying the notion that others now *know*, and is reveling in some self-indulgent form of "Ain't I special!" Whether I leave it in or not, I feel profoundly honored by that name. I also feel it validates my life-long quest and desire to share my knowledge and insights with the world. It is comforting to be seen.

In the days that followed the meeting, I felt deeply connected with Lama Satsang. His presence accompanied me nearly every minute of everyday. I carried his picture around, practiced what I remembered of Tsa Lung as well as of the meditations he had taught us. Then life, my grief, Richard and my lack of discipline took over again, and I let my practice slide.

In January of 2009, while on the East coast and in the hopes of reviving my connection with the energy of the Lama, I proceeded to read the notes from my encounters with him. Serendipitously, the next day *(the 11th)*, I was receiving my first email from the Lama's organization in regards to his upcoming events. Amongst dates in Switzerland, Spain and India, there was a five-day retreat planned to take place in Sedona the following April. I could not avoid reading into the magic of the timing and promised myself that I would find a way to be there. With considerable difficulty, I did.

Although Richard was not informed of my upcoming visit *(I had wanted to fully benefit from this gift to myself)*, I could not help seeking him out when I got there. And the state in which I found my beloved was deeply unsettling. I began the retreat with a heavy heart, torn between my commitment to it and my awareness of Richard's self-destruction just a few miles away. On the second day of the retreat, the heaviness was unbearable and I drove off into the desert to assess the situation. I eventually reached a moment of something that resembled inner stillness, managed to silence the voices of guilt about considering leaving the retreat *(which was paid for and non-refundable)*, and came to the conclusion that perhaps the retreat had brought me here so that I could be there for Richard. Slowly, I accepted the fact that life had happened and that it was okay to respond to change by readjusting my priorities. I drove back to the premises, peacefully packed my bags, informed the organizers of my departure, left, and went to pick up Richard. We headed home and did some more growth and healing.

That is the story of my relationship with Tulku Lama Satsang. Actually, that's almost it. There was yet another incredibly fated occurrence last August: After years devoid of interest or involvement on my part, I looked up his website one morning and to my great surprise, there was an announcement that he would be making his first visit to Canada in September by offering various workshops here in Vancouver! I was blown away and of course, signed-up for one of them. On the given day, I showed up at the location excited by the prospect of the reunion, wondering if he would remember me, only to become quite discomposed when I realized I was the only one there. An attendant informed me the event had been cancelled because the Lama had injured his foot in Europe, but that everyone had been informed via email, except me apparently. I drove back home slightly perplexed yet still grateful for providence's reassuring wink.

Now that is the full story of the relationship with my Lama. The future may hold more.

Death is a sublime event that awaits each of us at the end of our earthly journey; it is not a sentence that looms in our future.

Although grief and sadness for those left behind are legitimate and unavoidable, regretfully lamenting the departed "had so much to live for" is misguided: they are now living for so much more.

I caught a glimpse of the birth that is death, and I can assure you there is no reason to fear. What lies beyond may be unknown, but what I know for sure is that it is greater than our imagination. Let us manage the weight of our sorrow when a loved one leaves us, but lessen the load with the lightness of rejoicement for the one who has gone.

JANUARY 6TH, 2012

TOP PRIORITY

I am now dedicating all of my time to this book. I am engrossed in the process. I am constantly jotting down words and thoughts: I have scraps of paper and pens next to my bed *(for those middle of the night pop-up ideas)*, near the sink in the bathroom *(easy access for shower epiphanies)*, on the coffee table by the sofa *(for the thinking snow-ball effect of something spoken on TV)*, on the kitchen counter *(for inspiration born from savory emanations)* and of course, on my desk.

For some reason, I feel a sense of urgency in putting down on paper everything currently contained by my mind: like a purging of my headspace in order to make room for my new life's wardrobe. Somehow, I feel it must all be done before... soon. I don't know exactly what defines this illusive deadline but I sense some unknown event is looming on the horizon and that my writing must be done before "then". Or perhaps it is not about any particular event; perhaps my restlessness is related to a general feeling that my destiny will not find me until I finish this part of the book: as if my writing is holding back my future, as if its completion is a condition *sine qua non* to the rights to Part II of my life. I can picture a celestial assembly of producers gathered around a table discussing my case, and the head honcho – tapping his fingers on a document entitled *Annie's Life: The Sequel* – commenting: "We're just waiting for her to get done already. Only then will she get this next script where her aspirations are fulfilled and her life unfolds beyond her dreams."

This is why I am writing, writing, writing, like I never imagined I would.

Amidst my dedicated and attentive hurriedness, joyful satisfaction and fascination for what is taking place in my life are bubbling inside me. Now and then, this effervescence causes a slight overflow of excitement, which results in sudden bursts of elation, occasionally expressed in a little dance.

Only a few times in my life have I fleetingly experienced such excitement about my future, and in retrospect, they do not even compare to what I feel now. The day I was ready to present my fitness inventions was a moment charged with the promise of a dream: but this feels infinitely more real, more on target, more on purpose. This time, I am not offering a creation to the world, I am offering myself, and it feels utterly right.

EARTH : THE THEATER OF OUR SOUL

Once again, I take my cues where I find them: Yesterday's analogy to scripts and productions is my perfect lead-in for a personally memorable allegory I wish to share.

Sitting on a Florida beach in 1998, contemplating the ocean, a story-cum-poem-evocative-metaphor sprung to my mind. I imagined human souls as actors standing in the wings of Heaven, considering their next human role, and waiting to get into the skin of their next character.

I imagined that after having completed their previous performance *(a life)* as best they could, the actors *(souls)* could climb back on stage once they felt ready to perform again *(i.e. reincarnating)*. While waiting in the wings, their choice of role would be meticulously pondered with the express and paramount goal of broadening their repertoire, and of eventually claiming the status of "well-rounded accomplished actor".

What if these actors began their careers with small appearances *(an uneventful or inconspicuous life)*, then moved on to noteworthy but modest parts *(a life with a little more teeth)*, until they eventually tackled major roles of momentous scope *(a life in which the soul expands by leaps and bounds)*?

And what if, as conscientious and dedicated actors eagers to deliver their best performance – *Check me out in this role, I'm really gonna sink my teeth into it!* – they delved so deep into their character that they forgot it was a role and became that role?

If these actors did indeed forget they were actors, then they could not possibly savor their performance or understand the true value of their stage relationships with actors who may also, by the way, be there as fellow amnesiacs *(two amnesiac having a relationship looks a lot like the Lama's theory that we all live in a constant state of lying)*.

How interesting would it be if the actors could not only choose their roles and play them, but could *also* sit in the audience to view the scenes' playbacks? Together they could discuss, assess, and give credit to the richest scenes they delivered, joyful or sad, in comedy or drama – *Good job in that scene buddy. Yeah, I really got into that one. Really good script too!* They could also comment on those less noteworthy scenes: those where they did not fully engage their hearts and could have done better – *I was a bit of a slacker there; I may have to do it again.*

Which relationships would be the most authentic? Those on stage, between characters, or those between members of the viewing party – friends and foes of the stage – who after the performance, all get together and head to the local pub to share a celebratory drink?

And what if, when a final curtain came down – as death's shroud at last reveals the true value of a performance – everyone knew for sure the actor was merely returning in Heaven's wings to ponder his next role? Should this transient disappearing act cause anger and feelings of betrayal and injustice? Or should the performance be applauded with gratitude for the shared experience and the possibility of a reunion in a later production bring smiles and anticipation?

What if... we were celestial dust observing the stage and decided to come play on Earth?

Consider the possibility that we are souls who have come to the Earth stage and taken on roles as human beings. Let us remember as often as possible that all the while dedicating ourselves to perfecting our craft, we can maintain the awareness that this is what we are doing. Let us strive to understand that the depth of our being lies behind our costumes and the personality of our characters.

JANUARY 7TH, 2012

AIRING OUT

My head is feeling like a pressure cooker. My ears are taking sanctions against me and acting as if they were twenty feet under water: my tympanums are boycotting their current living conditions. Thoughts are bouncing around my brain relentlessly and I can't seem to do anything without having to stop and jot down a note. I just now interrupted my meditation to write down this pressure-cooker idea, which is neither clever nor important. As much as I would like to sit and write, the sensible and imperative thing to do is go out and play: I'm off to the mountain to air out my brain. See you!

Oh so pleased with myself! I did hop on the gondola in the pouring rain and up the mountain I went. Up there, snow was falling abundantly: it was winter wonderland. Being so frazzled this morning, my compassionate personal goal had once again been to simply get myself out the door to execute some rejuvenating nature breathing. A short, gentle walk would do just fine; no expectation of performance. But true to form, a quick dip in the waters of open spaces became a prolonged immersion. Once a guest in a mountain's temple, up there where land meets sky and the wind is free to blow and whirl to its heart's content, my heart expands, I feel alive, and time is no longer a notion that deserves attention. And if on top of that I can whip out my camera to capture the powerful display of the forces of nature, or snap the intimate portrait of a bashful fern hiding behind an icicle, I'm in heaven.

As I was shooting one of those frosted tiny twigs, guess what happened?

Drumroll.

A good-looking really nice man stopped and talked to me for a couple of minutes! OMG! Stop the presses! The earth's poles must be shifting! Yeah, I know, it was just two minutes, but his eyes were sparkling as he actually addressed me, "Isn't this extraordinary? It's just so beautiful, and you look like you're having a great time." Two minutes that made me feel really good and rekindled my hope that I will not forever remain invisible to the opposite sex *(this is quite pathetic)*. Unfortunately, as he was speaking to me I could not help but think that I probably looked like a pitiful wet rat. I quickly did an out-of-body evaluation of my appearance and saw my head wrapped in a poor-looking winter hat with the hem flipped up, my drenched bulky physique misshapen by six layers of ill-assorted clothing, and my mascara no-doubt running down my face along the trickles of melted snow. What a shame. At the end of our little chit-chat he continued on his way *(opposite mine)* and I wondered if maybe he discerned beauty behind the mess, and fantasized that he would await my return at the gondola, wishing to pursue our conversation *(Wow! Seriously desperate)*.

FINDING MY TRUE LOVE

As far as meeting my perfect-man-for-me goes, not only am I ready but, as you can see, I am also always on the lookout. I can't help it: I want it therefore I focus on it. Isn't that how we achieve our goals? That's why it ticks me off when people *(who themselves have a significant other)* patronizingly tell me that "It will happen when you don't expect it", or, "It will happen when you stop looking for it." Bull. Do they really think that it can slip my mind that I would like to find a partner? I'm 47 years old: Is there actually a possibility that the day I find my mate I will say, "Oh really? What an unexpected surprise, I wasn't even thinking about it!" Anyway, if there is any truth to their nonsense, I am doomed because I am anticipating it, willing it, affirming it, and I will always seek it until I get it.

Partners will come into our lives when partners come into our lives: there are no conditions to fill, no prerequisites. They may fill a void when someone is at their most vulnerable just as they may show up when one is fully empowered. The reason for a merge, and the moment in time when two stories intersect, is as case-by-case as can be. Any pretense of justifying why it hasn't happened is foolish presumption.

JANUARY 8TH, 2012

CRYSTAL-GAZING

MY PERSONAL COACH

I got up this morning after sleeping five hours in a row: fantastic, and a bit of a surprise, because the hours leading up to the night were sprinkled with a pinch of self-doubt. The hike was invigorating but the feeling of exhaustion that followed was a breeding ground for misgivings about my current situation and choices *(still not strong enough to withstand exerting myself)*. Fortunately, I was once again able to reel my thoughts in before they spun out of control *(practice makes perfect)*. When my negative thoughts began nibbling the bait dangled by my exhaustion, I first considered leaving my line in and catching whatever sorry fish would get hooked *(I mean, I hadn't indulged in the sport for a while – over a week now)* but then I reconsidered and wondered: What exactly would be gained? So instead, I let the voice of my wiser-self chime in. "Okay, so you're not so giddy tonight. You have to know it is again mostly the result of having pushed yourself too hard on the mountain and not eating enough before exercising, right? Presuming you are aware of this, what are you gonna do? Give into those feelings or shoo them aside for tonight and see if they're still there tomorrow?"

I made the smart choice and later tucked myself in with loving whispers: "Good night beautiful, you've done a great job today, get some rest now. You are doing so well, you are a wonderful woman; you are on your way." This may sound weird but hey, by now you must be getting used to that, and frankly, this pillow talk is very soothing to me.

This morning, my Mom told me: "Annie, if you keep going like this, your life has no choice but to change, it's a law of nature." I conquered.

I have recently really taken to this practice of coaching and pep-talking myself. It allows a separation between my inner being and my emotions. It's an observer's point of view, which provides a wiser more objective outlook on what is going on. In doing so, I stand back, take the long view, and get some perspective.

Putting a little distance between you and your story prevents from totally identifying and losing yourself into what's going on in your life. I have discovered that even in the midst of terrible times, a part of me is actually detached from my drama; and allowing my awareness to stand in those shoes for a moment can be quite helpful.

At times of deep sorrow, this practice of stepping aside has given me permission to fully give into my emotions all the while knowing I would not get lost in them; and both these aspects are crucial to the epic maneuvering of life. I can recall my wise observer saying: "Wow Annie, you're really sad right now. You sure are crying very very hard. This is a tough one. Go on, let it out, and we'll be fine later." These words were at once validating my emotions and reminding me of their impermanence.

As human beings, emotions are our lot and their existence is quite inescapable; they are an intrinsic dimension of our human condition, and to be honest, they are the spice of life. Emotions must not be denied or tethered: they require expression. But there is a nuance between letting them run free and unbridled, and going along for a lively ride with the reins in hands.

THE CHAPTER APPROACH

Last summer, a friend was going through the worst heartbreak of her life. She had never lived through anything like it before, never had had her dreams taken away from her in such a way, and she was sinking, fast. I must say that the older we are when we finally are within reach of our life-long dreams, the harder it appears to be to have them yanked, because we don't have the luxury of the bulk of our years ahead of us. So my friend called me in an utter state of distress. She literally could not function anymore, not for the last month or so. It was the first time I had ever seen her like that. She had always been a tough cookie, a person who could compartmentalize; a woman who could sweep things aside and go on with her activities (and enjoy them). She was the type who could not understand those who dwelled in despair after a heartbreak. She was never too analytical or tempted to swim in the waters of existentialism. But on that day, she needed a good pair of ears and a new set of tools. She talked, I listened, and I came up with a strategy and exercise to help her get though it.

"Darling, is this the thing in your life that will kill you? Are you going to let this do you in?" *

She managed to answer, "No, it will not kill me."

"Okay, so it means that one day, you will be on the other side of it, somehow."

---

* Note: Sometimes, the answer to the question: "Is this what will kill you?" can be "Maybe." If this is the case, a strategy other than the Chapter Approach is necessary. For example, when I got dangerously sick and despondent in 2009, my personal answer was, "It's a definite possibility." In this case, some drastic action was needed and my choice, as you know, was to take the gamble to fly to Arizona in the hopes of reigniting my life-fire. Luckily for me, it worked.

"Yes, but I don't know how I'll get through this."

"That's okay. But at least we know you won't die from it."

"Yes."

"I understand this is extremely sad, exceedingly hard and painful, and you should allow yourself to feel that. Hard not to. But, you should give yourself a deadline for getting lost in your sadness, and not being able to function. Give yourself another 24 hours, a week, or even a month during which you will let yourself be overwhelmed and cry your heart out. But when you reach that day, it's over. You begin anew."

She thought about it, and I was touched by her receptivity. Then she said:

"Until my birthday, in six days."

"That sounds good. You have a plan."

"But what do I do? This was my life, my future, all my dreams we shared, and we had the same goals."

"I know, it sucks."

And I continued with the plan.

"You have always said you would write your autobiography one day, right? Okay, so be your older self now, ten or twenty years down the line, and imagine yourself writing this chapter..." I allowed a pause for her to bring herself there. She said:

"It will be called The Biggest Heartbreak of my Life."

She was getting it. She was getting into it. She was already the calmer person (herself) who would be writing the story.

"Now from that perspective see this: you have made it through, you've survived. Now write the story with different outcomes: One where you get back together with him and learn great lessons from the experience and in which you are stronger and closer as a couple. Then write another one in which you continue your journey without him and learn great lessons from it. Now imagine you are the reader, what you would like to read. What would your heroine do? How would she deal with it? How did she come out stronger? How did this make her a better human being? What would you admirer reading, if it was someone else's story? What reactions from her part would inspire you and make you inwardly applaud her?"

I let this sink in.

"Can you feel it? That wiser older woman who can tell the story is *also* you right now; she's there. You are not only the emotion-ridden crumbling woman you think you are at the moment. Can you picture your book? Now do you see that this is only ONE chapter in your book? It's only ONE chapter darling, it's only ONE chapter."

She repeated after me and I could imagine her nodding her head, tears streaking down her face.

"It's only ONE chapter."

"And you know what? It's only a middle chapter in the book; granted, a pivotal one, but still only in the middle. You *will* live through this. It will be a horrid period, you will have devastating emotions, but you will live to write about it.

So live your pain because it exists. Allow yourself to be deeply affected. Give yourself a deadline. And *know* it is only ONE CHAPTER. Look at it, feel it, repeat it to yourself: 'It is only one chapter of my life, it is only one chapter in my book, it is only one chapter. One day, I will be able to tell the story, which means: I will survive this.'"

I am happy to report that this chapter of my friend's life will conclude with the two of them getting back together and growing from this difficult event. As a result, they have both looked within themselves, and at the dynamic of their relationship, and have uncovered great treasures they would otherwise have never looked for. They have embarked on a journey that will make their lives much richer.

In the midst of drama, taking a moment to write our story as if from a future standpoint is likely to be highly beneficial. First, it allows us to see that we will make it to the other side; two, it shows that whatever we are going through is only an episode in our life; three, by writing different outcomes, we envision that we will make the best out of whatever happens and that life will go on. This form of journaling is healthy and can be immensely helpful.

Sometimes we forget that we are not only the emotional-self going through an event. There is another part to us: the writer, the historian, the consciousness; the guardian that is the wiser observer of our eventful lives. In times of crisis, deferring to the voice of this inner-chronicler can give us access to a more objective point of view.

SCENARIOS: A DOUBLE-EDGE SWORD

In the context of the chapter approach, positioning ourselves in a future scenario can be a valuable practice. It can provide perspective by granting access to a wisdom that the emotions and shock of the moment deny. It allows a more rational and dispassionate glimpse into what is currently an overwhelming situation. Imagining ourselves at a time when objectivity will prevail is conducive to reconnecting with our center and bringing some clarity to the moment.

Another instance when creating scenarios turns out to be useful is for the purpose of visualizing where we want to be. Seeing ourselves doing what we aspire to do through our mind's eyes can be a powerful motivator when pursuing a goal. I have also found that at times, when I am afraid of failure or of a negative outcome, considering the worst-case scenario can defuse my fears by unmasking the monster under my bed. When I am consumed with worry or feel paralyzed by a choice I need to make, I ask myself: What's the worst thing that could happen? What's the worst-case scenario? Usually, although the answer consists of something that doesn't appeal to me, it also makes me realize that even the worst results would not be the end of my life, and are doable. Sometimes, this can take the edge off.

But as with many tools of the mind, scenarios can be used for good or bad. The lesser evil is when, in the midst of an activity, we allow our minds to be engrossed in the future recounting of our adventure while we are still living it, which takes us away from the moment. This is what I was referring to when I mentioned the annoying monologues that sometimes render my hikes as much a physical as a mental workout because all I can think of is what I'm going to tell someone else about it.

Higher up on the scale of negative uses is the endless replaying of mental ditties about the past or future. You must know what I'm talking about: Repeating conversations that have taken place or that we plan on having, over and over like a loop in our head or a needle stuck in a groove of an LP.

We *(I'm including you in the majority of humans)* do have the uncanny ability to produce hallucinating amounts of repetitive monologues. If I have a grievance with someone, for example, I can repeat the monologue I plan on having time and again *(and even the dialogue: I can very aptly put words in the other person's mouth and provide them with emotions too)*. I have, in fact, been doing just that with a delicate issue I want to bring up with a relative. The thing is that because it may rock the boat, I have been mulling it over for *(how embarrassing)*, five months. And the further irony that proves the point of the uselessness of this evil is that now that so much time has passed, I will probably never mention it. How foolish to have wasted so much of my brain-time.

So this is something else I am paying attention to when it comes to my consummate ego's ramblings. And the more I listen for these repetitive thoughts, the more I hear; and sometimes the only way to shush them up is by literally blowing a few loud raspberries.

Here is my advice: Say what needs to be said if a situation concerns you, but if you don't plan on doing anything about it today, stop playing it over in your head until the actual time comes *(if it ever does).* In reality, your inner parroting is probably not adding anything new anyway. And as far as scenarios of how your life should unfold or of what may happen in the future? Don't spend too much time holding on to them: The truth of the matter is, good and bad, our scenarios rarely come through the way we imagined. The constructs of our minds are indeed castles in the sand.

Use the power of future scenarios wisely:

As a focal point and visualization tool towards a goal: Good

To get perspective on what's happening now: Good

To take a step back from overwhelming emotions: Good

To show yourself that the worst-case scenario is not the end of your world: Good

To distract you from fully enjoying the present: Bad

To play back an old story over and over in your head: Bad

To conjure up an argument that hasn't happened yet: Bad

JANUARY 9TH, 2012

ON YOUR TERMS

When I was refused passage to the USA almost two years ago, I remember finding some solace as I practiced the skill of allowing my future inner-chronicler to be heard *(and it is a skill that does require practice because it may not come naturally when you are in the middle of the storm)*. It afforded me valuable peeks into a future that could be positively affected by the incident.

Through this event, as I mentioned earlier, not only was I taught to pay reverent attention to signs posted along the road *(the bold letters* and *the subscript)*, and ultimately understood that "The Big Guy", or providence, would intervene if I failed to do so, but just as importantly, I was showed that even when you think you have no options, you do.

LOOK AGAIN, YOU MAY FIND AN OPTION

Although months prior to being turned around at the border I had been receiving clear signs showing me it was time to get out of Dodge, USA *(end of relationship, gallery closing, denied visa, money drought, etc.)*, I had felt it was impossible for me to follow these signs because of my lack of financial resources. The more I searched for possible proactive scenarios that would allow me to act on these warnings, the more I inexorably walked into the same dead end. The conclusion of my perpetual brainstorm was always the same: There is nothing you can do without some money first.

With this rationale in mind, I spent days and months, obstinately pursuing ventures that could lead to "getting money", which was what I believed would allow me to move forward. Perhaps after endless failures I should have realized that what I perceived as noble perseverance was actually close-mindedness because the result was my immobility. My firm belief that I had no other choices was eventually disproved by providence, which, under the guise of a zealous customs' officer, forced a solution upon me.

Admittedly, moving-in with my mother *(whom I love dearly)* had not been a solution I had been willing to seriously entertain but a solution it was, and there I was. Just as the once immutable Berlin wall, the maxim "no money, no option" was being torn down from my belief system, and new horizons were being revealed.

Sometimes, despite what we believe to be an open-mind, it appears we still wear blinders limiting our peripheral vision.

Sometimes, the permanence of certain beliefs turns them into such fixed structures framing our minds that we forget to consider taking them down.

Sometimes, when we think we have no options, asking ourselves this question may be of help: Which wall's demolition am I not prepared to take-on?

LIFE AS WE KNOW IT

When you think you are stuck, trapped, and that alternatives are inexistent, do the exercise of imagining how life could force a change upon you *(to put it a different way, think of how you could be a victim of circumstances imposed upon you)*. If you are successful at finding such ways, it means options exist. They may involve risky moves, exist beyond that wall you did not want to tear down, or come in a shape you were reluctant to consider, but I can almost guarantee solutions are there for you.

In my case, although I thought I had understood this lesson with the border incident, I actually repeated the almost exact scenario, on two fronts no less, in the year that followed. First, I slowly resumed my habit of prolonged stays in FriHo, even thought I had had a deep sense I was supposed to stay in Canada. Two, I went back to the belief of "no money, no option" and for months, made my move to Vancouver conditional to having money. Not surprisingly, this relapse produced identical results : Nothing.

One day, pondering the risks I was choosing to take by insisting *(against my better judgment)* on spending time in the USA, it occurred to me that one way or another, things were going to change. They were going to change because I *knew* I was no longer where I belonged, and so I began imagining the no-nonsense ways destiny could take care of this for me : perhaps the house in FriHo would burn down, or some misunderstanding at the border would have me barred for five years, or I would get sick and have to return to my country.

And that's when the absurdity of perpetuating my behavior hit me *(and when I first formulated the question I mentioned in the story of the woman who was letting "The Big Guy" stop her through illness, instead of choosing to do so of her own volition)* : "If I know that things are about to change, wouldn't it be nice if I chose the terms rather than being victim of them ?" Light bulb. "If it's going to happen anyway, it means there is a way to do it."

From that day on, my passive waiting game was no longer acceptable. Even though I still did not know how I would achieve my goals, I began repeating to myself several time a day : I am planning my exit strategy, on my terms."

It is on the heels of this awakening of sorts that in April 2011, I finally made the decision to repatriate all my belongings and return to Canada *(on my terms)* and conceived my bold plan to move to Vancouver despite the lack of work or funds.

As I sit here today, I can tell you these lessons are worth learning. We are all prone to some degree of procrastination for a variety of more or less valid reasons (timing, finances, laziness, dejection, any and all fears). But being proactive is the rewarding way to go.

If you know your life cannot continue the way it is now, chances are it will not, and it would be easier on you if you were to determine the terms of the transition yourself.

Perhaps you can take my word for it: If the Gods of wind are pushing you in a certain direction, just say okay and steer yourself that way. If not, Poseidon may stir up a mighty storm that will leave you a battered castaway on the shores of your life. You'll end up in the right place, but your trip may be a fair bit more rocky. Memorable, but rocky.

Choose your move before it chooses you.
When you** know, **do. If you fail to, it may hurt.
Use life's winds instead of standing against them.

JANUARY 10TH, 2012

OUT WITH THE MIND, IN WITH THE HEART

Yesterday's text was a bit of a mind bender to write, and it's actually not sorted out yet. By the end of the afternoon, I just had to let it go and head for the Seawall; my mind had been fighting with my self with words and ideas in a bloody battle. Up to now, most of this book has flowed from self to paper, but for some reason, yesterday felt like an Osterizer was callously stirring my brain. I spent hours attempting to untangle a few different ideas I wished to convey. The difference between previous entries and yesterday's arduous one, is that with the latter, my mind was at the helm dictating what I *should* and *wanted* to write as opposed to my inner-self freely transmitting to my pen.

I experienced something similar back in December when I wrote about the water crystal. Then too, I had known what I *wanted* to say but the writing itself was a mishmash of thoughts until I went back and fixed it *(ditto for yesterday, which is why it hopefully sounded just fine to you).* It is obvious to me that the type of book I am writing requires my inner-self be in charge until my mind takes over for the proofreading and editing.

The two major phases of my art career illustrate a similar change of the guard from mind to heart. The first period – for which I received a measure of public acclaim in the contemporary art world – consisted of black and white, photo-realistic drawing-installations honoring the traditional canons of beauty. These works depicted a nude female body suspended in a surrounding white void and juxtaposed to various objects. These pieces demonstrated a seductive technical virtuosity *(I am still surprised to be their author)* and explored the then-popular discursive tactics and theoretical narratives. These intellectual socio-political comments were conceived in my mind and executed by my obeying hands.

Professionally, my mind remained in charge until, at the height of my career, I underwent the traumatic reconstructive surgery that changed the course of my life. As mentioned earlier, the physical procedure of removing parts of my body also resulted in the excision of the persona I had spent my life developing, and that changed everything. As a consequence of the surgery, I was left with the raw, unarticulated, and undomesticated essence of who I was.

The drastic inner shift that took place had a wide range of effects on my life, one of which being that the art I had been creating up to that point no longer reflected who I was. Not that it had fully corresponded with me before, but I had hitherto ignored and forged through the nagging feelings because of a sense of obligation for persevering in a direction that yielded success. But, with my persona out of the way, the mere thought of pursuing in the same vein was now utterly repugnant and unequivocally unacceptable.

Therefore, following my surgery, I stopped producing art completely with this silent radical assertion: *When I start making art again, it will be inspired, flowing, from the heart, without thinking, and in color.* My mind was being demoted and relinquished to its rightful place: not in charge. A new era was dawning.

But it certainly turned out to be a terribly long dawn because for the next 14 years, I did not produce any art, enter a single gallery or museum, or look at an art magazine. The sense of disconnect I had felt had been so deep that I could only avoid the entire art scene until I found myself again, which finally occurred in the Red Rocks of Sedona. Amidst these ancestral landscapes my spirit was freed, my heart expanded, and my creative energies flowed. Within months, I started to draw in color, without thinking. As I later prepared an expansive retrospective catalogue as part of my application for the American visa, I reacquainted and reconciled myself with my earlier art and the broken circle was at last fully mended.

This process of learning to draw from the heart was not without obstacles. The pathways of free artistic expression were still encumbered by debris that would require will, courage, and muscle to clear out. I knew what I wanted and was ready to do it. But in reality, I was not sure if I had that kind of talent – or even possessed the ability to access my inner artist – or could ever create from any other place than the mind. I had always been one to secretly admirer and envy artists who stood in front of their large canvas and threw wild instinctual strokes onto its surface; seemingly entranced by their inner life-force. I had also always thought this could never be me. But now, I wanted it to be me and was willing to give it a try.

It began one particular day, when spurred by some surge of bravery, out to the art store I went. I bought dozens of very colorful pastels and a variety of pads of paper. Once I returned home, I put them out on display in my office. For a while, all I could do was walk up to these intimidating foreign objects, take a few deep breaths, and walk away. This new environment I was planning on exploring required some serious acclimatization.

Then one day, in was D-day. I took the lid off the boxes of pastels, revealing a seductive rainbow of colors, laid a sheet a paper in front of me, and sat down: It was time. As crazy as it sounds, I was actually shaking, breathless, and perspiring. I took hold of my first crayon and drew a line, than a second crayon and a second line. I drew about five hesitant uncertain, pale, pathetic lines, and had to stop. Emotionally and psychologically, it was all I could take.

Although there wasn't much to show for, the process was initiated and I knew I would not turn back: the odyssey had begun. At that moment, I made a commitment to myself that for the next thirty days I would draw one picture a day, no matter what, without judgment, and without any expectations or pressure that these drawings had to look good in any way.

There were rules though: I would not be allowed to pre-think the composition, or consciously choose a subject matter, or be allowed to think about the colors I would pick up. I was to sit (on the floor) with my eyes half-closed and breathe calmly. Then, with an intentionally relaxed gesture, I was to pick-up (but not choose) a crayon, and in a continuous, sweeping motion, bring my hand over the paper and intuitively draw shapes and lines, and fill them up with pigment.

On the third day, I drew more than shy lines. As I was drawing, I physically felt my inner-self pushing through and victoriously emerging at last. When I saw the fullness of what I had drawn, I began to weep. A sense of relief, gratitude, exhaustion, and joy filled my heart. This image represented a milestone in my quest to access and release who I was: this picture was the manifestation of my true identity. For the first time, I saw ME, and I was beautiful, colorful, vibrant, inspired. I remember calling Richard and describing what was happening. In tears, I muttered, "You should see..." And that became the title of this work.

On day seventeen, a new kind of challenge was added to the mix. After driving all day to Ste-Ville for a visit with my parents, I was now faced with the prospect of having to draw not only exhausted, but in a whole new environment. Having grown accustomed to my creative surroundings at home, the change was profoundly unsettling. But faithful to my no-matter-what commitment, I whipped out my arsenal, which was now comprised of a few hundred pastels *(I had returned several times to the art store)*, and set-up on the dining room table. To my great dismay, both my parents decided to come and sit next to me and observe their daughter. I winced. In spite of my great strides, I remained the little insecure girl who despised creating in front of people *(from kindergarten right up until university)* for fear of performing poorly. Nonetheless, empowered by me recent discoveries, I decided to forge through and proceeded to draw, under their watchful eyes. The image that resulted is one of my favorites of the series and is called *Breaking Barriers.*

Gifts were abundant as I continued drawing for the thirty days of my regimen. Months later, back in Sedona, I shared my experience with a visiting girlfriend. Having mentioned that I had saved all these drawings, she asked if she could see them, curious as to the experience I was so enthused about. It took a lot of convincing on her part because the images felt very intimate to me. But, I eventually caved and spread most of the artworks on a white sheet laid on the floor. She contemplated the whole without a word, edited the selection, and then said, "You have something here girl. These are good." I honestly did not understand what she was saying. To me, these were only my self-discovery experimental doodles. But then I tried to look at them through her eyes, and saw what she saw.

A few months later I printed a limited edition of a selected few and designed a promotional pamphlet featuring the following meaningful headings: *Breathe..., ...Don't Think..., ...Create..., ...In Color.*

This revival of my art was a symbolic reflection of my inner transformation and a proud testament to my personal journey. I had gone from imposing, black and white, cerebral compositions that often made me cry from unspecified pain, to intimate, colorful, intuitive expressions that originated from my heart and made me cry with joy. Although my intellect can still be awed by the aesthetic experience of viewing my earlier technically proficient drawings, my heart rejoices when contemplating the inner freedom and liberated spirit that come through the pastels.

The ideas flowed naturally today. I am relieved to feel back on track. I had temporarily gone off in the wrong direction and it felt... like the wrong direction: moving forward was like pulling teeth and making me queasy as opposed to being a stimulating adventure.

Ego is a powerful entity whose role is to service our self on this material plane. He should only sit in the driver's seat when duly appointed and when his services are required to lead our *soultrain* ***to a destination purposefully chosen by our inner being.***

JANUARY 11TH, 2012

THE FEMININE PREROGATIVE

Restoring the flow from heart to mind yesterday had a tint of magic to it: I love being the instigator, witness, and experiencer of such alchemy. I love being fully present and aware as I go through these kinds of transformations. And yesterday's experience was heightened because it was a once-a-month special day.

[P]ARDON [M]Y [S]USCEPTIBILITY *

Yes, I am talking about my periods. Now, I'm not trying to spin a princess story here, when on a magical day, the little girl becomes a woman and she should be so grateful because once a month, she will be able to go horseback riding, swirl on a beach, go swimming, and do gymnastics in slow-motion with a smile on her face. Don't get your knickers in a bunch. I know very well what it means to have periods and I am not one of these women for whom it goes unnoticed either – I know cramps, and the impossible task of sleeping days prior, and the whole world feeling as though it is too much to bear. But. I think there is a serious misconception that needs demystifying, for women as much as for men. And if not a misconception, then at least a different aspect of the phenomenon that needs to be investigated and considered.

I personally do get my knickers in a bunch when I hear the pervasive mythos that all women become bitches for a few days, and that men should put up their arms in a cruciform in order to repel evil

* Other tentative titles included: **P**retty **M**agic **S**tate; **P**rotecting **M**y **S**pace; **P**rivileged **M**oments **S**hared; **P**ardon **M**e **S**ir.

and then run for the hills *(a misconception that gave rise to the* ***P****issed at* ***M****en* ***S****yndrome acronym).* That period lore is a crock and it needs to be exposed.

I can't deny there is such a thing as PMS – **P**robably **M**ore **S**ensitive syndrome. Yes, there is an increased emotional response but I also believe it can be tamed and even appreciated. I have learned to consider it as a different state of being rather than an irrational, unmanageable, and incomprehensible curse. There is a way to make it work for me rather than against me. During this time, it is not my experience that I become a she-devil but simply that I am ultra sensitive. My shields are down *(picture* Star Trek*'s Voyager)*: My ability to deflect exterior blows is diminished. The adversary's attacks hit with more force of impact and cause more damage. The ship is vulnerable. And it is the captain's duty to maneuver onto a course that will avoid aggressions and malevolent forces and, with the assistance of a supportive crew, no one will ever know that momentarily the mother-ship was an easy target.

ALTERED STATE

I have discovered just a few years ago that this *period* of delicate maneuvering culminates with a real gift *(back to the fairytale: Mother Nature unexpectedly shows up with a pretty little box tied with a red bow. Not. There is a twist).* On the first or most abundant day of the "red tent" period, I am included into a zone. My sensory perception network of organs is in a state of heightened perceptivity. My brain, my eyes, my ears, my touch, my soul, operate differently: they are tuned to a different frequency. On a day like yesterday, I could review my entire book and not get overwhelmed. Ideas flow peacefully, with enhanced clarity. I get the big picture of mundane and metaphysical issues. Events seem to occur more slowly, one after the other rather than one on top of the other, affording me time to act and react sensibly and even wisely. I live in the moment more than during any other day. On that day, I am an open vessel ready to receive all that comes my way. I am wide open. I see things in a new perspective, my intuition is greater, I can offer counsel with confidence.

There is a caveat though. In order to experience this state of openness, you must be able to steer your ship to a clear space: because being wide open to outside energies means to be open to all energies, good and bad. Therefore, the trick is to create a favorable environment where vulnerability is transformed into receptivity. You must avoid as many interactions as possible with people who are not aware of your state: you must try to eliminate irritants and abrasives from your schedule.

Try experimenting this awareness on a day spent alone, away from society's disconnectedness: I think you will be amazed by your discoveries and mourn years of opportunities missed. But it is never too late *(except if you are post-menopausal, of course, but then you could share this with a younger woman and let her benefit from this gift)*. I do realize it may be impossible for many women to extract themselves from the world for an entire day, and to those I say, do your best; perhaps, simply by carrying this new awareness, your experience will change.

And for the sake of evolution towards a world where the feminine and the masculine will be better understood and lived, the more women do change their experience of periods, the more the fallacy of "the curse" will be dispelled and the role of femininity restored.

For a time, I did have the truly great fortune of explaining and sharing this state with a man *(yes, Richard)*. He would observe, listen, be attentive, and curious. To be seen and recognized on such a day and encouraged to embrace and explore the possibilities it presented was exquisite. To be able to share in the mystique, having my insights sought and valued, connected us deeply. I believe that real "superior men"* can share the magic of such days, and the greater number of such men, the better.

THE FEMINIST MALAISE

Given today's first topic, this is the perfect opportunity to venture into more sensitive territory. At the risk of getting some people's goat, I would like to suggest that the feminist movement missed something. Out with my scandalous statement right off the bat: I believe some truth resides in the traditional roles of man and woman! Hold on! Let me continue.

I do not, in anyway, refute that the movement was essential to our society's evolution: It was born from legitimate unease and suffering in the face of blatant injustices and inequalities, as well as from a deeply rooted frustration from being considered and treated as second-class citizens by a male dominated society.** But I also recognize that the crux of the issue was involuntarily stifled in the mix and that this prevented the most deep-seated problem from seeing the light of day: What truly lay at the source of the revolt was that on the scale of value, women and their roles where not given as much weight as men's accomplishments. In a society putting ever more value on acquiring possessions, the forefront and active role of provider was elevated, and the one of nurturer, guide and home keeper relinquished as subaltern. Analogically we, as a society, tend to give recognition and idolize actors while the writers and directors mostly remain nameless.

---

* To use a connotation coined by David Deida in his book, *The Way of the Superior Man*.

** As a reminder, it is only in 1974 that women were given the right to obtain a credit card without having a husband or father as co-signer: and this, regardless of their wealth or profession. Another surprising anecdote is that the Boston Marathon only accepted women in its rank as of 1972. We owe these and other momentous milestones to pioneers such as Gloria Steinem who tirelessly dedicated their lives to the cause of women's validation.

That's why a few decades ago, women righteously gathered under the umbrella of feminism. Their collective cries needed to be heard in order for balance to be restored. Their united voice denounced the wrongs perpetrated by their masculine counterparts and was raised in claims of equality. The global message stating that women were equal to men was obviously on target, but the manner in which to prove and achieve this, denoted a collective ignorance of the essence of the problem *(or perhaps it was the necessary first step).*

As an unfortunate result, the message that emerged from women's groups was that "woman" needed to emulate what "man" did in order to be recognized rather than women needing to be recognized for what "woman" did. Certainly, it is not too late to undertake this next step: embarking on the quintessential path to equality by educating society until both roles are equally valued.

If men and women were aware and understood the inherent attributes of their respective nature, mutual respect would ensue, and the dissatisfaction that arises from not being seen, valued and respected would dissipate: That is the next step towards parity of the sexes.

I am not suggesting that women should return home, this ship has sailed *(although no woman should feel pressured to abandon her dream of being a homemaker if it is her calling – let's not allow the pendulum to swing to the other side)*, but for the love of Creation, let our future progress be in the direction of celebrating our differences and complementarity rather then attempting sameness.

This afternoon I caught a glimpse of a woman on a talk show who was half-jokingly boasting that soon, women would discover that men were obsolete. NO! Please no. There are two principles that make up human beings – the masculine and the feminine – and it would be a shame to attempt to erase the differences or take on both roles. There is a beautiful dance to be danced between two partners who, although partaking in the same dance, cannot dance the same way. Think of all the ballroom dancing we are privy to on television these days, how magnificent is it when the man, inspired by the woman, steadily and expertly leads with strength and gusto, and the woman shines as she exhibits the myriad facets of life itself. *

THE GREAT EQUALIZER

Being equal does not mean having to perform the same tasks and act the same way as someone else. Equality can only be found in the value we put on each other's worth. Is a gold medalist in one discipline more worthy than another? Should we all strive to compete in the same category *(how boring would Olympics be)*? Is a hammer more valuable than a nail? Should the moon try to become the sun in order to be recognized? Of course not. The tragedy would be to deny our true nature.

The Great Equalizer is the integrity of the performance. When a woman is fully aware of her true nature and holds the reins of its expression in the world, a real man will rejoice and embrace to fullness of her being. His heart will swell with gladness and it won't even occur to him to compare or evaluate the performance.

LADY LIBERTY

In this modern world, independence too often comes under the guise of a dollar sign. Unfortunately, the current structure of our society dictates that financial self-sufficiency is a prerequisite to autonomy. It makes much sense: if you are not financially secure, you will be dependent on someone (or something) for your daily subsistence. Once again, I would like to offer a twist on this reality. I would like to add that money is not an essential condition to achieving a status of independence.

---

* Of course I think women are great leaders too, but the minutia of the question is for another discussion.

Just as Nelson Mandela declared himself free while being in prison, a person can be independent without money. Radical isn't it? But I have recently discovered this powerful subtlety through my personal journey. Although I am living the epitome of financial dependence, I have never felt as independent as I do now. Granted, my index of feeling independent fluctuates daily, but at the core of my being I have achieved self-reliance. And I have done this by knowing who I am and acting towards the fulfillment of my calling. Through self-empowerment I have become an empowered woman.

Although I look forward to my day of financial independence, I will not draw my identity or determine my worth by the content of my bank account: it does not define me as an independent human being.

I am a fiercely independent woman who simply happens not to have money at the moment. And this is *not* an oxymoron.

At sunset tonight, I drove myself down to the beach with the intention of injecting some oxygen into my brain with a healthy walk. Instead, when I got there, I decided to treat myself to a five-dollar decaf soy *latte* and placidly accompany the setting sun into its descent. Bundled up in my down jacket and winter hat, I niched myself between two stones, leaned my back against one of BC's beaches notorious driftwood giant logs, and savored both the landscape and steamy cup of fancy Joe. Gazing to the South across the water appeared the shimmering lights of Vancouver's western suburbs; the East was decorated with the Lion's Gates suspended bridge jutting across the dark grey sky like a weightless streamer of lights, its southern tip extending into the ominous shadow of Stanley Park stalking the inky waters of English Bay. The inlet was spotted with the illuminated silhouettes of moored transatlantic vessels silently settling in for the night. The sky was painted orange and traversed with two long and narrow fumy streaks, and in the western distance, over the contoured ridges of Vancouver Island's procession of peaks, three puffs of somber clouds slowly drifted away. The composition was completed with the sound of gentle waves lapping the shore at my feet. Above, the celestial watching eye of the Northern star* overlooked this rich symphony of life. What a perfect way to end this day.

> ***Men and women are like two different species*** *(of the same genus)* ***and contribute to life's diversity. Let us strive to discover and appreciate their particularities and avoid bringing their unicity into extinction.***

JANUARY 12TH, 2012

12 DAYS OF JANUARY

There is a metaphysical theory that suggests that the content of one's twelve first days of the New Year acts as an oracle and provides clues as to the personal tone of the twelve months to come – meaning that January 1st represents the month of January, January 2nd, February, the 3rd, March etc. Many years ago, I took an amused interest in the idea and began diligently recording my thoughts every year, for the first twelve days of January. Through any given year, when I go back and test the theory, I tend to focus more on the frame of mind, type of energy, or overall dispositions I displayed on the particular

* It may have been Venus – I wish I had an iPad *(and an iPhone)* with the constellation app.

day I'm looking at. It is entertaining: kind of like reading your horoscope in a tabloid; some days, there seems to be a definite correlation. Needless to say that this year, I will have plenty of material to go over.

Since today, the 12th, represents December 2012, it is the occasion to perform a time-defying, back-to-the-future yearly review, and to look over my twelve days of January. Overall, the reading leaves me very hopeful. I have pretty much steadily maintained a happy disposition *(even busted a few jigs)*, I have been excited about the future, my wild ego never ran completely loose, and above all, I have dedicated myself to an endeavor that reflects my truth. Oh, and let's not forget that a nice man showed interest in me and that yesterday, I received an unexpected check in the mail. Yes, the year bodes well. You may have noticed that I choose not to attempt interpreting the mystery of the second hit on my car. I will leave this one be.

This exercise has put me in a retrospective mood and as a result, I feel like giving a shot at revising the early chapters of my manuscript. *(I'm either getting very good at going with the flow or I am very susceptible to autosuggestion. I'm not sure. But let's see where this leads me.)*

A LITERARY BEDLAM

Big mistake. I just spent a few hours poring over my earlier writing and it has pretty much flattened my spirits. Contrary to when I took my first encouraging cursory glance a couple weeks ago, today's sustained gaze was anything but uplifting. I was expecting a little chaos and some interesting anarchy of thoughts but what I have just come to face with is way beyond that. Before beginning this process of revision, my idea had been to leave the first portion of the book as close as possible to its original form as I imagined it would truthfully reflect my then state of mind, and be a great Point A (then) contrast with Point B (now). But my mind's recollections, as to the cohesiveness of my writing, were an illusion. Yes, the daily entries really do reflect my state of mind, but it's a little extreme: my thoughts appear dispersed, fractioned, and convey little continuity, and quite frankly, for the sake of hoping to write a good book, they cannot be left as they are. Although the raw material is all there, there is a lot of sorting out to do. And right now, it is the magnitude of the upcoming work that is overwhelming and demoralizing.

I guess it should not have come as such a surprise. How could I have expected coherence when I was in such a state of confusion, gasping for my very breath, and struggling to spot a buoy I could grab onto. I remember sensing that I was on the verge of clarity but mostly, that fear blurred everything. Furthermore, I had not yet figured out that I was indeed writing a book. So how could it read like one?

Editing there will be and rewriting too; I remain confident that regardless of an improved syntax, my evolution and transformation will still transpire quite clearly.

But right now, I feel ragged. It is as if I have spent the afternoon going against my own grain. Just as two days ago when I battled through a mutiny attempt by the controlling ambitions of my mind, so too now do I feel my latest misguided efforts have depleted me of my energy, motivation and joy. What I should at last understand is that what comes naturally to me these days, is allowing the flow of my thoughts to spill onto paper; anything else consumes me and requires vast amounts of effort. I should know by now that anytime I try to steer my activities away from the effortless lane that bears my name, I pay the price. At the moment, I am on a creative roll, and attempting to edit my work makes me feel off my game and upsets me. So, starting tomorrow, I will wisely do away with my experimentations and return to what feels right; I will resume writing those themes and stories I wish to include in my book.

If I wanted to find something positive about today's debacle, it is that by going over what I have written to date, I was able to observe the undeniable progress I have made. I have truly found my voice both figuratively and literally, as I have witnessed not only the evolution of my inner being but also that of my writing skills.

Different types of energies are favorable to different types of endeavors. When a task feels as though it is grating on your core, that the shavings are pieces of your equanimity, and the amount of effort required is disproportionate to the result, chances are you are going against the natural grain and squandering your energy wastefully. Redirecting your aim may be wise; there will be an appropriate time for whatever needs done.

JANUARY 13TH, 2012

HERE AND GONE

Well, I am just about ready to cry. I had been writing for hours this morning, having even chosen to forego a scheduled day off because I was feeling inspired and boasted a clear mind. I had successfully managed to pull myself out of yesterday's off-track slump and put myself back into the light of things. My message had been coming through with fluidity and shone with memorable metaphors and comedic relief. I had been feeling so proud and... vindicated, for not having crumbled under the anxiety that had overridden my hitherto positive morale. I had felt as though this was some of my best writing yet. All that had been left to do was write a closing sentence.

And that's when suddenly, as I was pondering this sentence, Word was invaded with a virus and transformed my document into forty-two pages of asterisks before my very eyes. I can only imagine what I must have looked like: eyes wide opened and gaping mouth.

I have just spent an hour with Microsoft: the virus has been eradicated but everything I wrote today is gone *(luckily, not the entire 42 pages).* I do want to cry. I had planned on rewarding myself with a hike, after a job well done. The sun is shining and rain is forecasted for days to come; it was a perfect time to seize to moment. But now, my heart is so not into it. All I want to do is try to recreate what I had so cleverly written but I don't think it is possible. What a shame.

Well this time, I really do have spilled milk to cry over. This is another one of these instances where crap happened and I can legitimately say, "This sucks." I am miffed. Please allow me a moment to bitch and sulk.

After doing precisely that for some time and also dutifully watching the last episode of *One Life To Live* – a soap opera that had been an on and off companion of my bed-ridden days for the past twenty-five years – I resisted the healthy idea of going for a hike. Really, all I wanted to do was stay home, wallow some more, and try to recapture my earlier literary brilliance. I eventually did manage to peel myself off from the sofa and up I went to the mountain *(but not before, as I hoped for a little pick-me up, trying on my favorite winter pants only to come to the unpleasant realization that they still did not fit).* But even up there, my mind did not find peace. I was and still am bummed. All along, shrapnel of my morning work kept coming back to me and I made every effort to hold on to them, jotting down words in the tiny notebook I carried in my pocket for exactly that purpose.

As I beat myself up for writing without making a backup *(which*

I usually do, diligently), I also wrestled with the fact that it was absolutely pointless to do so: The text is gone. Move on woman. I mean, how much spilled milk can someone really pick up, and what is the point in crying over it? None. And I must admit that, by now, I have had an appropriate amount of time to sulk. So, it is time to let go. *(And girl, for future references, try to keep in mind that the lesson applies whether the metaphorical milk is words, relationships or money!)*

Yes, time to let go. Except that I am not very successful at it today.

YOU DID IT THIS MORNING, YOU CAN DO IT AGAIN

As the evening falls, my core is still shaken by the emotional double-whammy I experienced over the course of the last days. The tremors have left me unnerved and my breathing is no longer supple. My head is painfully pulsating from the disquieting quakes, and the fear of aftershocks is registering as anxiety.

But amidst the unrest, I defer once more to the advice of my inner wise-one: "Just go to bed, read your Harry Potter, and start over tomorrow. You did it this morning; you can do it again. Now rest."

Good night.

Trying to hold on to something that no longer is, truly is futile. Time spent on our knees soaking up spilled milk will inevitably be disheartening and cause aches and pains. In the end, whatever is salvaged will probably not be appetizing at all anyway.

JANUARY 14TH, 2012

THIS LITTLE EGO OF MINE, IT REALLY WANTS TO SHINE

BEHIND THE SCENES OF THE LAST TWO DAYS

So the past twenty-four hours put me through the ringer. Actually, the onset was more like forty-eight hours ago when I ill-advisedly decided to review the early part of my book: Realizing that my preliminary writing resembled a chaotic jumble caused an upsurge of doubt and a breach in my confidence. Not only did it make me question my ability to bring it all together cohesively when the time would come, but it also allowed my insecurities regarding the validity of my book project as a whole, to resurface. Unbelievable. But, there I went again.

A RIVER RUNS THROUGH IT

Well, as you can imagine, this was the ideal terrain for my ego to hit the ground running. Admittedly, in view of my recent *(relative)* happiness and confidence, he had probably been feeling left out and neglected. In fact, he has lost some feathers in his cap. Needless to explain how, when my latest state of unrest arose, he seized the opportunity to reclaim some jurisdiction over my life.

So it was that, forty-eight hours ago, he started stirring up trouble by drawing attention to the existing rift between my creative writing and my attempts at structuring my manuscript. He deftly played up each side against the other until he got everybody riled up, and then cunningly fueled the hostilities between the land of my right-brain – ruled by my inner-self – and his own personal dominion: the left-brain. Up until two days ago, the energy had been running almost unimpeded in his nemesis's territory, but once the flow had been temporarily diverted onto his own, he wanted it all for himself. And so, he revived the age-old territorial clash: Who gets the river?

This initial uprising resulted in hours of grueling palaver during which feathers were ruffled but no one took arms. The morning after, an armistice was reluctantly reached wherein each side would not meddle in the other's business or interfere with nature's impetus. Parties came to this tenuous agreement by recognizing that the course of this energy-river would naturally alternate and irrigate both lands in its own time: for now, the creative inspiration-driven right bank would benefit from the rushing waters and later, the mind-structured left bank would have its turn. Suspicions still abounded, but for a moment, there was peace. This is how I was able to write undisturbed yesterday morning, that is, until the next computer-crash-bombshell dropped and eradicated my work.

I was a little dubious as to the probability that peacetime was haphazardly broken only hours after reaching a precarious truce. It smelled a little fishy to me. I know; it is rather farfetched to entertain the idea that my ego could actually have schemed to infect my computer... or is it? Do we really know the capabilities of this worthy adversary? Hem. He certainly did benefit from the mishap. I knew he was bruised by the terms of the armistice and I had expected a surge of counter-activity to erupt eventually. I had even warned myself to be on guard, knowing this was certainly not the end of the conflict and that future negotiation rounds would be plentiful. Perhaps my victory had been a little too easy in view of the crafty player involved? Perhaps I had been a little cocky thinking that I could mediate a timeless rivalry without collateral damage? Well, whether my computer crash was a coincidence or an underhanded riposte, the result was the same: Self-doubt. Was I doing the right thing writing this book, now? Was it worth writing? Was I hiding behind this project?

Oh Dear Lord. It was time to take a hike.

THE REAL SLIPPERY SLOPE

While on said weary hike yesterday – as I was trying to recuperate not only my words but also rebuild my bashed-in confidence – I became the unsuspecting guinea pig in a demonstration of the power of manifestation of our energy output. As I was gingerly walking down a steep icy portion of the trail, I noticed a secondary path to my right. It was more like a concave glistening groove perhaps imprinted by an earlier bobsled joyrider. Well, having a temerarious streak in me, I decided to venture onto it, sit, and slide down. Dumb move. I slid so fast I nearly lost control and actually hurt my wrist and bruised my well padded behind *(time for a quick dose of Arnica).* Checking each of my limbs upon stopping, I picked myself up while silently moralizing: "This is what happens when you let Ego lure you aside or get on board with Doubt and Uncertainty: it's a fast and dangerous ride downhill."

THIS MORNING

As I pulled up the curtains this morning, I was greeted by a land peacefully shrouded in snow and took it in as inspiration: Peace can descend upon me once more. I prepared myself a luscious *latte*, lit a candle, and began a gentle meditation, prompting myself to reconnect with the feeling that all is well. *(A very gentle meditation indeed, partially induced by the emanations of a steamy* latte.*)*

The stillness, in and around me, opened the stage to my wiser-self. Graciously, I surrendered the pulpit and listened in deference:

> "You wonder if perhaps you are fooling yourself with the illusion that writing this book is the right thing to do? You wonder if perhaps you are using this as an escape to avoid facing the reality of getting a job and settling for a mediocre life? You may have good reason to do so, after all, you are still not earning any money. But.

"If you were not doing the right thing, do you believe that you would be sleeping better? That your life-long sordid nightmares of savagery, combat and terror, rivaling with the best horror movies, would have disappeared? That your health would be improving as it is? That you would have had such a good run of inner peace and wellbeing that looked a lot like happiness? Do you really believe that if you were not operating from your truth, that these changes would be happening?

"Let me remind you of the place of knowing you come from: For over ten years, something has been speaking to you about writing this book. For months now, you have been realizing that all the obstacles, blockades and derailments have led you to this endeavor, and that you were being divinely granted the time to write. Also, writing has come to you with surprising ease and has procured you with great joy and satisfaction.

"Let me remind you that these imperfect circumstances correspond perfectly with the unusual task of writing-from-the-middle that you have defined and undertaken. You have felt that your calling was to write from within the tunnel, before reaching the end and basking in the light. You have chosen to chronicle a "live" account of your journey, and if you did not go through tests of fire, where would your teaching dwell? What example would you be?

"And as for your doubt in your ability to organize your book into a cohesive whole? When the time comes, you will be inspired, and it will sort itself out with ease as well. When it is time, your left brain will take over and perform splendidly.

"Let me reassure you, your truth is still true. You have been provided with plenty of proof to support that, and you can rely on those manifestations. This is where your focus should be. Keep doing what feels right and life will unfold as it should."

So it is that after clamoring uncontrollably for two days, the unruly crowd in my head started settling down. I may have buckled under the unending chatter of my ego, his relentless remonstrance and fear-monger's ways, but this is not my first rodeo and I will not be so easily unseated. He may stir me up and make me work up a sweat, but I will triumph. With yet more practice, I will turn this bully into an industrious ox.

With my composure regained, I got up to my desk and cleared the dozens of scribbled scraps of paper strewn upon its surface. The act of uncluttering my working space, I used as a symbolic ritual to consciously clear my mind. The peaceful flame of the candle glimmered gently and illuminated my thoughts as I took a deep breath and started writing anew.

To be honest *(needless to say)* I remain feeling slightly daunted by the magnitude of the task ahead. But for today, I am peaceful and okay. Compassionately, the Universe flutters an eye in my direction: my shuffling iPod randomly plays Bet.e & Stef's *I Take It Day By Day.*

Ego is a crafty and vocal fellow; being outspoken is in his nature. But there is another voice in our head that can, if given a chance, supersede his untamed expression. By taking a moment to allow peace, stillness, and quiet to set in, this sage presence can be heard.

JANUARY 16TH, 2012

SLUMBER PARTY

Obviously, by now, you have abundantly noticed that sleep has long been a foe I still hope to befriend. Sleeping five hours in a row *(including moments of half-conscious awareness, mind you)* is about a once-monthly occurrence; and the miracle of going to bed at night and waking up in the morning oblivious of time having passed, happens once, or twice a year if I'm lucky.

Over time, I have devised and experimented with a few sleep-facilitating tricks, and although they are no panacea, they do occasionally work *(if they were miraculous, sleep could now be my BFF, but as it stands, we remain barely courteous towards one another)*. So, for all the other insomniacs out there, I will share their gist.

Before I describe these various stratagems, there is one generic practice that seems to initiate relaxing *(though even this simplest one is not always achievable)*. It begins, inescapably, with establishing a slow breath. The next step is to consciously transfer the center of perception from the head to the heart: Instead of the head/mind being the most active transmitter and receptor of the body, the idea is to try to lower presence and awareness to the chest/heart level, and get away from the hustle and bustle of the mind. In fact, we should probably aspire to dwell and function from the heart regularly, day and night.

THE TRICKS AND TIPS

The first one is the sleeping baby. We have all seen pictures or videos of exquisitely and peacefully sleeping infants. When attempting to fall asleep, imagine this baby, totally relaxed, no tension existing in any of his muscles: the eyes, the mouth, the cheeks, the fists, everything is peaceful. The only movement is the hypnotic gentle rhythm of his breath, which seems to reach and nurture even his tippy toes. Imagine his soul, unencumbered and still unblemished by earthly life, blissfully able to return to its place of origin and rest in God's loving and protective arms. Not a worry to have, knowing that all is well. Now focus on your face and mimic this state of absolute peace, and feel the arms of God around you. All is well.

For the more active types, a more physical imagery may work. Imagine your brain as a muscle: its weightlifting exercise being intense curls of mental activity that repetitively contract the tissues. Now imagine releasing the mental activity as you would the tension in your leg or arm after a particularly strenuous routine that made you feel the burn in a certain muscle. Imagine catching your breath in relief.

This is the one that actually worked for me last night. I managed to shut off my mind's chatter by feeling my brain cooling off *(steam rising)*, relaxing, imagining the frontal lobe gently leaning against the back lobe, which in turn rested on the back of my head, just as I would lean against a wall following a sprint.

A slightly trickier possibility is focusing on the images appearing on the inner screen of your mind when your eyes are closed. Focus on the sequence of usually unrelated various images that come up, and when you find one that is innocuous enough not to get your mind going, project yourself into the screen so that you become part of the environment you see. I have found that I can become involved in the storyline of my choice and start interacting with the scenery or a particular character. Once I succeed in doing that, I am already in a world of semi-consciousness. My mind lets go of my reality and slips into Lalaland.

And if all else fails, play a make believe game with yourself and pretend this is one of those high school days *(way back when)* when you have had to get up way too early for your teenage body. But, on this particular morning, fortunately, you found out that a snowstorm *(or whatever works from your childhood memories)* has closed all schools for the day and you slumped back into bed. Remember how good your bed felt, the guilty pleasure of getting a reprieve for an exam and of slipping back under your covers? Remember how quickly you fell back asleep? If you can fool yourself and recapture that feeling, you will drift right into Morpheus's arms.

Although too often unacknowledged and undervalued as such, the heart is the true central system of human beings. The problem is that our current logical, rational, and intellectual way of life has falsely led us to believe that we are first and foremost thinking-beings rather than sentient ones, thus misguidedly favoring the mind. Descartes' *"I think therefore I am"* ***could perhaps become, "I am aware of my mind's thinking, therefore I am."***

JANUARY 17TH, 2012

TIME FOR ANOTHER PARADIGM SHIFT

This is now mid-January, and the grace period afforded by my previous paradigm shift – whereby I would not look for a job until I completed certain portions of my book – has, as far as I am concerned and for all intent and purposes, elapsed.

At the time of this decision, I mentally granted myself permission to write *(relatively)* guilt-free for a couple additional weeks. But that free pass has expired and I am not where I thought I would be: there is a lot more that remains to be done. And pressure is mounting and being compounded by my unyielding inner conflict between feeling right about my dedication to my book, and my monetary sense of urgency, which is furiously re-arising. This one just keeps on giving and it is getting excruciatingly redundant and sorely irksome.

Although I understand that extreme pressure creates diamonds... hem... hold on just a minute... is this what I actually believe? That in order to produce a gem of a book I need to submit myself to extreme pressure?

Without being able to put a finger on it, this is the precept that has been nagging at me since it appeared in my wiser-self's broadcast of a few days ago. What I heard was that I am the one who defined the terms of a story-from-the-middle, claiming that my calling was to write a "live" account of my journey – before reaching the light – and that without the continuous tests of fire, any pretense of teaching by example would be fraudulent. It is not the first time, within or before this book, that I have made such claims, but it is beginning to seriously bug me.

Although I understand that my trials and daily woes have made my journey a universal one, and that this commiserating is my way of offering support and guidance, I believe I have allowed my ego to slip one past me. I've allowed him to masquerade a personal belief as inner wisdom. This is definitely something to watch for when you listen to your inner voice: there are loopholes through which your swindler of an ego can sneak-in a few counterfeit pearls of his own wisdom.

Truth be told, as of now, if my current struggles were removed from the equation *(strictly speaking, the financial ones)*, all that would be lost would be a few choice sound-bites of my ego: "You should be looking for work! You're not doing the right thing. You should not feel so good. You're gonna crash and burn. You're gonna have to go back and live with your Mom. You're being irresponsible! You're being foolish! What if this doesn't work out or takes a long time to bear any fruit? Everybody says it's almost impossible to get published and if one does, it can take up to two years! What will you do then? You're gonna be miserable."

My experience of struggle is already plenty rich and abundant, and it really does not have to go on. The real problem, I guess, is that I believe it does. I believe that unless my situation generates immense pressure, worry, insecurity, pain, or fear, my experience is not laudable or worthy. And this is the antiquated paradigm that needs changing.

The truth is not that hardship is a necessary condition to accomplishment or worthiness but that *I* need adversity to feel worthy because I don't know any other way: The problem is my inner belief, not my inner voice.

This reminds me of a moment in *Finding Sarah*, the televised journey of Sarah Ferguson on OWN. On the show, she sets out on a trek across the Arctic to, ultimately, prove something to herself. In a conversation, Oprah insightfully and humorously tells her that although she is free to choose to go trudging across the Arctic with 40 pounds on her back – and find she will receive the assistance of the universe through her journey – she really doesn't *have to* carry 40 pounds across the Artic to prove anything! Indeed. And I don't have to struggle financially (or health wise) for my story to be worthy of sharing, or to live a valuable life.

I'm thinking of a four-prong approach to remedy this damaging, erroneous belief, and to enter this new paradigm where struggles and pain do not equal worthiness.

1 — EGO SENSE

The first step is to recognize the value of my ego *(demeaning him is unproductive)*, heed his warnings, and engage him respectfully. "Yes dear, I hear you. I do need to earn money. But instead of using up your time and energy to yap my head off, please use them to go seek an adequate or even great job, or other source of income. I will remain receptive and open to your suggestions."

2 — SELF TALK

Next. Have a conversation with my Self. "Girl, you don't need to suffer to complete your book. You have learned enough from suffering to talk about it competently; you have even earned a Masters and PhD on the general subject of struggling. You can now use you education to teach but you don't have to keep studying."

3 — I DECLARE

Third, make a declaration to said Universe. "I Annie, declare that suffering is no longer my path for learning and accomplishing. The opposition is dismantled. Resistance is futile. I allow sanctions to be lifted and blockades to stand down. I declare all access to resources reestablished and free circulation of abundance to be restored."

4 — LOOKING FOR ALL IS WELL

Finally, meditate until the feeling of everything-is-all-right returns. If I were to tell the tale of such an endeavor, here is what it may sound like:

Happy Kitty

I have a lovely little ball of fur named Mr. All Is Well
Happy Kitty, to his buddies, is his sobriquet as well
Over the years and now and then
Precious time together we've spent
Until this wounded heart is on the mend
Never enough is what is meant

When we do my heart patters and pelts
And all with the world indeed seems well
But when Ego, our foe, his antics out belts
Sadly our bliss he is gifted to quell

Soon skittish Happy Kitty off and away strays
For easily spooked is part of his ways
And in the morning I find myself alone
And without my furry ball to fill our happy home
Ego soon turns it into a wretched place to roam

High and low in search of him I go
Below the bed and under the covers
High up in trees and down in the gutters
My quest is meticulous and thorough
Frenzied and fraught and hopeful also

Throughout the search I call and yell
Where are you Happy Kitty, Mr. All Is Well?
Come back I miss you, return to my heart's swell
Without you it is true, I am simply not well

When at last reunited are we
Into my bosom he is home safely
Into his ear I whisper gently
Happy Kitty, now stay here with me
Filled is my heart which sings like a longspur
My dearest furry friend, purr, purr, purr

Often behind a clever camouflage that make them difficult to discern, our personal beliefs are usually, perhaps always, reflected in our lives. If we believe overcoming hardship is honorable and want to live an honorable life, then our life will be hardship. If we believe that enduring pain and conquering fears make us worthy, then pain to endure and fears to conquer we will find. Let us unearth the assumptions that create obstacles in our lives, replace them with healthy core-beliefs, and see how our future then unfold under the auspices of a new paradigm.

JANUARY 18TH, 2012

JACKHAMMERS AND SCREECHING BRAKES

A headache that has been building up amidst the last few days' fracas has now shown up in full force. Acetaminophen and ibuprofen are having no effect whatsoever. And atop the repetitive impacts of these jackhammers, the unremitting sounds of screeching train brakes, metal to metal, are endlessly reverberating in my head: Those are the strident notes of my tinnitus, 24/7. Although the painful digging of jackhammers certainly undermines my day(s), I know the excavation will be done eventually and that the quiet of the neighborhood will at some point be restored. On the other hand, the never-ending hiss of the tinnitus is... never-ending and dangles no respite at the end of its stick. It requires that a part of my brain constantly stand guard and fence-off madness at every moment, and this sustained attention is like an unmended leak steadily draining my vitality.

Anyway, I have kind of accepted it. No, not really: I have learned to live with it because I don't have a choice – sleeping with a white noise maker and keeping a fan on at all times in the house. Unfortunately, oh so unfortunately, silence is the enemy – for now. In the early years, when I was still getting acquainted with this long-term cuffed companion, I went for a canoe trip down Maine's Allagash River, and on the third day, park rangers had to be called-in to get me and my friend out of the park because the nighttime silence had proven unbearable and had brought me to the edge of insanity.

Regardless of the history, I remain steadfast in my belief that, just as so many other ailments are resolving themselves as a result of living in my authentically, I will find the key and end this undesirable pairing. This too shall pass.

But for now, these physical afflictions contribute and demonstrate that I still believe that difficulty and praiseworthy go hand in hand, and that suffering is the honorable way to go. Obviously, I still harbor doubts regarding my ability to dissolve all resistance against the Universe's inherent goodness; obviously, my core belief remains that life is a hard, upstream battle. One sign of personal progress though, is that at least by now *(since my big OMG The Universe IS Good epiphany)*, I understand that it is *I* who fights its generous flow and not *it* that conspires against me. I therefore consider myself that much closer to stepping onto the raft that will take me on an invigorating ride down the Universe's mighty river.

In order to work on my imperfect belief, I have been attempting to write a new affirmation poster-card about this bountiful Universe, and I am encountering complications. I want to state that the Universe is abundant, that I am a fully-fledged constituent, and I also want to remind myself that struggling is no longer necessary. The problem is that affirmations should not include what you shouldn't do or what you don't want – the brain does not know how to *not-do*, it only understands how to *do*: that onto which you bring your attention, is what your brain will remember. It will not differentiate whether you are telling it it's good or bad. It's like praying. If your prayer sounds like: "God, please, I don't want to suffer anymore, I don't want to be poor, I no longer want to be sick. Help me!" what is it you are actually focusing on and feeling? The answer is: your suffering, your lack of money, and your illness. This is what is being put out into the Universe or reaching God's ear. What we invest our energy in will grow: good or bad. So we must be very aware of what our thoughts, prayers, and affirmations are made of.

So when I try to write this poster-card, I keep running into the same problem. I keep including words like, "there are no obstacles", "all resistance is gone" or "I do not need to struggle any longer." The closest I get to is this: "The Universe is abundant. I surrender freely and completely, without interference." But I don't feel it, and the word "interference" is in there too. Wait, I think I have it. How about this: "I am a constituent of a generous Universe. The easiest path is the path of abundance."* I think I like it.

I really do get that my natural state is joy and abundance. I got a keen sense of it for a few weeks following my arrival in Vancouver. During that time, I was exuding joy and the world was responding in kind. I had discovered my pleasure and ability to socialize, I had gladly realized I still new how to have fun, and I was profoundly gratefully for reclaiming my long-lost self. I was a little beacon of light bouncing around the city; and it felt as natural as breathing. It seemed so obvious at that moment that this was the natural state of life. The feeling was exhilarating and the exhilaration generated more goodness. *(We know how the story went: "...and then, once I started worrying, it was gone, and the roller coaster ride began" – but I'm just making a point.)*

I also got a sense of how disturbing it was for some people to even witness abundance in action. This distrust and disbelief in the generosity of the Universe is perversely pervasive. One particular anecdote is very telling of this malaise. Sitting on the beach one sunny afternoon, I shared with a new (very new) friend how things were coming together rather magically for me in my new town. I told him how I had gotten great deals and freebies for furniture on Craigslist, how I had found a beautiful suite, was being treated to lunch and afternoon tea, and how farmers were giving me free veggies and berries. I was unpretentious but glowing, and doubtless appeared convinced that this streak of benevolence would continue. The man looked at me begrudgingly and said, "What makes *you* so special?" It was obvious he did not agree with my good fortune. For some reason, this was

---

* Iteration #2: "Life is good. I embrace easy. The Universe is generous."

rubbing him the wrong way. I answered something short like, "Well, I just am", and did not offer any further explanation or argument. I was encountering a different wavelength and harmonizing would not occur. Silently I told him, "You haven't seen nothing yet. This is just the beginning."

> ***Our natural state is joy; and joy builds upon joy. If it is eluding you in your life, create feelings of joy in your inner world in order to begin the process. Since you know how joy feels, meditate until you generate that feeling inside you, without cause. Invent reasons; happy hormones won't know the difference. Pretend until your belly is smiling. As you go about your day, you can build on that joy with little things like putting on your favorite sweater, eating out of your favorite bowl, laughing at you cat's mannerism, or loving a tiny flower blossoming in an unexpected place. This will lay the foundation onto which more joy can build.***

JANUARY 19TH, 2012

IT'S JUST A RIDE

This road from Alaska to Happy *(an elusive city perched on the mountains of Peru)* sure is a bumpy ride. The number of uphills and downhills, of fallen trees blocking the road, of floods and flat tires, is astounding. Yes, there are astonishing views as well, but at the moment, I am having a difficult time appreciating those: it is the washed out road ahead that is preoccupying my mind, and the constant brush of empty pockets on my thighs forever reminding me of the upcoming trouble of filling up the tank that I am concerned about.

My ego is still being rowdy and I can't seem to settle inside. I wonder what this travel would be like if I had unlimited gas-money; if I didn't have to worry about stalling in the middle of the desert, or in the heart of a virgin forest, or half way up a mountain. What kind of pleasures would I experience if I could zoom on these roads with unbridled enthusiasm and carefree attitude? Same views, but I bet I'd discover a new dimension to them and enjoy them even more.

Here's a truth: regardless of what *(most)* people *(with money)* say – that their affluence is unrelated to their happiness – it is definitely a most precious commodity, and the highest interest it generates is basic peace of mind. Until you know what the lack of it deprives you of, you have no idea. As Morgan Freeman insightfully said, *"Money is unimportant unless you don't have any"**. And if the peace of mind provided by a plump bank account was to relieve my tinnitus and nausea, I may be one to preach that money does indeed buy happiness.

THE ART OF MINDFUL MINDLESSNESS

Despite all the bellyaching I've been doing about those same few torments endlessly going 'round like carousel horses in my head, I am actually in rather bright dispositions lately. I am still energized by the fact that I am writing a book, pleased with its overall content, and both cognizant of, and grateful for the various milestones punctuating the road behind me.

In order to spur my spirits further along, I began this morning with a long meditation consisting of ohm chanting. I have a twenty-minute recording of a congregation of Tibetan monks voicing an entrancing ohm; and at times when I feel the need for a potent brand of tonic,

---

* In an interview on CNN's *Piers Morgan Tonight.*

playing it is almost inescapably transforming – that is: if I can muster the discipline to play the tune, conscientiously listen, and ultimately accompany them with my own sound. If I keep at it long enough, even looping the song on my iPod if necessary, it will inevitably work for me. The secret is to stick with the chanting until I feel the vibration of the sound expand from my throat to my chest, reaching the extremity of each limb, and enfolding each organ. Once this vibration fills every space of my body, it acts as a tuning fork and resembles a rallying cry for all my cells to join together as members of one orchestra, performing in unison; rather than having disparate preoccupations, each cell then becomes a member of one team, taking one concerted action, towards one goal: supporting me.

How wonderful that I was able to find enough determination to do it this morning *(almost like discipline isn't it?)*.

Today, this practice has allowed me to reconnect with the fact that all is well *(Hello Kitty! Glad you're back!)*, and that I am on the right path. I have also decided to extend my grace period a while longer; I will take the time to write those portions of my book I endeavored to complete before looking for a job. I am very much aware that although sometimes tempting, returning to worrying would yield nothing I want. Another way of saying this is that I understand that if I were to tune-in again to WORRY 105.5 F.M., I would not be listening to JOY 99.6 F.M..

I was introduced to this radio-tuning metaphor when I was about ten years old. For a while there, my parents, who had had a falling-out with the direction of the Catholic Church, opted for a home version of Sunday service. Once a week, my father would sit the family down on the kitchen floor *(our kitchen was carpeted – yes it was, with an orange-ochre quasi-psychedelic pattern)* for Sunday discussion. He would pick a topic based on some book or the other he was reading, such as *The Secret to Happiness* or *The Power of Your Subconscious*, and share with us the lessons he was himself learning. One of these teachings addressed the idea that if you tune your inner radio to the frequency of GLOOM or FEAR F.M., you should not be surprised when you don't receive the joyful music broadcast of HAPPY F.M.. During these sessions, we would practice telepathy, train our intuition with cards, or work at finding answers with a pendulum.

In retrospect, these were pretty radical Sunday teachings for the time. The funny thing is that later in life, my father, who had a second change of heart towards the values of the Church, had a difficult time reconciling with the fact that all of his children were spiritually rather marginal, and rejected religious traditions. One day towards the end of his life, as he was deploring this, I reminded him lightheartedly of his Sunday teachings and that his children were precisely the intrepid, free-minded, nonconformists he had raised. As if just grasping this, I remember him looking at me with a quizzical half-smile, repressing a chuckle, and flaring his nostrils : an involuntary telltale sign of mischief; my father could never pull a prank, his nostrils always betrayed him.

MATERIAL GIRL

Right now, I see no washed out road ahead and I am uneventfully driving on a smooth, freshly laid coat of asphalt on a scenic road of Costa Rica. I am enjoying the lush surroundings and I am not even concerning myself with the gas gage. Nice. I am perfectly aware this is but a stretch of the road but this most recent personal belief paradigm shift – whereby suffering does not equate worthiness – is moving me along as I am journeying towards my Peru *(and traversing Costa Rica means that I am getting closer to the equator and that the road behind is much longer than the one ahead).* Of course, I really look forward to the day this inner metamorphosis actually translates into the material world. Plainly speaking, I look forward to having not only all the gas-money I need but also the luxury to put my bare feet up on the dashboard, watching the world go by, as my perfect-man-for-me takes his turn behind the wheel as I finally cross into Peru. Picture perfect.

Not resisting involves effort.
Letting go entails grasping what matters.
Relaxing takes awareness.
A quiet mind necessitates forethought.
This mindlessness business requires quite a bit of mindfulness.

JANUARY 20TH, 2012

IN GOOD COMPANY

Last night, as I was pursuing my reading of the last installment of the Harry Potter series*, I was amused to see how universal second-guessing yourself really is. I mean even Harry Potter does it! In the story, Harry is essentially fighting dark forces outside and inside himself while on his quest for identity and purpose *(sounds very familiar)*. At some point, he is faced with a critical decision and, listening to his intuition, elects to continue on his initial path and thus chooses *not* to act on another front *(kind of like choosing to write my book and not look for a job!)*; But he is filled with doubts *(I can relate)*. The author enumerates the various "what ifs" haunting him. Basically, these "what ifs" make him question whether he was supposed to have understood something and acted rather than not, and whether working out some particular issues was *meant* to make him "worthy" of following the other path *(a very common theme I hear)*. "What ifs" further make him wonder if the choice he made may have actually been

---

* *Harry Potter and the Deathly Hallows,* by J.K. Rowling.

madness *(fair question, again I relate)*, if he might have misunderstood the intention behind the trials *(uh-huh)*, and whether or not he had misread the signs *(uh-huh, uh-huh)*. He is even tormented when trying to satisfactorily explain to himself why he had made this crazy choice in the first place. And yet in the end, this hero does rely upon his intuition and ultimately reaps the rewards *(I'm counting on that)*.

It sounds to me as if there is some universal akashic reserve where a world of second-guesses is stored and from which everyone draws bountifully throughout their lives, real or fictitious.

We are all heroes, and despite flare-ups of self-doubt and second thoughts, we shall continue on the courageous path traced by intuition, and in the end, reap the rewards of a fulfilled heart and purposeful life.

JANUARY 21ST, 2012

SIMPLE DAYS

Gentle day of bits and pieces for the book, the house, and myself. I am feeling positive, peacefully energized.

Sometimes, we just need a day off.

JANUARY 22ND, 2012

LIFE: A MOVING PICTURE

Yes, sometimes a simple day is just what Mother Nature prescribes. In the wake of an event that has sent shockwaves through our belief system, emotional make-up, or life situation, it is often wise – or even unavoidable – to slow down, take a breath, and smell the gardenias. Some days are meant to let the dust settle so that we can catch a clearer view of what our new environment looks like.

Whether we embrace it or not, we must accept that the landscape of our life is constantly changing and requires we adjust our gaze at every moment. Failing to do so will maintain us in a perpetual state of disappointing illusion. In a universe that is in permanent flux, aspiring to hold on to sameness, expecting things to stay as they are, or pursuing a fixed goal, are all exercises in discouraging futility. This is why, although setting goals is important to provide momentum and direction, the goal itself must always remain malleable: the very nature of life demands it. As narrated in the television series *Touch*, *"Humans try to cling to snapshots when life is a moving picture."* *

The ineluctability of change may explain why people's ambition to "arrive" in life, is never really fulfilled. The dilemma, or catch-22, is that the set of conditions that, at one moment, lead us to define our point of "arrival" is already obsolete the instant the moment has passed. This is also why any quest for perfection is vain: the gauge by which we measure our ideal is irrevocably reset by new inputs day after day – minute by minute – and so, what was once defined

* This quote comes from an episode that aired later in the year.

as perfection can never satisfy later. Furthermore, perfection is the antithesis of change: it is the epitome of fixity and can only appear in a snapshot, and therefore, is contrary to the moving picture that is life.

There is a dual principle of physics that illustrates this paradox eloquently: "static equilibrium" versus "dynamic equilibrium". Static equilibrium is a state in which there are no changes, disturbances, movement, or input: It is a self-contained system. Dynamic equilibrium is a steady state that occurs when corresponding forces balance one another, resulting in stability: It is an open system that is in constant movement and is thus a work endlessly in progress. Life is a dynamic equilibrium: In the wake of each event of disruption and incoherence (an arrhythmic phase devoid of stability), it perpetually adjusts as it seeks to recreate the steadiness of harmony.

This question of dynamic equilibrium was discussed in a website's daily communication I subscribe to.* It insightfully mentioned that since an input of new elements and energies was necessary to trigger the instability in the first place, every new state of harmony differs from the preceding one. Therefore, the universe, Earth, and humans alike, can never recapture or "return" to a previous state of equilibrium but rather can elevate themselves to meet the new existing frequencies.

Who we are today is just for today and is not who we will be tomorrow. So when someone asks you *(or you ask yourself)* if you have achieved balance in your life, you can accurately and honestly answer, "I'm working on it."

---

* Terralive.net reports daily on events such as earthquakes and solar flares (data is extracted from scientific sources such as nasa, noaa, usgs and neic). It provides an intensity index as an indicator of how the concomitant modulations of Earth's magnetic field may affect the various aspects – physical, emotional, behavioral – of our lives. When activity is high, I find it most fascinating to have these disruptions brought to my awareness and establish correlations with my state of being.
Note: As brilliant as I believe this to be, I shall be upfront and tell you the author is my brother.

And by the way, let us all relieve some undue pressure from ourselves and forever forget this doomed pursuit of perfection.

In our life's quest for stability, let us remember that the balance we achieve today will inevitably require adjustment tomorrow; and depending on what new element was added to the mix, this adjustment may consist of a subtle tweak or a total redo. Expecting each day will inevitably dawn a new normal will spare us a lot of grief.

JANUARY 23RD, 2012

YOU ARE THE CENTER OF THE UNIVERSE

To celebrate the Chinese New year, let me reveal a hidden secret. You have all certainly been told, at some point or another, that you were not the center of the universe *(or you told someone they were not)*, and that the world didn't revolve around you, right? One day, when you were making everything about yourself, someone got really irritated and told you off. Well, I am here to tell off these people myself and announce that they were wrong: You are the center of the universe*! Yes, really, you are. To be precise, you are the center of *your* universe. Sounds selfish doesn't it? But let me explain: being self-centered is exactly the point.

* Apologies to Copernicus who toiled to dismantle this model!

First, I must pull this statement back to slightly more modest dimensions. Maybe we are more accurately the center of our solar system *(still pretty impressive)*. But I had to head up with the catchier phrase because the solar system bit doesn't roll off the tongue as well. And frankly, when I want to play with this metaphor, I like to think of being the center of my universe – it caters to my megalomaniacal penchant. But for now, in the name of accuracy and global imagery, I will explain with the solar system model.

THE PHYSICS OF LIFE

Have you ever wondered why some people, who were at some point intrinsic to your world, inexplicably disappear out of your life ("Why don't I hear about so and so anymore?")? And similarly, why others suddenly, and even mysteriously, just appear ("Where did this one come from?")? Of course, as thinking logical beings, we construct rational explanations for these phenomena: something our limited human brain can grasp and hold on to.

For example, if a lover or spouse exits someone's life (without mutual consent), the injured party will find justifications for the dramatic move in either a quarrel that occurred, perhaps fault a newfound love, or blame an intentional attitude of indifference from the other. In many cases, the poor "victim" may even cry in despair and ask acrimoniously, "Don't you love me anymore? Why have you fallen out of love?" The thing is, the real reason, the nucleus, the nub of the issue, may be that the person has simply fallen out of gravity! It may be that "irreconcilable differences" are actually the result of real, sub-molecular, physical, incompatibility.

SUN, PLANETS, MOONS AND EVERYTHING IN BETWEEN AND BEYOND

Let me paint a very simplified picture of the solar system. This rudimentary fresco, I hope, will provide you with the perfect backdrop for the parallels I wish to make with this analogy. Once you see it in your mind's eye, you will be able to enjoy drawing your own correlations with life.

First thing to establish: as the center of your solar system, you are the sun *(not sure I had to specify that, but just in case)*. Now the astronomy class:

The solar system is mainly comprised of planets, moons, asteroids and comets. Everything in the solar systems revolves around the sun *(you!)*. To emphasize the importance of the sun *(you!)*, it contains 98% of all the material present in the system; the sun is definitely the big kahuna. Because of its massive presence, it exerts massive gravity: it attracts all the objects in its vicinity (for billions of miles around) towards itself. Solar winds also push out particles and gases out of its space, which affects the various fields surrounding the planets orbiting around it *(your actions affect others)*. Although our solar system only has eight main planets *(representing the principle people in your life)*, it contains over a hundred worlds *(minor planets and moons)*. There are also other areas that compose the solar system such as the Asteroid Belt, the Kuiper Belt and the Oort Cloud. The belts are composed of millions of objects that also orbit around the sun *(still you)* and, interestingly for my metaphor, some of these comets occasionally get thrown off the orbit, and either fly away or burn up: either way, they disappear! *(Disappear for us, that is, but perhaps end up in another sun's orbit!)* Lastly, the Heliosphere is considered to define the boundaries of our solar system: it is the place where our solar winds mix with the winds of other stars.*

Do you see it? Do you see the limitless possibilities of correspondence? In everyway, we are a microcosm in the image of the macrocosm: As above, as below.

Returning to how this relates to life, the sun (us) and whatever it is composed of, determines what (who) will orbit in its (our) world. Like

---

* Note: Please forgive astrophysical incongruences.

magnets, we either attract, repel, or have no effect on matter traversing our space: At some level, the component atoms that make-up our core will exert magnetism on certain types of alloys only, and not others. In life – as we grow, heal, evolve and transform – our core composition changes. Consequently, it will be impossible for some existing objects (people, circumstances, events) to remain in our gravitational field since the bond no longer exists; the interaction will have dissolved.

This process is reflected perfectly in relationships: as personal changes occur, the result will either not affect the attraction between two people (particles involved in the attraction were untouched; the couple stays together), intensify it (new particles generated new affinities; the couple grows and evolves together) or eliminate it all together (particles lost their interaction factor; in this case, even if someone wanted to stay, they couldn't: "I want to still love you, but I just don't", "I would really want to stay, but I'm unable to"). Life is change, and change breeds change. Blaming someone for changing is a painful and useless accusation, telling someone you don't want them to change is unfair, and preventing someone from changing is cruel and goes against nature. Immutability is a physical impossibility.

Within these hundreds of worlds in our solar system, occasional explosions, flare-ups, or collapses, may create temporary chaos and set things flying off in random directions. And this is why I have to believe in accidents, luck, and other imponderables.

As a powerful sun, we all shine brightly: illuminating, creating, and directing our world in each moment. Our aura acts both as solar winds and gravitational field. It is the composition of our personal core that determines which planets revolve around us, which stars illuminate our skies, which asteroids bounce off our atmosphere or crash our surface. And the power of being sovereign ruler of a solar system comes with the responsibility of the effects our make-up has on the rest of the cosmos. The waves that ripple off our shores will erode somebody else's coast; our earthquakes and tectonic shifts will create a sidereal tsunami in another galaxy. The inner flutters or our being will cause the universe to tremble: such is the Butterfly Effect*.

Let us be responsible rulers of our own world. Let us beware of our power and be aware that we are accountable for the universe. Let us always be conscious that at the fringes of our solar system, the breath of our being mixes with the winds of the soul of other stars.

JANUARY 24TH, 2012

IT COULD HAVE BEEN SO MUCH WORST

This morning, as I turned around from my desk to return to my yoga mat *(I had, once again, interrupted my routine to jot down a note)*, I stepped precisely on the open glass-case I had left on the floor while performing my exercises. A fortunate reflex made me lift my foot before all my weight had pressed on the case, and although the glasses went flying, no damage was done. Spontaneously I exclaimed, "Lucky, lucky, lucky me! Thank you, thank you, thank you!"

It is occurring to me that in the past few months, since my general change of attitude and embrace of a good Universe, whenever some glitch happens – if I cut myself cooking, I drop a hot meal on the

* Butterfly Effect: In chaos theory, it is the phenomenon whereby a minute localized change in a complex system can have large effects elsewhere.

floor, or forget something on my way to an appointment – my immediate thought is "Oh thank you, it could have been so much worse." I instantaneously imagine how my finger could have been further under the knife, how my bowl of soup could have hit the carpet instead of the wooden floor, how I could have been further along the road before realizing I had forgotten a crucial piece of paper, etc. This change has taken place without me thinking about it or making a conscious effort towards it. And it is comforting to know that my hard work is paying dividends for which I don't have to lift a finger. I am making a plan to acquire a profusion of such shares to insure my cozy retirement.

A slight adjustment in attitude can alter what part of an event will be in focus. Turn the lens to the right, life is a bitch, a little to the left, you're one lucky SOB!

JANUARY 25TH, 2012

DO YOU BELIEVE IN MAGIC?

Why has the magic disappeared from the hearts of so many people nowadays? Were we told too early *(or too late)* in life that Santa Claus does not exist, that the Tooth Fairy was our Dad, and that dreams should be kept to oneself – and that if you do choose to have dreams, you do so at your own risk and perhaps should not dream too big either? Is life's suffering simply too much for most people and as a result, the safest way to live is to renounce your dreams and minimize your expectations? It sadly appears to be so. As Max, the sarcastic character from the television series *Two Broke Girls* would say: *"This is life, lower your expectations!"*

And yet, most of us are still moved by movies, books, and reality-shows in which an unsung hero is celebrated, lost lovers are reunited, or a burrito slinger achieves his unlikely life-long dream of making a living from his singing. Despite evidence that too many dreams are vacating the hearts in which they once dwelled, the fact that such uplifting stories still harp at the strings of sensitivities of millions denotes the amaranthine nature of human hope. As much as the dream of a happy ending is gnawed at throughout our life and leads to bitter disillusion, the hope that it may one day come true against all odds, is never fully eradicated.

It does sadden me at times to live amongst a ruck of down-to-earth, pragmatic, disabused beings. It inevitably brings me down. I need to rub elbows with kindred spirits and find my tribe. I remember writing a paper on the Laws of Attraction in a philosophy class in college *(not a good idea)* and being failed on it. The teacher wrote that I was naive, that my views were simplistic, and that it was time for me to grow up. I can recall being angry, as if she was soiling something precious to me – like being told all over again that Santa Claus wasn't real. She certainly succeeded in dousing my fire that day, but the light never completely went out. In the course of my life, I may have suffered my share of disillusionments, dwarfed hopes and battered dreams but still, part of my heart doesn't know we are not supposed to believe in magic. Quite frankly, if there really is no magic in the world, I'm not even interested.

Now, why am I bringing this up this morning? Because last night, after sharing my publishing dream with a friend *(in recent days, I have finally begun telling people closest to me that I am writing a book)*, I was reminded again that I should know that writing this book will not put butter on my table. I was told I should be aware that many people before me have written books that certainly never bought them the table onto which they'd hope to place the plate that would hold the toast to spread some butter on. And yet, this friend is addicted to American Idol, which to me is precisely about people believing in the unlikely chance of making it where most fail, about individuals often risking everything and pressing on against all odds, and who ultimately see their stubborn belief rewarded. So it appears to be okay to applaud the perseverance and unreasonable boldness of strangers and the miracle of their improbable new-found success, but believing that someone you know might be at the receiving end of good fortune or life's magic, is not. Of course I know that in this particular case, my friend simply wants her friend to find autonomy and security because she has seen her suffer for too long. She would like for me to bet on a horse with better odds. Nonetheless, doubting someone's passion has never helped anybody become all that they can be. So I'm a little cross right now.

Living life as a stubborn and tenacious believer does come with a price, but occasionally yields its rewards. I have a good story for that *(surprise, surprise)*. Several years ago, I was given ninety days to move out of my then apartment. After searching in vain for a new place for weeks to no avail, I eventually had to schedule a moving truck for eight o'clock on the very last morning of the ninety days, without providing a drop-off address. The closer the deadline, the more my friends and family urged me to settle for acceptable lodging and to just sign a lease, any lease. Being who I am, I wouldn't settle.

As it turns out, I escaped the forewarned catastrophe by the skin of my teeth. The day prior to moving-day is when I "miraculously" found an exquisite house with expansive views along the St-Lawrence River. As my sister and I were driving up and down streets of a potential neighborhood, we saw an old man mowing the grass of a house sitting on a fabulous property at the end of a cul-de-sac. Not only was the house for sale and not for rent, but its size and location made it obvious that it was out of my price range. Sitting in the car, my sister and I fantasized for a moment about what it would be like to live there, then drove away. Half way down the block, as we were both feeling uneasy about leaving the house behind, we turned to each other with an equal look of Why not? "What have we got to lose? Let's give this a try", I said. With a swift U-turn, we made it back to the house and off I went to see the man. After a quick introduction, I made the suggestion that perhaps he could rent his property until the market got better *(it was in a slump then too).* To make a story short, he agreed to the amount I was willing to pay and I moved-in the next day. Later, after hearing the story, visitors could only shake their heads and say to me, "You are so lucky!"

Well, I have something to say about that *(surprise again).* A more rational non-believer would have never taken the risk I took and would have never experienced the magic (luck) I experienced. Sometimes, it takes balls to have faith. Magic comes to those who dare to believe and dare to act accordingly. It is improbable that one will find a treasure if they are unwilling to live as a treasure hunter.

So it may be safer not to cultivate dreams but my middle name is not "Safe" and I refuse to live a safe, meek, life. I like the fireworks and in order to partake in the best shows, you have to stay up through the darkness. So I will keep on jumping fences, on taking gravity-defying crazy leaps of faith, and on foolishly continuing to be bold and dream big. No guts, no glory.

Just as it is a fine line between genius and madness, I believe it is too between faith and naiveté. And frankly, I would rather consider myself living as a faith-filled genius than as a naive madwoman.

One thing is for sure: magic has less of a chance of coming into your life if you don't dare seek it.

JANUARY 26TH, 2012

A FINELY THREADED NETWORK

EVERYBODY IN THEIR OWN LITTLE WORLD

I remember being at the beach last September and observing people around me. It was fascinating to witness the different realities unfolding next to one another. For a while, I amused myself by delving into the minds of a few stars of their own world, and imagined what living this moment was like for them.

There was this little boy, just a few feet away from me, who was selecting and intently moving small rocks one by one. He was earnestly at work digging out some stones and with significant effort, was throwing them a couple feet away. I could see the stern expression on his face; the boy was very focused. Obviously he had a very specific plan in mind, although it was invisible to me. His moment had purpose, he was building something, and in his eyes, his creation was of vital importance. The world around him did not exist; my world was invisible to him.

Then I watched this older man walking along the beach. As he reached the edge of an eight feet tall seawall standing along the length of a waterfront property, he paused. Since the tide was coming in, the small waves were now crashing against the base of the concrete wall, thereby covering the man's path with turbulent waters. I saw him stop and ponder for a moment, assessing the risks of crossing this area, and eventually deciding to go for it. Very slowly, he gingerly walked along the wall, the water nearly up to his knees. The passage was tricky because the ground was made of slippery stones. I imagined his attention focused on each step and his thoughts about the fact that this was a rather perilous escapade. I also heard his self-motivation and determination to follow through with his exploit. "I'm doing this", he seemed to think.

Looking out towards the ocean, there was this young girl of twelve or thirteen, standing on one of the posts at the end of the pier, in her sporty bikini. She was looking down in the water at her friends who had obviously already jumped. Her mother was there with a video camera, ready to capture the courageous leap of her daughter for posterity. Two other girlfriends were standing next to her, also poised to jump. The group in the water was cheering her on; voices enthusiastically shouting she could do it. I think I watched for at least twenty minutes. She would nod meaning, "Okay, I'm doing it now", than back away. She would swing her arms back and forth readying herself, and stop short of jumping. A few times, she stepped down the post, almost capitulating, only to come back up, seemingly more resolute than before. She was scared but determined to do it... the audience was growing. Finally she did jump and I could imagine her satisfaction, relief and pride, and what she would get out of this experience. It would leave an imprint for the rest of her life. Another world was happening on that pier.

Finally, just in front of me, another story was simultaneously taking place. There were two Asian teenagers – who definitely looked like tourists *(I could tell, being a local and all!)* – attempting to get into a miniature inflated dingy, both at once, all the while carrying a crab-cage they were planning to drag with the hope of a miraculous catch. They had huge safety jackets hindering and making awkward all their movements. They must have attempted at least a dozen times to sit inside this unstable contraption before they actually succeeded. These guys were silly and goofing around, possibly experiencing the ocean for the first time in their life. They were having a ball without a second of care for what a comical spectacle they were putting-on for us bystanders. Yet another world.

The exercise was engrossing. Something felt at once innocent and awry in this concurrence of seemingly unrelated realities. Although unable to put my finger on the reason for my fascination, I decided to save this cluster of stories by recording them on paper, sensing there would be a meaning to them someday.

Five days ago, glancing through my notes, I wondered again why these stories continued to captivate me and how they could be integrated in my writing. Did they offer any insight? What was their relevance? Since no answers were volunteering themselves, I made-up a sign onto which I wrote the following question: What is the point of *Everybody in Their own Little World*? Today, I received my answer: it's an illusion. The perception of separateness is a fabrication of our ego.

WEB DESIGN

This answer came to me as I watched the pilot episode of the new television series *Touch*, in which a young autistic boy sees the world as a mathematical lattice of interwoven events, and attempts to communicate, through numbers, the roadmap it reveals. The visual of the opening credits presents an image-sequence of nautilus, sunflower, pineapple, and galaxy; and through semi-transparent layering, juxtaposes points and lines that reveal the geometric relationships governing the intrinsic patterns of each of those elements. I was transfixed: not only have I mentioned some of these same images just recently in the book, but I have also produced subway and train station posters celebrating the Year of Mathematics fifteen years ago that also featured the same visual. Understandably, I was immediately hooked: They had me at "nautilus".

An upsurge of emotion arose as I watched. I felt thankful and relieved that this hitherto arcane knowledge was at last going to be disseminated in a public forum. I felt excited that this principle of interconnectedness would now enter the realm of pop culture and would undoubtedly become part of the vernacular through the interest generated by what promises to be a successful television series.

A few years ago, the movie Avatar opened the door to such heightened awareness by appealing to, and awakening a universal and innate knowing that we are living parts of a greater whole. Today, this new series presents a mathematical approach to the same ideas and has the potential of drawing-in and opening the minds of multitudes in our greatly right-brained, individualistic society. I hope it takes off into the stratosphere.

It is time for the truth of the kinship of all creation and of our interrelatedness to be brought to light. The world needs to know and have its eyes wide opened. For too long these notions have been jealously guarded in hermetic gnosis, and in recent times, have only been timidly brought forth by the brave, though scanty, attempts of a few. The fortress surrounding the false belief that our individual existences and actions are divorced from that of others, and inconsequential to the rest of humanity, must be torn down. It is time for the isolation to end. Right now, most of us are oblivious to what is truly at play; in fact, we are pretty much unaware there is even a universal game going on. The truth of the big picture lies like the three dimensional scene hidden behind the illusion of the two dimensional image of an autostereogram; our brains have yet to develop the ability to overcome their limited way of viewing the world. Most of us remain too focused on the individual dots of a pointillist picture.

We are on the eve of a game changer; we are being gently introduced to notions that will become common knowledge; not unlike the discovery that the Earth was round, or the early days of baseball, when people didn't know about the game and wondered what the hoopla was about. Once they did though... well, that's history. Let's not be bench-players: Let's play ball.

INTENTS AND SIGNS

Riveted to the screen, I watched the pilot episode. I reveled in the clever twists and turns of the international storylines that skillfully revealed unexpected connections and demonstrated a global design most inhabitants of the world never even suspect exists.

I was thrilled to witness the plot exploring, and somewhat elucidating, the realm of intent and signs. As we follow the disparate stories of various characters – and witness the personal motivations behind their actions – we are not only made to understand that they are connected, but also that the intent, or impulse, that drove each of their actions in the first place, was not, in the end, the "real" reason why something was done. This, the characters and viewers only discover as the final scenes play out.

Similarly, we are also given to observe that signs posted along the way, although undoubtedly there for a reason and warranting attention, are perhaps not the signs one might think they were. Although a sign is indeed a sign, the interpretation one makes of it may not correspond to the unfathomable encoded writing. The "real reason" of a sign may only be revealed in the end.

The existence of signs suggests we wisely sharpen our intuition and awareness; and the surprise of where they lead, that we surrender the outcome to faith and destiny.

Prompts of our inner-voice and cues from our gut-feelings can be relied upon to direct our actions. We can also keep our eyes peeled for signs to point us in the right direction. While their guidance is trustworthy, we should not assume the destination we are being ushered to will resemble our intended objective.

WORLD WIDE WEB

As popular shows and movies are now introducing the hidden principle of non-separation to the masses, so too are the new tools of this age of telecommunications. To the faultfinders of an ever-growing presence of communication technologies *(including myself on occasions)*, I present a redeeming, and even commendable, aspect to the epidemic. A noteworthy benefit (beyond the obvious) of these devices and practices is that they allow people to experience "live" our state of interconnectedness.

It has actually just occurred to me that this surging trend of Tweeting, Facebooking, live chatting and blogging, is in fact teaching millions how each one of our actions (posts) influences others and provokes reactions globally. This hitherto unseen immediacy of communication is an introductory course in the principles of oneness and instantaneity. This social media savvy generation is the first to experience a world where one is nearly indivisible from the other and where a tag such as "This is so 4 seconds ago" is considered life as usual. The social media enthusiasts live in a world more attuned to the new quantum realities of a universe where the frontiers of distance and time are collapsing.

The significance of this evolutionary leap remains unclear. But although we may not be privy yet to the surprising denouement of this particular plot, one thing is certain: This collective movement is, beyond the shadow of a doubt, part of a greater design.

Despite the apparent segregation of our stories, there exists a connecting thread that unites us in fundamental oneness. Regardless of our delusion of separateness, our isolated stitches are made by one thread that weaves our individual design into a global web of sublime interrelatedness.

JANUARY 27TH, 2012

DARE ALLA LUCE *

There is a lightness that has been gently infusing me lately. Not only has giving myself permission to continue writing a little longer allowed me to relax and enjoy coasting along the allegorical roads of Costa Rica, it has also further reinforced my faith in the value of my book. And as far as value is concerned, the further understanding that hardship does not equal worthiness is beginning to really set-in this time.

From this quiet stillness, I am drawn again this morning to reflect upon this personal belief that life must be hard in order for it to be honorable. As I contemplate the notion, I realize that I have always, on a subconscious level, made sure that any accomplishment, joy, or reward came at a hefty personal price. I see that growing up, I was taught that blood, sweat, and tears would warrant a good living – which was to say that pain reaped rewards. I carried this imbedded belief into some relationships, which made me accept the lows of lows in order to be granted access to the delights of the highs: it did seem natural that the crests should be matched by their corresponding troughs. This fallacious belief, of course, transpired throughout my professional life as well. In this arena, it translated into never getting a job or contract with anything that resembled ease: the process always turned out to be complex, laborious, and usually followed being turned down many times prior. Once, a great paying job came my way with relative ease, and on some level, I felt I did not deserve it. A frame of mind such as this one has generally meant that when I have witnessed people obtaining good

---

* In Italian, *dare alla luce* is "to give birth" and literally means: to give (bring) to the light.

money for their work, I have either judged that they had not paid a fair price or, felt jealous this kind of prosperity eluded me. In any regards, in my view of the world, a painful transaction at the cash register must always preclude enjoyment of life.

THERE IS NO PRICE TO PAY

This was my first meditation-induced illumination this morning: THERE IS NO PRICE TO PAY. A part of me has probably always known this, which would explain why I have always been, and still am, reluctant to use the word "deserve", as in "with all the trouble you've gone through, you deserve some happiness." "Deserve" inherently implies that you have done something to merit your good fortune and that you have previously "paid your dues". I have always been uncomfortable with this concept, even though my journey is a testament for living by it. And obviously, it appears that I still don't think I have paid the full admission price to the fair because I'm still standing behind the gate, longingly watching the fun rides from a distance.

This idea that there is no price to pay made me take another look, this morning, at my current state of affairs. Even though I know I will get through it – because I am familiar with seeing through massive projects that initially seem unconquerable – I do feel overwhelmed by the gargantuan task ahead of me. And right now, this process of letting myself feel engulfed appears to fall into the category of semi-intentionally making things hard for myself in order to "deserve" later success.

As I became aware that I was perhaps perpetrating unnecessary hardship just as a conscienceless habit, I momentarily began to blame myself for my lack of alertness. And since I was in the vicinity of guilt, I also began chastising myself for not handling this stressful situation gracefully at all times. And that's when something else clicked, and my wiser-self exclaimed: "Whoa girl! Don't get carried away. This *is* a big job and you are within your rights to occasionally feel overwhelmed."

LABOR PAINS

"Annie, you are giving birth to yourself. It IS a big deal!"

Another light bulb. Of course I am, and of course it is! Didn't I write back in October that I was in a pregnant pause and that I was hormonal? After a gestation that lasted decades, I am now preparing to give birth to all the thoughts, experiences, and insights that have formed my whole, purposeful, true self. And it should be expected that the pregnancy will be accompanied by morning sickness and that every second of the delivery will not be performed with grace. I am beginning labor and it is intense. It is not a walk in the park. But if I accept the intensity, breathe with and into it; if I cease resisting the fact that it is not easy or effortless; if I just stop fighting it, I can experience the process fully, in all its intensity and glory.

IT'S A BEAUTIFUL THING

Birthing a great project is a beautiful thing; any major undertaking we commit to in life may qualify as one. We should be forewarned though there will be discomfort along the way and labor pains will certainly accompany the crowning moment. But all of it can be embraced if we are aware that we are carrying our creation, nurturing it to term, and that we are about to give it life.

The belief that worthiness is something that is earned is false. It does not come with a price tag of pain, struggle, hardship, adversity, blood, sweat, tears or otherwise. The only label worthiness may come with is that of an open heart. We are deserving of life's consideration simply because we are, not because of something we do. Being worthy is our natural inheritance.

JANUARY 28TH, 2012

PROOF OF LIFE

I have been waiting for proof from life for months now. Actually, it's been years, but I have been more sanguine about it since daring the great leap of faith of moving here. In fact, my hopes were stirred even further when I uncovered the benevolence of the Universe, and further yet as I discovered my purpose with this book, and earnestly embarked upon the journey of writing it. Somehow, I did feel as though I now "deserved" it and waited with bated breath.

I have said on several occasions that if only I was offered an occasional reassuring two-thumbs-up from the Universe, and particularly if I was shown concrete support in a form that would alleviate my financial worries, my load would be lightened and my faith replenished to the rim.

Proof Of Life: This chapter heading has been sitting on my desk within a list of unused titles, awaiting the blessed day when some grand life-changing event would occur to assuage my wearied heart, mind, and bank account. I have been expectantly waiting to share the good news and thus provide you with faith renewing evidence that, indeed, the Universe will support you once you make a decision that follows your heart and your soul's purpose.

But despite my recent "material girl" wishes, I have been considering letting go of this unanswered prayer for a while, in order to free my mind of the cumbersome clutter of oft-dashed expectations.

WITHOUT FANFARE OR FIREWORKS

I almost did not notice. It nearly evaded my vigilance and virtually eluded my awareness. I could have missed it.

This morning, it occurs to me that the Universe has indeed been right there, as promised, supporting me in my endeavor, from the very beginning. The truth is, that ever since I made the decision to undertake the writing of this book, I *have* been able to do so uninterrupted. Other than a day here and there, regardless of circumstances, I have been writing continuously. Discretely and unnoticed, life has in fact been enabling my journey all along. I simply had not seen it. I did not recognize the assistance because it did not come in the form I had been expecting. I had envisioned an absence of monetary concerns and what I was given was access to loans, credit and gifts, affording me the luxury to live in a beautiful home, amidst the grandest of my beloved nature, with time on my hands, dedicated to writing.

LIFE SUPPORT

Through the grace of God, a conspiring Universe, an occurrence of life's magic, karma, or a manifestation of my will: I have, in fact, been living on life's support.

This is a humbling lesson.

> ***Even though focus is an admirable virtue, sometimes softening our vision may be beneficial. We might just realize that what we needed and asked for had been there all along but just didn't look like we thought it ought to.***

JANUARY 29TH, 2012

MAMA PROVIDENCE

The recent discovery that I am in the process of giving birth and should therefore accept the intensity that I am feeling, has been quickly gathering momentum. In fact, it has had a snowball effect of increasing my peace of mind. In turn, this peace of mind has steadily gathered me into the present moment. I am here, and at the moment, this wave of intensity is cresting and I am skillfully surfing it. Hence, the anxiety-filled anticipation and fear of it crashing down on me, has been relegated to a minor concern. I have gleefully adopted some of the nonchalant demeanor of a surfer-dude and it's working out nicely for me. My thoughts are clearer, my actions more focused, and I seem to have found a way to enjoy not only the waves but the quiet between the waves. Very cool.

Another contributing factor to my quasi-hedonistic attitude lies in the choice I made ten days ago – when the trepidations and money-concerns started creeping-up again – to grant myself yet a little more time to write certain portions of my book before seeking work. The laxity provided by these extra days, along with the effects of pseudo-pregnancy hormones, has resulted in the surprising experience of something akin to a beach-bum attitude *(well really just akin– let's just say I still aspire to experience this fully one day, when I grow up).*

This peace of mind that keeps rolling down the hill has now reached even bigger proportions and has resulted in providing me with a wider outlook on my situation: Just as I knew Providence had spoken through the customs officer who turned me back at the border nearly two years ago, it is occurring to me that perhaps this

Providence character – a woman of action and few words – has been keeping a diligent eye on me and has even been patiently *(or maybe not so patiently)* nudging me in one, single, very specific direction: "Write your book!"

I know this does not news make; I have already broadcasted this many times before. I know I have said that life seems to be insisting I do this, but it appears that I am somewhat of an inattentive viewer *(good news for the broadcasters, they can feed me the same material over and over)*, or if you will, an obstinate child, who needs to be told the same thing again and again, in various creative ways, until she gets it. *

By now, I am hearing Mama Providence's firm, insisting voice, "Child, what's the matter with you? What is it you don't understand?" I picture this stout black Southern woman – still dubious as to whether I have heard her or not – acting out a little skit in the hopes of finally getting through to me. As a show of her determination in preventing me from being distracted, she mimics standing in a doorway, blocking all access, and pretends to turn away an invisible someone whose intrusion could sidetrack me. "Nuh-uh, Annie's not seeing anybody right now, come back later." Mama knows best. Since she notices that I am still looking puzzled, she makes a rare exception and goes on to explain her position with more words than she is accustomed to:

> "Here is what I have been trying to make you understand: Complete your book. It is what you are supposed to be doing. Once this is done, you can go out and look for work. At that point, if work comes knocking at the door, I will warmly invite

* Note: "Dear Mama Providence. Please keep in mind that I have not always been such a stubborn child. Last year when you whispered that I should move to Vancouver, I complied without question." Just sayin'.

it in and bring out the biscuits. But not before then. You need to stop fighting me on this girl. It's for your own good. What else can I do to make you understand? I have thwarted every one of your business proposals, sabotaged every job attempt (didn't even let you become a barista); I even regretfully made you feel sick to keep you at home, writing. To entice you and help you understand, you were provided with a deep sense of satisfaction and even happiness when you dedicated yourself to writing. All this, I did, hoping you would have the good sense to stop questioning me. Yet there you are, nagging me again, wondering what you are really supposed to do! You are smarter than this girl. Now get to it!"

Wow! I think I heard her. I am on the verge of surrendering to her will. She does present a convincing *(relentless)* argument. Did I hear her right? Did she say that the past several years of fruitless searches for an opportunity to launch my fitness products have been aborted through her own doing because I am supposed to write this book *first*? Wow again.

If I consider the situation from her point of view, what are a couple months more of borrowing money in order to fulfill my destiny *(and get her off my back)*? At this point, if I crash and burn: I crash and burn. If I can't reimburse the debts I have incurred to date, a little more will not change the outcome: crashing and burning there will be. And really, time wise, it is not such a big deal; I predict it is only a matter of weeks before I am done *(okay, maybe more than two months, maybe 12 weeks or something)*. I realize I have been playing games with myself ever since October when I accepted that I was unable to work, and even those times when I chose not to work. I did it piecemeal, right up until recently when I decided to grant myself a few more days still. I have never embraced my book completely. I have been living on one short reprieve after another, constantly keeping guilt in my back pocket; never maintaining a clear conscience for very long. And I think I have also been fooling myself believing I could actually finish this book while looking for a job, or working, even part-time.

The reality is that I am breathing, eating, dreaming this manuscript. I see it in my soup, in my coffee, in my bathtub, in a bird, in the rain; I see it in Santa Claus and Harry Potter for God's sake! I am living this book 24 hours a day and the only way it will get completed is with 100 % dedication.

Her message appears to be unequivocal: "Girl, it is time you contemplate getting this book done completely, not just parts of it, and trust life to unfold as it should after that." This is something I will seriously think about. Very seriously.

Mama Providence is a very clever woman and one should not attempt to argue with her. Everyone could certainly benefit from learning not to talk back when she speaks; it would make life much easier. When Mama Providence tells you something, shut up, listen, and say "Yes Ma'am".

JANUARY 30TH, 2012

'YES MA'AM'

How dense can I be? *(no answer please, this is a rhetorical question).* I mean, what's my problem? *(again, rhetorical).* I have been thinking about her message, and I think I get it now. I actually get it.

I've embarked on this journey willingly months ago and I now know that I have incredible roadside assistance services. I have a whole team looking out for me: A Benevolent Universe is tracing my itinerary, Life Support is providing me with the necessary funds as I go, Mama Providence is my cheering squad, my Wiser-self is coaching me along, and even Ego is finally on board lightening up on his doomsaying and helping in organizing my thoughts.

So why don't I stop talking about getting out of the car before reaching Peru? I should realize that I am past the point of doubting my travel plans. How foolish is it to think of slowing down, getting distracted, and loosing focus, as I am crossing into Panama and getting ever closer to my goal? Months ago, I set out on this perilous journey and I have already covered much of the distance: overcoming difficult obstacles, completing challenging legs, and seeing wondrous views. Peaks of the Andes are almost on the horizon and completing this book, although not the destination in and of itself, is intrinsic to reaching my Peru.

I know this because the theme of my journey was to find my voice; and this book *is* my true voice. And I have come to the understanding that one must first find, express, and live their Truth before experiencing the success of a fulfilling life.

ANGEL DIVE

It is almost decided. Actually, I *have* made the decision: I WILL take the time needed to complete this project fully.

Although I have made the choice, I still need a few deep breaths to integrate this major decision 100 % in order to eliminate any trace of second thoughts, doubt or guilt.

I want this choice to inhabit me completely.

I want to experience the freedom of this angel dive into the mystic lake of possibilities and enjoy the sensual pleasures of swimming naked in the waters of my destiny.

[...]

It is done. It is so. I am free. This book will be.

> ***If you*** *know* ***what you are supposed to do, do yourself a favor: Dive-in wholeheartedly and whole-bodily. Avoid testing the waters with your big toe or conclude to wait until the water is warmer. Climb up a path to the edge of the majestic cliffs lining the shores of your lake of choice, take a deep breath, and launch yourself into the most gracious dive you have ever attempted. You have it in you, just do it.***

EPILOGUE

JULY 2012

From that moment on January 30th, my resolve did not waver once. I may have been exhausted at times from the unimagined amount of work I had undertaken, but doubt never visited me again – I would not stop until the book was done. Since I knew for sure that nothing would divert me from seeing this book through, my ego's foreboding was shushed completely.

Throughout my months of writing and editing, the regular occurrence of "coincidences" supported me. Now and then, the Universe spoke to me through serendipitous signs and synchrony. Subject matters I was writing about would show-up in a book, on television, or in a movie ; a writer's blocks would be answered by the sight of a poster on the street. On a few occasions, a theme I had decided to forego would appear in one of those same ways, and this would prompt me to bring it back. One day in early spring, I had temporarily decided my book wood be called *The Runaway Mind*; the very next day, I overheard a conversation between two guys at the beach, one telling his friend, "Really ? You haven't heard of the book *Runaway*?

Incredibly, on May 8th, I began to revise *December 27th* – the day I tell the story of Richard and I – only to realize it was his birthday.

One evening in February, looking up at the stars, I was overcome by a feeling of absolute certitude that, with this book, I was on my way to living my full potential : I had finally reached the point where all the pieces were coming together and where elements of my destiny were converging. I profoundly understood that to present this book was the reason for having been who I had been, and that my life had been lived for this very purpose : for my story to be shared. My lifetime of questioning, of trials and inner struggles, only made sense if it could be used to serve others; and now was the time, finally. I knew in that moment that my life was never going to be the same and that I was about to shine my brightest light. This feeling that I was at last in my rightful groove was truly blissful.

In February as well, I heard that Richard was seriously ill and that he had a few months to live. The news did send shockwaves through my whole being and there was no point in trying to deny its impact by rationalizing that is was to be expected. It took me a day to process the information and for my energies to reconcile with the impending change in the state of our union. The thought of him no longer being on the planet was something I needed to gently assimilate. I also knew that he would be an infinitely better guardian angel than he ever was a life-partner.

Faithful to our history, some magical anecdote happened that day: In order to get assistance in fixing a bug in my computer, I called Apple's technical service and was put on hold until a tech was available. After a few minutes, a super enthusiastic man greeted me, "Good day to you! My name is Richard, what can I do to help you on this beautiful day". I was flabbergasted and it took me a few seconds to recover. Typical.

The following day, Richard and I talked peacefully, acknowledging the time had come. He said he would leave this Earth sober and I told him I would see him before he left. A few weeks later, I heard from his sister that perhaps his death was not so imminent after all. I have not heard from him since.

As weeks went by, and as the sense that I was in the midst of accomplishing my purpose grew ever stronger, a new serenity came over me. I realized that whatever happened after I had completed this seemingly preordained endeavor, was okay with me. Whatever came after was no longer critical to my fulfillment. My exhausting quest was over. I no longer had to seek meaning in my life; I had found it. Now that this peace was at my core, working in a coffee shop, if necessary, would be a pleasurable exercise in simplicity. Furthermore, I felt that any challenge or difficulty that I may encounter would no longer be the Universe's response to some personal off-kilter vibes, but rather, something that was part of my highest destiny and aligned with my spirit. I even accepted the possibility of having to move away from this part of the country I have grown to love dearly. In the most important way, Vancouver had served its purpose and I was grateful.

On Easter morning, as I took a moment to reflect, I realized I no longer ached in prayer. It was almost as if I no longer had reason to pray, in the sense of asking to be found. Now that I was doing what I was meant to do, all that was left were devotions of gratitude and desire to honor my newfound path.

From the beginning, writing this book became the most important thing in my life and I became a total recluse. For the past nine months, my only socializing has been one business meeting, Christmas dinner upstairs, one lunch at the restaurant, and one shared coffee. And I have guarded my words preciously: until a month ago, no one had even read a single paragraph.

Since January's commitment, I have gone to bed every night looking forward to the morning, so that I could get back to my book, often beginning at 4 or 5 A.M.. Of course, I now realize how naive it was to think that twelve weeks would be sufficient time to complete it. It is turning out to be more like twenty-five plus. And for those last twenty-five weeks, I have barely taken a day off: my dedication has been feverish, as if on a mission, which is what this project has become.

Sometime in May, I began to get a little impatient and wanted this crazy endeavor to be done already. But, more than once, I gently reminded myself that this experience of delving into my purpose for the first time was a once in a lifetime event and that I should be fully present in it, savoring every moment, not wishing it would go faster; one day, I reckoned, I would look back fondly at this exquisite period of transition and appreciate that I did not try to hurry to the finish line.

One particular morning, I woke up entirely discouraged and decided to practice some of my own preaching. I meditated that having one bad day was okay and that I could embrace it for what it was. Not only did I succeed but as soon as I accepted it, the dispiritedness disappeared and I was clear-minded and joyful for the remainder of the day.

From the time I wrote *Dare alla luce*, I symbolically contemplated my book-writing process as a pregnancy. I eventually consulted a due-date calendar and determined that, with the conception having occurred on October 1st, my due-date was June 23rd. Whether the book or my true self were to be the fruit of the gestation was intertwined, and perhaps amounted to the same. Obviously, what I thought of as labor pains back in January were mere Braxton Hicks contractions – I was nowhere near the final event.

In the weeks prior to the forecasted day, I saw that I just might serendipitously complete my book on time. But as the date got nearer, it became clear it would not be so. I accepted this with equanimity and figured my baby may be a few weeks late. So it was quite unexpected, when on the eve of my due-date, I was presented with an early gift: an ultimate transcending epiphany. Up until then, my plan had been to complete my book, send out a few copies of the manuscript to key people, and wait for someone to show interest in publishing it. What was revealed to me was the realization that I was about to repeat the exact same process I had followed all my life: after doing all the work and bringing a creation to the edge of seeing the light of day, I was going to wait for someone else's favorable vagary to birth it. Incredibly, I had not even seen this. In a dazzling flash of light, the magnitude of this revelation descended upon me, and in a matter of minutes, I made the decision not to wait for anyone to deliver *me*. No more. The power to do so was, and should rightfully be mine. I would assist my birth with my own hands. I would launch my book myself, put who I was out for the world to see, and only then, let the invitations come to me. I had built it, now they could come. This intimate process would finally bring me into full self-empowerment.

Time to push this baby out of the nest.

Here we are. With my book in your hands, I present to you, my IPO: Annie's Initial Public Offering.

My story-from-the-middle has been told but remains...

... to be continued.

UPDATES ON THE LIGHTER SIDE

—I did not broker peace between my neighbors.

—I did not attain consistency, which was my goal of January 1st.

—My body is not yet "healthy, lean, limber and strong", but I still believe it will eventually.

—I did have to go back to some medication because of a pinched nerve in my neck that radiated pain in my arm and kept me from driving or walking for more than ten minutes at a time, for nearly three months. Obviously this did not help with my sleep-challenged condition. I am much better now.

—On April 14th, a man initiated a real conversion with me as I was standing on the pier! I don't even know his name, but this consisted of a noteworthy event.

—My nausea and vertigo did not subside, but the past few weeks have definitely seen an improvement.

—My tinnitus is through the roof.

—My bank account still isn't plump, but *I believe.*

—I still pinch myself for the good fortune of living in such a beautiful part of the world.

—I am planning on hosting my Book Launch at "THE" Coffee Shop...

The End

Coffee Time

Once I held the first printed proof of the book in my hands, I felt confident enough to contact the owner of "THE" Coffee Shop and boldly put forward my plan of launching my book there.

Over the phone, I gave him a brief overview of my story and background, and, prompted to cut to the chase, proceeded to tell him what this call was about, mentioning that time was of the essence.

Graciously, sight unseen, he agreed to support me although he had never – despite numerous requests – agreed to this type of on-site involvement. We met an hour later to iron out the details and satisfy his curiosity as to who was that person who had made him deviate from customary behavior.

After chatting for a while, he asked, "What made you think that I would agree to this?" My only, very unprofessional reply was, "I felt this was written in the stars."

The place is called Delany's Coffee House. It is a five-location family owned, socially conscious local business, and the founders believe in giving back. They promote Organic and Fair Trade coffee, give their used grinds to local farmers for composting, donate their less-then-perfect beans to charities and are active within the communities they serve. In fact, the first musical event I attended here was a free outdoors concert they sponsored. As a spokesperson was addressing the crowd, my Vancouverite companion of that evening asked me if I knew who were the Delanys. Being fresh off the plane, I said I did not. After hearing his praises, I shared my appreciation for this kind of business spirit – success *and* generosity – and foretold that one day, I would rub shoulders with them. It appears the day has come.

As the first person to extend a concrete gesture of kindness and faith in sending my book off into the world, I wish to thank Mr. Robin Delany for his receptivity, support and hopefully, his intuition.

ACKNOWLEDGMENTS

Although this book was written quietly, remotely, and for the most part, without anyone knowing it was being written, I was not alone on my journey.

First and foremost, my mother was there for me, everyday, in spirit as well as through the magic of virtual face time. She was an unwavering supporter, a tireless cheerleader, and a steadfast believer in my dream and mission. In order to hone her hesitant knowledge of the English language, and in preparation for my book, she has been reading English novels out loud for an hour everyday for the past two months. I consider this remarkable motherly love and dedication.

From a different plane, now and again, I have felt my father approach this earthly dimension and give me strength and guidance. Aside from his ethereal presence, I thank him for being an exemplar of integrity, for instilling in me the virtues of conscientiousness and perseverance, for opening the doors to nature's kingdom, and for fueling my spirit's appetite for freedom from my earliest days. This innate, nurtured and insatiable hankering for boundlessness has come at a price but I would not want to have gone through life any other way.

As for the unavoidable material plane, I would like to thank Gary whose contribution in the funding of this unreasonable quest gave a whole new meaning to "friendly banking". He has been a constituent of the *Life Support* team sent to insure that I would see this adventure through, and has also always believed me to be a woman capable of extraordinary feats.

I want to thank my mother's clan of sisters and brothers who have wholeheartedly included me in their daily prayers for so many years.

I also wish to acknowledge my own smaller clan of sisters and brother – Michèle, Nicole and Benoit – with whom, throughout my life, I have shared the particular closeness that can (almost) only result from the bond between siblings. Our experiences together have run the gambit from spending riotous evenings – silliness unleashed – guffawing until our bellies and jaws hurt, to the intimacy of long critical conversations at various dolorous times of our lives. I thank them for being who they are.

I send my love to my friends Christina and Rusty and thank them for always being my friends.

I wish to acknowledge Rod who was the first person to read portions of my book and kindly begin the process of proofreading.

Although I feel slightly awkward doing so, I sincerely wish to thank Oprah for her many "classes" both on OWN and 'live' online. I am especially grateful for the timing of her *Oprah's Lifeclass* series last October, which perfectly coincided with the timorous emergence of my long-awaited literary journey and fanned the embers of my soul's desire.

Generally, I thank all the people who have crossed my path through the years and became unsuspected collaborators. Some provided me with the perfect anecdotes to illustrate my reflections, and others supplied material that prompted me to reflect. Throughout the book, I have called them friends and acquaintances and to be honest *(until the last line is written)* some of those may have been family members, though I chose to avoid specifics.

The few particulars I have chosen to keep, I was granted permission to do so. In my last conversation with Richard, I asked him if he wanted me to use his name, and jokingly said that if he did not, I would call him Bob *(not – I would have selected something grander).* Predictably, he gave me his blessing, proud to be known by his name in our exceptional love story.

Finally, and oh so importantly, I express my immense gratitude to my niece Maude. She is both a wise and gifted human being as well as a talented graphic designer. At the eleventh hour, her unexpected offer to get seriously involved in my project – revisions, proofreading, book design, website, posters, business cards – flabbergasted me and moved me. And so, after eight and a half months of flying solo, she was the first person to eagerly read my book in its entirety. As her reading progressed, she would send me comments of how certain parts made her laugh or cry or think, making my heart sing with gratitude to whatever or whomever had inspired me to write such a book. Once she was done, her final feedback was that she believed in this book, she believed in my success and above all, she believed in me. As if being this great "Mastercard" collaborator *(priceless!)* was not enough, she also took on the roles of consultant and counselor. At times when I was running on fumes, I have reached out to her and she fueled me with her enthusiasm and energy. I don't know what I would have done without her, and I will never have to find out because she was there.

In the spirit of my own lessons, I would like to recognize myself for my courage, faith and perseverance.

Ultimately, it is *you* that I wish to thank with my whole heart *(the bottom of it is simply not enough)* for taking the time to read the many words forming the stories and reflections of an unknown author. Hopefully, I have given something back and contributed, somehow, in lending my support for a few of your own courageous steps, or perhaps in providing ideas that will cause you to pause and make you go hmm.

Despite the diversity of our stories, we are the same in our human experience and I feel privileged to have had the opportunity to share mine – it makes so much sense to have done so.

Thank you, thank you, thank you.

CONTENTS

NOVEMBER 2011
MEADOW REPAIR

DECEMBER 2011
THE RUNAWAY MIND

JANUARY 2012
SOULSHINE

INTERIOR PAGES PRINTED ON ROLLAND ENVIRO 100™ BOOK WHICH:

Contains FSC certified 100% Post-Consumer Fiber

Is certified EcoLogo

Is processed Chlorine Free

Is manufactured using Biogas Energy

Is a Permanent Paper

ENVIRONMENTAL ATTRIBUTES

For every thousand books printed, compared to its 100% virgin fiber equivalent, here is what will be saved:

12 trees
44,811 L of water — 128 days of water consumption
1,496 lbs of waste
3,889 lbs CO_2 — 7,333 miles driven
20 GJ — 92,254 60W light bulbs for one hour
11 lbs NO_x — emissions of one truck during 16 days

Dear God

I will do my best

You take care of the rest